Why Did the Vatican Honor the Swastika?

A Catholic Couple's Five-Year Search for Understanding

Stephen & Diane Galebach

ISBN 978-0-578-14371-2

Published by Galebach Law Office

Amazon international edition

A companion publication for this book, the Timeline of Events and Documents, is accessible online at the Galebach Law Office website: http://investigation2.galebachlaw.com/itimeline.html

Copies of this book, and quotations for bulk order prices, may be obtained from Galebach Law Office, 9-11 Touro Avenue, Medford, MA 02155 USA; email: books@galebachlaw.com; telephone 781-874-2270.

Table of Contents

Chapter 1. A Bizarre Discovery

This is a story about discovery. The first discovery, the one that led to all the others, was unintentional. Neither of us ever thought of looking for a photograph of a Catholic Bishop blessing a swastika flag. Steve was not the most prominent Catholic in the Reagan Administration of 1980s America. But he was one of the most involved in policy initiatives that were important from a Catholic perspective – issues ranging from religious liberty and rights of the disabled to child exploitation, alternatives to abortion, and immigration policy – both as a legal policy advisor on White House staff and then as a senior aide to the United States Attorney General.

When he happened upon that first discovery in 2009, Steve was already well aware of the controversies swirling around the Catholic Church and Pope Pius XII from World War II and the Nazi era. After his service in President Reagan's government, Steve was invited by the founder of the Catholic League for Religious and Civil Rights to join its board of directors. During his two years on that board, the League published and distributed materials defending the reputation of Pius XII. Steve knew the Vatican had made questionable compromises with Nazi Germany. He figured they were done at a time of immense pressures. Surely approving Nazi ideology was not one of them. If an Archbishop blessed a swastika flag, the symbol of that ideology, it could not possibly be done with Vatican approval.

Diane grew up in a large Catholic family in the suburbs of Chicago. From a young age she experienced God as love, mercy and grace. Her faith has flourished through an adventurous life that has included bearing and raising ten children. As our children got older, Diane got into social entrepreneurship. In 2004-2005 she headed a group of tech-savvy young people to develop a pioneering website. VictimPower.org enabled anyone in America to report crimes anonymously to local police and prosecutors in every state. Though the online service worked well during its two years of operation, and no one's anonymity was ever compromised, we learned two things that surprised us. First, while U.S. Justice Department officials were initially welcoming and supportive, the top powers of our government had already resolved to eliminate anonymity on the Internet. Second, law enforcement authorities often needed to be held accountable and pressured, typically by phone calls from Steve as the group's legal counsel, before they would effectively serve the interests of victims and witnesses.

We have long taught our children that living under authority includes holding authorities accountable to serve. In a family, that involves recognizing our wrongdoings, saying we are sorry, and forgiving each other. Parents and children are on equal footing when it comes to repentance and forgiveness. We have found this is the key to peace within our family. For many years, however, we did not think of the applicability of "holding authorities accountable" within the Church, much less with respect to Pope Pius XII (1939-1958).

Some years ago for Christmas, Diane gave Steve the book *Pope Pius XII: Architect for Peace*. It was a glowing biography by a nun, Sister Margherita Marchione, countering some of the attacks on the wartime Pope. Steve thought some of the book's arguments were not entirely convincing, but he did not look further. Books like *Hitler's Pope* were not on our Christmas list, or in our personal library.

Steve was troubled when he returned in summer 2009 from an afternoon in the Harvard Library near our home. He told about a picture in a German Nazi newspaper showing the Archbishop of Buenos Aires ceremonially blessing a large swastika flag in the mid-1930s, at a time when Pope Pius XII was still Cardinal Eugenio Pacelli, Secretary of State of the Vatican. Steve was looking for something entirely unrelated, in a World War II restitution case he was handling for clients.

The Nazi newspaper he was looking into, *Der Stürmer*, described the swastika ceremony as occurring at a Eucharistic Congress. There was indeed an International Eucharistic Congress in Buenos Aires in 1934, and it occurred during a Holy Year proclaimed by Pope Pius XI (1922-1939). Diane had gone to an International Eucharistic Congress, in Lourdes, France, in 1981. We had taken our whole family to Rome for a Holy Year, in August 2000. How could a symbol of evil, the most profound evil of the 20th century, be blessed or honored at such an event?

2. The Photograph in *Der Sturmer*

Yet there it was. The picture Steve came across at Harvard was less distinct than the image on the cover of our book, because it was on microfilm. But the message it conveyed was crystal clear. The caption said, "An Archbishop Blesses the Swastika Flag." The subcaption added more details:

> At the Cathedral in Buenos Aires Archbishop Dr. Luis Copello blesses the Swastika Flag of the German Pilgrim Group that had gone to the Eucharistic Congress in Argentina. This ceremony was attended by the German Ambassador and the Argentine Foreign Minister.

The caption made the ceremony seem official, authoritative. The aspergillum in the Archbishop's hand is easily recognizable to anyone who has attended a Catholic Mass at Easter. It is used to bless the congregation by sprinkling holy water on them. The priest typically walks throughout the church using it, so that everyone is touched by the blessed water.

Theoretically, albeit rarely, holy water might be sprinkled to cast out evil, as in an exorcism. But if that was the intention here, why was the German Ambassador invited? It took just a moment online to find that Ambassador Edmund Baron von Thermann had a reputation as an enthusiastic Nazi. He was an officer in the SS, the elite *Schutzstaffel* whose members later formed Hitler's cadre for carrying out the Holocaust.

The caption's venue for the ceremony, the Cathedral during the Eucharistic Congress, made it appear all the more authoritative. The International Eucharistic Congress of 1934 was a huge event, comparable in its day to the World Youth Day 2000 that we attended in Rome. Between one and two million people attended the six-day event in Argentina. About 70,000 of them were from overseas, an impressive figure for such a remote part of the world before air travel.

A closer look at this issue of *Der Sturmer* showed it was designed to leverage the photo for maximum propaganda impact. The article above the photo was entitled "Hatred Extending Beyond the Grave." It told about a Nazi leader who was denied a Catholic funeral just because he was a Nazi, a man who struggled against the Versailles Treaty, against the Jews, and against the "Jews' lackeys."

An article to the right of the photo made it clear who the "Jews' lackeys" were: the Communists. The article was entitled "Who Governs Russia?" It claimed that 447 out of the top 550 Soviet officials were Jews. That "proved" the Jews were the real power in Communism. Never mind that Stalin was absolute dictator, non-Jewish, and antisemitic.

Another page of *Der Sturmer* contrasted "Priests and Pfaffen." Priests, it explained, help their fellow human beings in their sufferings and sorrows and "do not make common cause with Jews." By contrast *Pfaffen*, a German slang word for clergy, are hypocrites and egotists who "have no qualms about exalting the Jewish people as the people of God."

The entire issue was full of articles, pictures, and slogans demonizing and dehumanizing Jews. That was true of every issue of *Der Sturmer*. The name means "attacker." It was the Nazis' most vicious propaganda attack weapon against the Jewish people. *Der Sturmer* regularly portrayed "the Jews" as a vast international conspiracy aiming to destroy Germany and Western Civilization. The page with the swastika blessing photo, for example, quoted the leader of the Hitler Youth denouncing the conspiracy of Jews, Jews' lackeys, and Masons.

Der Sturmer was so vile, and so effective as a propaganda weapon, that its editor was convicted at Nuremberg, after World War II, for crimes against humanity. The Nuremberg Tribunal's judgment against Julius Streicher was based largely on the content of *Der Sturmer*. That judgment, which condemned him to death, included this passage:

> In his speeches and articles, week after week, month after month, he infected the German mind with the virus of anti-Semitism and incited the German people to active persecution. Each issue of "Der Sturmer," which reached a circulation of 600,000 in 1935, was filled with such articles …

The swastika blessing photograph appeared in *Der Sturmer* nine months after the Eucharistic Congress of October 1934. The photograph did not appear contemporaneously in the Buenos Aires newspapers we have checked. Surprisingly, as far as we can tell, it never appeared anywhere except *Der Sturmer*. How did this photograph find its way to the most murderous of all the Nazis' antisemitic propaganda organs?

3. What Does It Mean?

As we delved into the historical context of the photograph, we encountered a further surprise. We could not find any historian who had written about it. Nor could we find references to any Catholic Bishop, anywhere, blessing a swastika.

We looked into the various possible innocent interpretations of the photo. Over the course of a year, one fact after another ruled them out. Was it a blessing of one national flag among many others? No. The swastika did not become the national flag of Germany until September 1935. Starting soon after Hitler came to power in early 1933, the swastika was flown alongside the black-white-red German tricolor. It was widely known that the tricolor was the traditional flag of the second German Reich, or empire (1871-1918), and the swastika was the flag of the Nazi Party.

Was Argentina so far away that Rome might not know about this? No. Quite the opposite. In 1934 Rome went to Buenos Aires, in the form of a Papal representative called a "Legate a Latere." The Legate was treated as if he were the Pope, personally present. Accordingly, the Legate received a 21-gun salute from ships of the Argentine Navy, as would a head of state, when he arrived in the Rio de la Plata estuary aboard the Italian liner *Conte Grande*.

Heightening the stakes in our historical inquiry, the Legate was none other than Cardinal Pacelli, the Vatican Secretary of State. It was the first time such a high-ranking Vatican official had come to any part of the New World. He was a sensation. Not only huge crowds, but the President of Argentina, General Justo, came each day to the Congress.

Was the Archbishop of Buenos Aires, Santiago Luis Copello, perhaps just a rogue Bishop? Was he the sort of renegade who could bless a swastika on the sly without involving higher authority? No. Facts ruled out that possibility as well. Archbishop Copello was elevated to Cardinal by Pope Pius XI in December 1935. That was more than a year after the swastika blessing ceremony. What was more, the Vatican bestowed this honor five months after Copello's deed appeared throughout Germany in *Der Sturmer*.

That newspaper was not only the most vicious Nazi paper, it was also the most widely viewed. Hitler made sure of that. He had display cases built expressly for *Der Sturmer* in every town across Germany. Cities had multiple *Sturmer* cases, located strategically at busy pedestrian spots. The Vatican's top representative in Germany lived and worked close to one of those display cases in Berlin, and there is evidence that he monitored it.

If Copello's swastika blessing might possibly have been secret when it occurred, it was not secret when he was selected for Cardinal. And Copello's elevation to Cardinal was far from automatic. The Archbishop of New York or Paris or Milan almost always becomes a Cardinal. But Copello was the first Archbishop of Buenos Aires to become a Cardinal. No Spanish-speaking country of South America, in fact, ever had a Cardinal until Argentina with Cardinal Copello.

What would we think if we were members of the German pilgrim group? Fall 1934 was a particularly incongruous time for a swastika blessing at a Catholic event. Erik Larson's best-seller *In the Garden of Beasts* graphically presents the scene in Germany leading up to the Night of the Long Knives on June 30, 1934. Larson tells how Hitler's henchmen killed the leadership of the *Sturmabteiling*, or SA, the Nazi stormtroopers. He also tells how they killed dozens of people on Hitler's personal kill list.

An aspect known better to Catholics, not mentioned by Larson, is the large number of prominent Catholics who were singled out that day by the Nazis. The Berlin-based head of Catholic Action, the most important Catholic association in Germany, was killed. So was the leader of the nationwide Catholic sports association.

An even more prominent Catholic in Hitler's cabinet, Vice Chancellor Papen, was held under house arrest in imminent fear of death. Papen's two top staff members were killed. The others on his staff were arrested, except a few who managed to flee. These were almost all Catholics, and mostly from the nobility, including a Countess. German Bishops did not bless swastikas. Why would an Archbishop at an international event do so after such outrages?

As Catholics, what would we have thought if we learned in late 1935 that Archbishop Copello became a Cardinal? The Nuremberg Laws had been enacted three months before that, two months after the swastika-blessing photo appeared in *Der Sturmer*. Those laws are infamous for depriving all Jewish Germans of their citizenship. It was the first part of the three-part Nuremberg Laws that decreed the swastika the national flag of Germany. Had Copello's photo helped pave the way? Whether it had or not, why choose this point in time to make him the first Argentine Cardinal?

4. Looking for Answers at the Holocaust Museum

After we started talking about these issues with friends, one of them sent a photo. It was from Eugenio Pacelli's coronation as Pope Pius XII in 1939. Our friend found it online. There at Pius XII's right hand, standing by the Papal throne, at the moment of his coronation, was Cardinal Copello. This, like other facts we were accumulating, only made the questions look more serious and important to resolve.

Then another friend suggested visiting the U.S. Holocaust Memorial Museum. Having moved our family from the Washington, DC area to Boston before the Museum opened, we had never been there. Wondering how to make contact, Steve did some Internet searching. One of his fellow editors from the Harvard Law Review appeared to have a connection with the Museum. Within hours of receiving an email from Steve, he proved to be a good entrée.

Soon we had an email from the Director of the Museum, telling us when to arrive for a meeting with the Museum's chief photo archivist. We set aside a full day, in order to have time for the sobering and thought-provoking exhibits. The enormous bin of condemned persons' shoes at the Museum was emotionally overwhelming. In the exhibit about Nazi propaganda, we came upon a full-scale replica of a *Sturmer* display case. It supplied a realistic framework for appreciating the contemporary impact of the Copello photo.

But we needed most of the day, as it turned out, for talking with the Museum's staff. We had some trepidation, having no idea how they would react to a Catholic couple bearing a photograph of a swastika-blessing Archbishop. The head of the Museum's extensive photographic archives was surprised upon seeing the photo.   While she was familiar with an immense range of Nazi era photographs, she had not seen or heard of this one. She immediately began calling in other experts, including Ph.D. historians, from the Museum's staff. The photo was equally new to them. They understood the possible innocent explanations of the photo, and they suggested avenues for research to test those explanations.

Museum staff showed us other photographs of clergy and churches in close association with Nazi symbols. These photos included a church decorated with a swastika flag, an Archbishop shaking Hitler's hand under two swastika banners, and clergy giving Heil Hitler salutes. Each of the pictures could be explained in light of Nazi era pressures. The Nazi regime required churches to display flags on national memorial days. Clergy, like other Germans, were required to give Heil Hitler salutes, and some of them shook Hitler's hand on occasion without necessarily indicating agreement with him. None of the pictures showed a Catholic Bishop or priest blessing a swastika flag. Of the people we talked to at the Holocaust Museum, no one knew of any Bishop ever blessing a swastika.

We were impressed by the diversity of Museum staff. Dr. Suzanne Brown-Fleming, a Catholic, had written a book entitled *The Holocaust and Catholic Conscience* and was doing research into documents from the Vatican Archives. Dr. Victoria Barnett had authored a book on the Confessing Church in Nazi Germany. She also edited the works of Dietrich Bonhoeffer, the Lutheran Pastor in the Confessing Church who was killed at Hitler's command just days before the war ended. Dr. Jürgen Matthäus, a German, knew about *Der Sturmer* and its practice of publishing doctored photos for propaganda purposes. The doctored photos were relatively easy to spot, he said, and the swastika blessing photo did not look like one of them.

The research suggestions from Museum staff occupied our spare time for several months. The Museum housed a collection of microfilm reels of Vatican Archive documents from the Pontificate of Pope Pius XI. We made return visits to examine the documents from the early and mid-1930s. They showed the German Bishops resisting pressures during 1933, the first year of Hitler's regime, to approve swastika blessings. Apparently, the lack of historical references to any Catholic Bishop blessing a swastika was the result of deliberate policy decisions by the German Bishops.

Museum staff gave us introductions to other historians, including several Catholic experts on issues of the period. Consultations with experts led Steve back into the Harvard Library to read the extensive literature about the churches in the Nazi era. Among the primary source documents in the library, he found explicit policies of German Bishops Conferences *against* showing favor to the swastika. These dated from the mid-1920s and early 1930s as well as 1933. There was nothing to show swastika blessings were authorized in 1934 or later years.

So why would Vatican authorities countenance a swastika blessing in fall 1934 or promote a swastika-blessing Archbishop in 1935? No one had an answer.

5. The World War II Restitution Case

Some of the staff at the Holocaust Museum were interested in the story of how Steve came upon the photograph. Anyone could be excused for wondering why someone would browse through *Der Sturmer*. As the American counsel in an international World War II restitution case, Steve was doing research in the Harvard Library. His clients were the American grandchildren of a Czech industrialist named Jan Antonin Bata. Steve was researching how their grandfather was attacked as a Jew in the Nazi press during the 1930s. The case gave him an opportunity to use his German in the course of his legal work.

Jan Bata was not, in fact, Jewish. He was Catholic. So were his ancestors, shoemakers for generations in the Moravian town of Zlin. Today Moravia is the eastern half of the Czech Republic. Together with Bohemia and its capital city of Prague, the provinces of Moravia and Slovakia comprised the nation of Czechoslovakia, formed in 1918. Much of the impetus for the new nation came from Czechs and Slovaks in America.

Self-determination for such ethnic groups in the defeated Austro-Hungarian Empire was an idea that American President Woodrow Wilson pressed at the Paris Peace Conference after World War One. The first President of Czechoslovakia, Thomas Masaryk, was married to an American citizen and made a declaration of Czechoslovak independence from Independence Hall in Philadelphia.

Why did the Nazi press attack Jan Bata as a Jew? Nothing personal, a Nazi official told him in the late 1930s, after the damage was done. Bata stood at the forefront of Czech and Slovak entrepreneurship in the 1930s. Astonishingly, he expanded the Bata shoe enterprise six-fold in the Great Depression. By the end of the decade he had over 100,000 employees in more than 100 countries. By branding him as a Jew, the Nazis subjected Bata's German operations to their nationwide boycotts of Jewish businesses.

Bata reacted against the Nazis in two noteworthy ways. First, he gave "no surrender" speeches in Czechoslovakia during the lead-up to the Munich Conference of 1938. Munich was where British Prime Minister Neville Chamberlain gave fresh meaning to "appeasement" by giving the Sudetenland to Hitler. The Sudetenland consisted of the ethnically German border regions of Czechoslovakia. It also contained the defensive perimeter of forts that Bata had exhorted his countrymen to defend.

The second thing Jan Bata did, soon after Munich, was help his Jewish employees get out of harm's way. The Bata company gave dozens of its employees new positions in far-off locations, from the Americas to India to Singapore. Bata paid for the families to travel and provided stipends for them to start new lives. By March 15, 1939, when Hitler invaded and took over in one day what still remained of Czechoslovakia, all but a couple of Bata's Jewish employees were safely working abroad.

Bata's relations with the British Government that sold out his country did not mend well. In 1940 the British put him and his company on their blacklist. The United States followed suit even before entering the war. Bata ended up in exile in Brazil. As Communist elements were vying for power back in Czechoslovakia in 1947, a Czech court condemned Jan Bata in absentia as a Nazi collaborator. The verdict enabled the confiscation of all his business and personal property with no compensation.

In 2007, the Czech Government reversed the conviction and restored Jan Bata's reputation, though not his property. Steve learned of this while waiting for a jury to return its verdict in a case he was trying in Springfield, Massachusetts. He was with two grandsons of Jan Bata through two weeks of trial. They were working at a small Lexington company that was battling a major international tech company over trademark rights. Diane had already heard their story, because she was the scheduling and logistics coordinator for our side, working with all the witnesses.

Bata, it turned out, was also a familiar name at the Holocaust Museum. The reference librarian, a Czech-American, was aware of the Bata heritage. So was a Holocaust survivor who regularly came to share her experiences with Museum visitors. Her brother worked for Bata at one point in the 1930s.

The story of Bata's actions to save Jewish employees and their families long went unpublicized because of the stigma of his post-war conviction. Pieces of the story are still coming to light. For example, Tom Stoppard, the Academy Award-winning scriptwriter and playwright, escaped from Zlin, Czechoslovakia on March 15, 1939 with his parents and older brother. His father, a key doctor at the Bata hospital in Zlin, had not left with other Jewish employees. The invading German Army took great efforts starting early on March 15th to prevent anyone from leaving Czech territory. Bata's effort to get his own wife and children across the border to Poland that day failed. Somehow an effort to get one of the last remaining Jewish employees out, with his wife and two young sons, succeeded.

6. Publishing a Historical Article ...

At the urging of Holocaust Museum historians, Steve turned the central elements of our research into an article. It was nothing lengthy. Just enough to present the photograph in its basic historical context. We expected historians would take it from there. They could analyze the controversial issues that radiated out from the basic facts.

The first part of the context was Argentina. Argentina's history before the 1930s differed from our expectations. Argentina had constitutional democratic government, with freedoms of speech, press, assembly and religion, patterned on the U.S. Constitution, from the 1870s through the 1920s. Military coups and financial collapses were not a feature of those years.

By 1929, Argentina was among the most prosperous nations in the world, measured by per capita income. Economic opportunity, combined with religious freedom, made it an attractive destination for Jews fleeing persecution in turn-of-the-century Czarist Russia. The Argentine Government actively encouraged Jews and others to immigrate in large numbers.

Argentina changed drastically during the 1930s. That decade, known to Argentines as the "Década Infame," or infamous decade, began with a military coup. The mid-1930s saw a veritable explosion of antisemitic propaganda. Jewish immigration was effectively halted. By the 1940s Argentina became a welcoming destination for Nazis rather than for Jews.

What role, if any, did Cardinal Copello play in these changes? Histories of Argentina said little about him. There was no indication that he made antisemitic or pro-Nazi statements. But the explosion of antisemitic propaganda occurred in large measure in Catholic publications. Some of the authors were priests under Copello's authority. Was he asleep at the switch? Or pulling levers behind the scenes? We did not know. Did his swastika blessing signal a need for more research into his role? Steve's article left that for historians to assess.

The second part of the context was Germany. The article described the German Bishops' policies against blessing swastikas and allowing them into churches. Bishops' policies from the mid-1920s to the early 1930s condemned Nazi ideology and forbade Catholics to join the Nazi Party. A group of Bishops denounced the swastika in 1931 as "the battle standard against the cross of Christ."

Even when the Nazis came to power in 1933 and their flag began to fly jointly with the German tricolor, the German Bishops resisted pressures to authorize Church blessings of swastika flags. The article presented the German Bishops' stance as the probable reason why there were no pictures of German Catholic swastika blessings. The article also posed the question about the ceremony in Buenos Aires: Why did a Bishop there, far removed from Nazi pressures, do what his brother Bishops in Germany steadfastly refused to do?

The article also addressed the question, why would Nazis *want* swastika blessings? Hitler encountered early resistance to the swastika flag. When he tried to make it the national flag in March 1933, two months after becoming German Chancellor, President Hindenburg and Vice Chancellor Papen stopped him. At a Cabinet meeting, they invoked the memory of the millions of Germans who fought and died under the tricolor in World War One. For the next 30 months, even though Hitler gained absolute dictatorial power, he did not decree the swastika the national flag. An authoritative-looking photo of a Roman Catholic swastika blessing, displayed nationwide two months before the swastika was decreed the German national flag on September 15, 1935, was certainly helpful for paving the way.

The final questions Steve's article posed for historians concerned the Vatican. What interactions did Cardinal Pacelli have with Copello in Buenos Aires? What Vatican policies in the mid-1930s could possibly explain Pope Pius XI countenancing a swastika blessing by an Archbishop, much less elevating him to Cardinal? As with the other questions, we intended to leave these to historians. When Steve finished the article, we both felt we had finished our inquiry into the photograph.

7.   ...or Not

Holocaust Museum historians put us in touch with two journals that seemed appropriate for publishing the article. One was a Church History quarterly. Its staff replied, however, that it was too late to get the article into their next issue. The other was a journal on Jewish-Catholic relations co-edited by Father Kevin Spicer, who has written on both the dark side and the brighter side of Catholic clergy in Nazi Germany. He encouraged Steve to submit the article for publication in his journal. Father Spicer quickly sent it out for peer review by two historians. We eagerly awaited their comments.

The results were not what we expected. One reviewer wanted to trim the article to focus only on German policy toward the swastika, "rather than try to provide an analysis of Pacelli and Copello." That would remove the most historically significant issues, at least as it seemed to us. Eugenio Pacelli had advanced a major step toward Catholic sainthood in December 2009, when Pope Benedict XVI signed a decree certifying his "heroic virtues." Shouldn't a historical article present questions about him *before* that process advanced further? The alternative was to risk a supreme embarrassment to Catholics if Cardinal Pacelli were found complicit in the swastika blessing *after* being declared a saint.

The other peer reviewer objected to our assumption that the Archbishop was really blessing the swastika flag. "Maybe he is but I cannot see it." This reviewer insisted that other sources must be found describing the photo, rather than relying only on the infamous *Der Sturmer*. Father Spicer agreed. He informed us, accordingly, that unless we did extensive further research, including in Argentina, the journal could not publish the article.

We knew this was a show-stopper. One of our children, during a two-month Spanish immersion program in Buenos Aires, had looked at all the newspapers from the time of the Eucharistic Congress. None of them contained anything like a photograph of a swastika blessing ceremony. If publishing required other sources than *Der Sturmer* to confirm the photograph, we were facing an insuperable obstacle.

Steve set about to change what he could, in response to the peer reviewers, hoping to negotiate an agreement to publish some scaled-back version of the article. Diane expressed concern about protracted delays in getting the photo and related issues into public view.

8. Self-Publish Online!

Surely, Diane urged, there must be a way in the Internet age to present the photograph to the public. With basic information about the historical context, anyone, whether a historian or not, could consider the issues. That could open up discussion, lead to new sources, and identify further information. Steve was skeptical about publishing the photo online. Anything about Nazis will be relegated to the fever swamps, he assumed, unless validated by a trusted academic or mainstream source. When Steve asked several historians about it, they reinforced his aversion to self-publishing online.

Diane persisted. Her experience developing the online website for victims and witnesses of crime had alerted her to the value of interactive communication over the Internet. She was convinced that Internet self-publishing, with opportunity for interactive comments, was the way to proceed with the photograph. So, with help from a tech-savvy son, Steve published the photo online with several pertinent questions:

Could anyone find a source, perhaps in Germany or Argentina, mentioning this photograph or event?

What mitigating factors might be relevant? A doctored photo, a blessing of many national flags without distinction, an unawareness of the threat of Nazism at a relatively early stage in its development, etc.

We published the photo and questions online in October 2010, and this early stage effort can still be viewed today. It was easy to share a link to it, by email, with historians and other interested persons. These included a number of Catholic writers known to Steve from his Reagan Administration days in Washington, and since.

Soon we received a suggestion from two Catholic friends: Share the link with Ron Rychlak. Steve had read *Hitler, the War, and the Pope* by American law professor Ronald Rychlak. It was the most detailed defense of the reputation of Pope Pius XII published up to that time. An email produced a courteous response and led to a telephone conversation shortly afterwards. Professor Rychlak passed along some thoughts about the photo from Father Peter Gumpel and suggested that Steve talk directly with Father Gumpel.

Father Gumpel's name is recognizable to anyone familiar with the literature about Pope Pius XII and the Catholic Church during the Nazi era. A German Jesuit based in Rome, Father Gumpel has been centrally involved in the canonization process for Pius XII over the past several decades. Books both favorable and unfavorable to Pope Pius XII include acknowledgements of the generous time and assistance given to researchers by Father Gumpel.

Within less than a week of his talk with Professor Rychlak, Steve received a call from Rome. It was Father Gumpel. His English was flawless, and his thoughts were well-organized and clearly presented. There were many reasons not to be troubled by the photo, he said, many reasons why it did not affect the reputation of Eugenio Pacelli or the reputation of Cardinal Copello:

It is doubtful that Copello knew much about the Nazis and their dangers at this point in time, a little more than a year after Hitler came to power.

It was four years before the Anschluss in which Germany took over Austria, five years before Germany invaded Czechoslovakia.

It is possible that someone from the German Embassy gave this flag to the pilgrim group, who put it in front of the Cardinal.

Quite likely the Cardinal was unaware of what it was, and unanticipated things can happen in such circumstances. Living in Argentina, Copello was thousands of miles removed from events in Europe. Moreover, his concern may have been simply not to cause a scene by refusing a courtesy to a group of foreign visitors.

The swastika was not the national flag of Germany at the time. It did not become that until 1935.

The photograph could have been doctored. *Der Sturmer* doctored photographs on some occasions, and this could have been one of them.

It is absolutely certain that Cardinal Copello did not intend to bless Nazism. There is no indication that he had any sympathy with Nazi or Communist dictatorships.

This may have been a trick to give the impression of a Catholic Bishop approving the swastika, when the Bishops in Germany had said no to the swastika.

These seemed to be plausible arguments, calmly and persuasively presented. Father Gumpel described his role with the Vatican. He was a consultant for 12 years before being named by Pope John Paul II in 1983 as the investigating judge in the sainthood cause of Pope Pius XII. He was not an advocate. He was obligated to be impartial. "If I had ever found anything to make me hesitant, I would not have signed" to further the cause of Pius XII. "I never found anything."

9. The Photo Is Authenticated

As we continued into 2011, following various research paths in our spare time, Father Gumpel's points were ever-present in our minds. They helped focus the inquiry.

Steve had been working on his Spanish and Italian. One of our sons, who learned French from Steve, spurred him on. Steve's Italian had been good enough to meet our needs on two family trips to Italy, and he had taught introductory Spanish to some of our children. When Steve asked for help from two sons who studied Italian and Spanish in college, he got a strong reaction from his former French student. Come on Dad, once you know French, Italian and Spanish are easy. Get to work.

Spanish was the essential language for looking into several of Father Gumpel's points. Steve examined what Argentine Catholics knew about the swastika and Nazism in the early and mid-1930s from journals of the time. The Harvard Library had two very useful sources for that purpose. One was a glossy Argentine weekly magazine, *Caras y Caretas*, comparable to *Time* magazine. *Caras y Caretas* covered Germany in surprising detail. The Night of the Long Knives received a two-page pictorial spread, showing which top Nazi figures were killed, and which remained in power. The Nazi assassination of Austrian ruler Engelbert Dollfuss in July 1934 received equally dramatic play, with a pictorial depiction of the murder. The tone in both cases was shock at Nazi brutality.

The second source was a Catholic weekly journal, *Criterio*, published in Buenos Aires. One scholarly work describes it as a semi-official publication of the Archdiocese of Buenos Aires. *Criterio* covered events in European countries regularly and extensively, as if they were next door. Germany, France, Spain and Italy received far more coverage than any of the countries of Latin America.

Criterio attacked Hitler before he came to power, describing him as a demagogue opposed to human rights, natural law, and Christian morality. In June 1933, five months after Hitler came to power, *Criterio* wrote that Catholics in Germany had no obligation to obey Nazi authorities in their policies of "racial purification and hegemony."

Criterio was equally clear on the meaning of Hitler's swastika as early as 1932: "His cross is the swastika, and this cross is anti-Christian, for it is opposed by its design and by its spirit to the Catholic symbol of redemption."

On August 30, 1934, *Criterio's* front page was devoted to a passionate denunciation of Hitler's Night of the Long Knives and the Nazis' murder of "the great Austrian chancellor," Engelbert Dollfuss. "The shooting of the President of Catholic Action of Berlin, Klausener, and of other Catholics, the imprisonment of dozens of priests, the closing of nearly all the press, the destruction of the youth associations, have taken matters to the extreme of a real persecution."

Argentine Catholics, as it turned out, were better informed about Nazi Germany than Father Gumpel posited or we expected. The detailed Argentine coverage of German events in mid-1934, by secular and Catholic Argentine journals, made it hard to understand why Archbishop Copello would bless a swastika flag just weeks later. So was it a doctored photo?

It was soon after Steve translated these passages from Argentine journals that Diane decided to come along on a business trip to Washington, DC. It was a three-day trip with two of Jan Bata's grandsons to the National Archives. Diane had already helped Steve in their World War II restitution case. Now, as the men pored through boxes of World War II-era documents at the National Archives in College Park, Maryland, Diane took a side trip to the Library of Congress in downtown Washington.

Approaching a reference librarian in the periodical reading room of the Madison Building, Diane asked if the Library of Congress had any newspapers from Argentina in the 1930s. Learning that *La Prensa* and *La Nacion* were in the Library's collection, she ordered the microfilm rolls for October 1934. Soon she was looking at *La Prensa*. Steve had suggested she start with October 1st and continue on through the Eucharistic Congress days of October 9 to 14.

Diane's Spanish was limited to what she learned with our youngest children from beginner's Spanish CDs. But she was able to recognize four words in a small headline on page 12 of *La Prensa's* October 1st edition. "Benedicas" looked like the word for "blessing" in Latin, a language Diane had studied in college. "Aleman" looked like the word for "German" in French, a language she had also studied. "Las Banderas" was right out of the children's CD, "B is for bandera." And "Copello" was, sure enough, Archbishop Copello. There was no photograph of a swastika blessing. But the full headline read, "The Flags of the German Section of the Congress Were Blessed by Archbishop Copello."

The text of the article concisely described a formal, obviously deliberate, preplanned ceremony:

> In the sober setting of the Church of St. Ignatius, yesterday shortly before noon, occurred the blessing of the flags and standards of the German delegation to the Eucharistic Congress, which were displayed in the great ceremonies of an international gathering. The former colonial edifice had been decorated for the occasion with red drapes and Argentine flags, and the main altar was brightly illuminated with candelabras and lights.
>
> During a mass, in which a choir performed a program of sacred music, a sermon was given by Father Jacob Wagner, president of the German delegation to the Congress. After prayers, seats facing the main altar were occupied by the Minister Plenipotentiary of Germany, Mr. von Thermann, and by the sponsors designated to act in the consecration of flags, the Argentine flag, the German flag, and the Pontifical flag, as well as the red flag with swastika and pendant, which had been placed in the sanctuary.
>
> Moments later Monsignor Copello, Archbishop of Buenos Aires, recited the customary prayers to consecrate the flags, and then solemnly blessed the faithful with the Most Blessed Sacrament. With this and a hymn sung by the congregation, the event came to an end.

So, the photograph was not doctored. It was not a spur-of-the-moment courtesy or indiscretion. *Der Sturmer's* notorious editor had gotten only one small element wrong. The ceremony was not "at the Cathedral"; it was at the *former* Cathedral. St. Ignatius is the oldest church in Buenos Aires. The rest of the caption was accurate. But how could such a ceremony come to pass? *Why* would Archbishop Copello do it?

10. Vatican Policy Toward Nazi Germany in 1934

The central question concerned not just Archbishop Copello but his superiors as well. Why would Pope Pius XI and his Secretary of State take the first Bishop known to bless a swastika, and make him the first Cardinal of Spanish-speaking South America? How could a deliberate swastika blessing in September 1934, three months after the Night of the Long Knives, two months after the Nazi assassination of Dollfuss, and the very month after Hitler's usurpation of absolute power in Germany, be regarded by Copello's superiors as anything but an outrage?

We had followed up Father Gumpel's statements about Copello's likely state of knowledge and disposition toward Nazism by examining the semi-official journal *Criterio* from his Buenos Aires Archdiocese. What could we learn about the disposition of his superiors by looking at documents and publications issued by or supervised by the Holy See?

Widener Library at Harvard had three primary sources that were relevant. First was a three-volume set of diplomatic notes between the Vatican and the German Government, beginning in 1933. Almost all the Vatican's notes were signed by Cardinal Pacelli. Second was the Vatican's own daily newspaper, *L'Osservatore Romano*, meaning *Roman Observer*. Widener had a set of yellowed but well-preserved hard copies from the 1930s.

Third was a twice-monthly journal, *La Civiltà Cattolica*, meaning *Catholic Civilization*, published in Rome by a select community of Jesuit priests. Ever since the journal began in the mid-19th century, the content of each issue has been supervised by the Vatican Secretary of State in a formalized pre-publication review process. Because of that supervision, *Catholic Civilization* is an influential source in the Catholic world.

In addition, there was the U.S. Holocaust Memorial Museum's sizeable collection of 1930s documents on microfilm from the Vatican Secret Archives. These were mostly cables and other communiqués between the Vatican's Berlin and Munich Nunciatures, or embassies, on the one hand, and the Vatican Secretariat of State on the other.

Patterns emerged from these documents. In the first half of 1934, the Vatican protested many Nazi regime actions. Cardinal Pacelli sent an average of three protest notes per month. He spent six days in face-to-face negotiations trying to secure a German Government commitment to protect Catholic associations.

The Vatican-Germany Concordat of July 1933 was supposed to protect the Church in Germany, but Hitler was not honoring it. Pope Pius XI said of the associations, "their cause is Our cause," and his words appeared in *Catholic Civilization*. The pages of that journal and the *Roman Observer* also featured repeated attacks on Nazi neo-pagan ideology.

One of Cardinal Pacelli's diplomatic notes, in May 1934, backed the German Bishops in their resistance to the swastika. He complained to the German Government that the swastika was connected with "meanings and missions whose anti-Christian tendency offends the faithful." The Bishops themselves wrote a joint pastoral letter in early June, registering complaints against Nazi propaganda and neo-pagan ideology. They made a point to tell Catholics that obedience to government stops short of requiring violations of conscience and God's commandments. When German Vice Chancellor Papen critiqued Nazi excesses in a speech that same month, the *Roman Observer* and *Catholic Civilization* gave him prime coverage.

Finally, in the last week of June, the German Bishops reached agreement with Hitler and his top officials for implementation of the Concordat. Purely religious associations would be protected, provided they were under the umbrella of Catholic Action, an overarching group controlled by the Bishops. Hitler agreed to stop anti-Catholic, neo-pagan propaganda.

The ink was barely dry on the June 29, 1934 agreement when Hitler struck in the Night of the Long Knives. The targeted killing of the Berlin-based head of Catholic Action made a mockery of the Nazi regime's agreement, the day before, to protect that association.

Despite Hitler's attacks on multiple Catholic association leaders, on Papen's Catholic staff, and on other prominent German Catholics, the Vatican refrained from protest. Cardinal Pacelli made no diplomatic protests over the murders. The Vatican newspaper did not criticize Hitler. It published the Nazi regime's justifications for the bloodbath without question or caveat. It repeatedly printed descriptions of overwhelming popular support for Hitler in Germany. *Catholic Civilization* followed a similar approach, mentioning the killing of Catholic leaders only in a footnote.

The pattern developed further in late July when the Nazi coup attempt in Austria killed the Catholic ruler of that country. Instead of criticizing Hitler, the *Roman Observer* and *Catholic Civilization* gave front page coverage to his ploy to quell international outrage. Three days after the assassination, Hitler appointed Germany's most prominent Catholic layman, Vice Chancellor Papen, as his new ambassador to Austria. The *Roman Observer* published

"Hitler's Letter to the 'Most Esteemed' von Papen" in full on the front page. *Catholic Civilization* reported that a "great impression" was made by Hitler's appointment of Papen and by Hitler's expressions of peaceful intent toward Austria.

The pattern continued in August when Hitler usurped absolute dictatorial power, upon the death of President Hindenburg. While Hitler had come to power constitutionally, he now abrogated the Weimar Constitution and became the country's "Führer." The Vatican's newspaper described his absolute power, but did not criticize. *Catholic Civilization* mentioned Hitler's "radical modification of the constitution," but also did not criticize. German Bishops continued taking the Concordat's oath of loyalty and obedience to the "constitutionally formed government," even though Hitler's absolute dictatorship made it anything but constitutionally formed.

Equally surprising was the pattern that appeared in September 1934. The *Roman Observer* covered the Nazi Party's annual "Congress" in Nuremberg that month in glowing terms. Articles puffed Hitler personally, every day for a week. Church bells rang for him. A paean of "eternal gratitude" to Hitler by a Nazi official was featured. The front page described Hitler's "vibrant appeal to loyalty, discipline, obedience and devotion" from his Nazi leaders, with no reminder that he had recently decimated them. In the days immediately following the Congress, the Vatican Ambassador in Berlin exchanged publicized visits with Hitler.

The most notoriously pro-Nazi priest in Germany, a Benedictine Abbot named Albanus Schachleiter, attended the Nazi Party Congress and was photographed with Hitler.

In the midst of its coverage of the Congress, the *Roman Observer* began to present a pro-Nazi Bishop, Alois Hudal, as a favored spokesman about Germany. On September 28th, a lengthy article conveyed Bishop Hudal's message that Germany has a "mission," to be a "trusted bulwark against Bolshevism."

A photograph appeared inside the article. It was Cardinal Pacelli aboard ship, departing for the Eucharistic Congress in Buenos Aires. Hudal is better known for helping Nazi war criminals escape Europe after World War II, and for boasting about it, than for close association with the Vatican in the 1930s.

In October 1934, Bishop Hudal met personally with Pope Pius XI and discussed his idea of Nazi Germany's "providential mission." A *Catholic Civilization* article in November portrayed Bishop Hudal as a great German patriot. That probably enhanced his credibility in Nazi Germany. He was actually a life-long Austrian citizen.

In October and November, *Catholic Civilization* ran a two-part series on Nazi antisemitism. The articles criticized German antisemites for their attacks on Catholicism, but not for their antsemitism.

Then, in December, the *Roman Observer* praised a new book by Bishop Hudal for showing the "congruence and harmony, rather than division and irreconcilability," between the Catholic Church and the German "race." The book said German Catholics have a religious obligation to obey and serve the authorities of Nazi Germany. Bishop Hudal longed for the German and Vatican flags together to "wave over the whole German country." This would bring an "auspicious future" to the "German *Volk*." The word *Volk* means "people" in German, but in Nazi usage it meant Aryans only, with no Jews included.

In mid-January 1935, shortly after Catholic Bishops helped produce an overwhelming majority vote in favor of Nazi Germany in an important referendum in the Saar District, Pope Pius XI wrote a letter to Hitler. The content of the letter confirms that the pattern of friendly outreach to Hitler and the Nazi regime over the preceding months was in line with his own thoughts. The Pope wrote the letter in German, addressing Hitler as "Du," the familiar term of address that Germans reserve for close friends and family. Saying he wanted "true peace" between Church and State in Germany, the Pope concluded the letter with a promise: "We will most eagerly strive that, after overcoming the still existing difficulties, so far as it is within Our power, Your desire for the common good will be crowned with auspicious success."

11. Cardinal Pacelli's Outreach in Buenos Aires

Cardinal Pacelli conducted an outreach of his own in Buenos Aires. In a historical work that mentions Archbishop Copello, Steve found a passing reference to Cardinal Pacelli relating to German Ambassador Edmund von Thermann during the Eucharistic Congress in Buenos Aires. Von Thermann, a German Baron, was described in the book as a conspicuously enthusiastic Nazi and an officer in the SS. Thermann made a splash when he arrived in Argentina in December 1933. His predecessor was highly regarded, but the Nazi regime fired him for being Jewish. Thermann was greeted by pro-Nazi Germans as he debarked from his ocean liner in Buenos Aires wearing his SS uniform. Together they sang the Horst Wessel song, the Nazi anthem named for an SA thug who died in a street fight.

Thermann set to work "harmonizing" the many German associations in Argentina to the Nazi agenda. His wife did the same with German women's groups. They were effective enough to draw considerable attention. The daily German language newspaper in Argentina, *Argentinisches Tageblatt*, which was anti-Nazi, openly opposed the Thermanns' endeavors.

On the same trip to the National Archives that occasioned Diane's visit to the Library of Congress, Steve requested documents about Thermann. Soon he was looking at official U.S. interrogation reports from the second half of 1945. Thermann returned to Germany before the end of World War II and was captured by the Allies at the war's end. Thermann told his interrogator about his goals as ambassador. One of his goals was "to establish good relations with the Catholic Church."

Thermann said his relations with the Church were "somewhat strained" until the Eucharistic Congress. But when Cardinal Pacelli visited Buenos Aires, he "attracted wide attention by inviting the Thermanns to social functions and conversing with them in fluent German." This established Ambassador Thermann's relationship with the Catholic Church. Thermann said that after the Congress "Archbishop Copello had been a frequent visitor to the German Embassy." Thermann also said he put a German Junkers airplane at Cardinal Pacelli's disposal.

Thermann is not exactly what we would consider a trustworthy witness. But we found two confirmations of his credibility on these points. As to establishing a relationship with Archbishop Copello, a second interrogation report proved decisive. The report, based on documents from the German

Embassy to Argentina, showed that the newspaper *El Pueblo* received regular German propaganda subsidies. *El Pueblo* was the Catholic daily newspaper of Buenos Aires. A scholarly work on the Catholic Church in Argentina identifies it as a semi-official publication of the Archdiocese.

Second, Thermann's claim about the Junkers airplane is confirmed by photographs. In the copies of Argentine newspaper pages Diane made at the Library of Congress, a photograph shows Cardinal Pacelli climbing out of a seaplane. A similar photograph can be seen in the Official Proceedings of the Congress. The corrugated metal fuselage and other features of the plane readily identify it as a Junkers JU-52.

Why would the visiting Papal Legate go out of his way to fraternize with a notoriously enthusiastic Nazi and SS officer? Thermann wasn't even a Catholic. The SS were Hitler's lead hit men in the Night of the Long Knives. Hitler publicly promoted the SS and its head, Heinrich Himmler, in July 1934, in grateful recognition of their murderous services.

And why accept a public favor from such a figure as Thermann? Savvy diplomats do not do such things lightly. One aspect that all writers about Eugenio Pacelli agree on, from the severest critics to the fondest admirers, is that he was the savviest of diplomats.

12. What Have Historians Said About This?

Widely read historical works about the Nazi era, from William Shirer's *The Rise and Fall of the Third Reich* (1960) to Erik Larson's *In the Garden of Beasts* (2011), pay little if any attention to church-related issues. The same is true of Hitler biographies by authors such as Bullock, Fest, Kershaw, Toland, and Wilson. So it is not surprising that these authors have little or nothing to say about Vatican policy toward Germany during the mid-1930s.

It is more surprising that books about the churches during the Nazi era overlook the pattern we found in September 1934 to early 1935. There are dozens of these books, and Steve has examined all the ones he could find in English, German, French and Italian. None of them mention the pattern of Vatican outreach to Hitler and Nazi Germany. Many authors say the German Bishops, and other religious leaders, made no protest about the Night of the Long Knives. But they do not mention what the Vatican *did* to favor Hitler and Nazi Germany in the months following that event, much less analyze why the Vatican did it.

A number of historians have written about Vatican efforts to reach a *modus vivendi* with Nazi Germany at other points during the 1930s. They generally understand those efforts to flow from a concern to protect Catholics in Germany. John Cornwell, a severe critic of Eugenio Pacelli, argues he was working to enhance Vatican power over the Catholic Church in Germany. But Cornwell's *Hitler's Pope* does not accuse Pacelli of embracing Nazi ideology or promoting a "mission" for Nazi Germany. Even though Cornwell covers Pacelli in Buenos Aires at some length, he does not mention Thermann. The only history we found that does mention Pacelli's interaction with Thermann focuses only on Argentina, not on Vatican policy.

One historical work stands out for its detailed focus on Vatican policy toward Nazi Germany in the mid-1930s. A work of seemingly meticulous German scholarship, its German title describes its subject: "The Position of the Vatican toward National Socialism as Reflected in the *Roman Observer*." The book focuses at great length on the *Roman Observer's* criticism of Nazi measures hostile to the Church, including the articles Steve found in the first half of 1934: calling out the Nazi regime for neo-paganism, anti-Christian propaganda, and attacks on Catholic associations and schools.

But the book tells nothing of the Vatican newspaper's coverage of the Nazi Party Congress, or its favorable treatment of Hitler, in September 1934.

The author mentions one of the three articles promoting Bishop Hudal, the one in December 1934. But he says only that the *Roman Observer* praised Hudal for critiquing Nazi neo-paganism. The author, Fritz Sandmann, does not mention the Vatican's praise for Hudal's concept of mutual compatibility between Roman Catholicism and the "German race." Nor does he touch upon the Vatican newspaper's promotion of Nazi Germany's "mission."

Herr Sandmann's book may help explain why historians have missed the disturbing pattern we found. His work certainly appears scholarly. Historians have cited and relied on it through the decades since it appeared in 1965. That is how Steve first came across it, in a historian's citation to the Italian translation of Sandmann's book. No one has done a similar study that we could find. Historians tend to rely on each other's books and articles rather than duplicate each other's in-depth research. Dissertation topics, like law review articles, are considered to be pre-empted if a scholarly work has already covered the topic in detail.

13. Vatican Policy Toward Nazi Germany in 1935

What about 1935? The swastika blessing photograph appeared in July that year. Archbishop Copello was announced as a new Cardinal in November. He was formally raised to that title in December at a Consistory in Rome, a special meeting of the Cardinals with the Pope. What do Vatican-supervised publications tell about Vatican policy during that period of time?

The very next issue of *Catholic Civilization* that the Vatican reviewed and approved after the photo appeared in July 1935 featured an article entitled "Gold, Money and the Jews." It was an enthusiastic review of a new two-part Argentine novel. *El Kahal* and its sequel *Oro* incorporated the basic themes of the *Protocols of the Elders of Zion* and presented them in a fresh and terrifying manner to the people of Argentina.

The invidious message of these books, published simultaneously in 1935, is apparent to anyone who gives them a casual glance. The cover of *El Kahal* features a serpent, the symbol used in the infamous *Protocols* to represent the "worldwide Jewish conspiracy" that aims to destroy Christian civilization and take over the world. The title page quoted the *Protocols* to explain the serpent to the uninitiated: "A little longer and the Serpent, the symbol of our people, will tighten its coils and strangle all the nations."

El Kahal made the message of the *Protocols* more contemporary and more dangerous by presenting the Jewish world conspiracy as *Communist*. The antisemitic propagandists behind the original *Protocols*, writing more than a decade before the Russian Revolution, branded the Jewish world conspiracy "Masonic," with the Jews controlling the Freemasons. The Communist aspect in *El Kahal* lent immediacy and power to the Jewish peril. The book's introduction sums up its message about Judaism and revolution:

The Jew foments it, directs it, subsidizes it, and after making a *tabula rasa* of the Christian state, suffocates it and installs himself in the empty capital, to govern under the inspiration of the Kahal, the precursor of the Antichrist. The Russian Revolution is a current and complete example.

The introduction also presents the final solution: "And this is the reason that among all the peoples, the cry 'death to the Jew!' has almost always been synonymous with 'long live the Fatherland!' Because two nationalities cannot coexist in the same nation."

In a five-page article, reviewed by the Vatican Secretariat of State according to the long-established review process, *Catholic Civilization* praised the two-part novel as "not unworthy to be compared with the *Utopia* of St. Thomas More." Author Hugo Wast, the journal affirmed, was a "profound believer." The article declared: "This is not an antisemitic novel."

That authoritative statement effectively shielded the book from criticism in Catholic Argentina. When a widely-read Catholic author in Argentina attacked the book as an invitation to massacre Jews, it was he who suffered, not the book. Manuel Gálvez was immediately sacked as a regular contributor to the leading Catholic journal in Buenos Aires, *Criterio*. *El Kahal* and *Oro* became best sellers. Authority and influence exerted from Rome had impact in far-off Argentina.

The next month, on September 15, 1935, the Vatican featured an endorsement of the Jewish-Communist conspiracy theory on the front page of its own newspaper. Under the heading "Goebbels Against Communism," the *Roman Observer* printed the Nazi propaganda chief's denunciation of Judaism as "the original cause of Bolshevism." It also published his accusation that "in all the countries where there are revolutionary disorders, the Communist tendency of the Jewish elements has played an important part in their preparation and their execution."

Rather than critique Goebbels' antisemitic conspiracy-mongering, the *Roman Observer* endorsed it. Invoking religious terminology about "mission" just as in 1934, the Vatican paper concluded its front page article with these words:

> Keeping up its battle against Communism without ceasing and without compromise, Germany and its leader are carrying out a mission that deserves the gratitude of all nations. The period of Communist revolution continues to be a menace for all peoples. Without proposing to intrude in the internal politics of any country or to give advice to any government, Germany raises its voice of warning to all nations against the gravity of the danger that Communism, of Jewish inspiration, represents for their culture and their existence.

This endorsement could not have come at a more fateful moment. September 15, 1935 was the day Nazi Germany enacted the "Nuremberg Laws." These laws consisted of three parts. The first part proclaimed the swastika the national flag of Germany. The second part stripped Jewish

Germans of their citizenship. And the third prohibited marriage and sexual relations between Jews and non-Jews in Germany.

Hitler, Goebbels and Göring all made speeches explaining that the main rationale for enacting the laws was the Jewish-Communist conspiracy that threatened Germany and all nations. Hitler said it was appropriate that the original symbol of the Nazi Party became the national flag that day, because the antisemitic laws fulfilled the original program of the Nazi Party. If the new laws did not suffice to protect Germany against the Jewish-Communist threat, Hitler declared, further steps would be taken.

The *Roman Observer* covered the implementation of the Nuremberg Laws in the following days and weeks in many short articles. None of them contained any criticism.

Meanwhile, Bishop Hudal came out with a new book in fall 1935. With an imprimatur dated September 24, 1935, the book endorsed the Jewish-Communist conspiracy theory in these terms:

> Wherever revolutions and governmental upheavals come to pass, Moscow has a hand in the act. It is the religious and moral dregs of Judaism, coming forth from Moscow today, that keep the Christian peoples of Europe in constant unrest, in order to prepare the way for the worldwide dominion of a race …

14. What Historians Have Said ... or Not

What have historians said about these materials from 1935? Historians recognize *El Kahal* as a book that did immense harm. A leading history of the *Protocols of the the Elders of Zion* describes how *El Kahal* popularized the invidious message of the *Protocols* in Argentina. The danger inherent in the *Protocols* is recognized in the U.S. Holocaust Memorial Museum exhibit called "A Dangerous Lie."

A history of Catholic antisemitism in Argentina describes the widespread dissemination of *El Kahal* and *Oro* and their impact in that country. This history also notes that the author of the novels served as Press and Publicity Chairman for the International Eucharistic Congress of 1934. Yet neither these histories, nor any others we have found, mention the *Catholic Civilization* article puffing *El Kahal*.

What about the Vatican's front-page endorsement of the Jewish-Communist conspiracy theory on the day the Nuremberg Laws were enacted? Steve reviewed more than three dozen histories that mention the Nuremberg Laws. Many of them say the churches, the German Bishops, and the Vatican were silent and made no protest. One historian who researched extensively in German Catholic Diocese archives in the 1960s, Guenter Lewy, describes a German priests' journal affirming the Nuremberg Laws. Lewy also describes Bishop Hudal approving the Nuremberg Laws as a "self-defense" measure. But neither Lewy nor any other historian mentions the Vatican newspaper's endorsement of the conspiracy theory on which Hitler and Goebbels based and justified those laws.

What about Herr Sandmann's study of Vatican policy as reflected in the *Roman Observer*? Sandmann says the Vatican took a position of "extreme reserve" toward the Nuremberg Laws. He does not mention the front-page endorsement of the Jewish-Communist conspiracy theory at all.

Obviously, there is a disconnect between what many historians have written and what the evidence shows. Nor is this an insignificant matter. The Nuremberg Laws were a crucial step in Nazi Germany's dehumanization of Jewish people. The Jewish-Communist conspiracy theory updated a "dangerous lie" and effectively weaponized it at a fateful time.

We found one historian who *did* describe Bishop Hudal as the Vatican's favored spokesman on issues concerning Nazi Germany in the mid and late 1930s. A French Sorbonne history professor, Annie Lacroix-Riz, identifies

Hudal as "the spokesman for the Vatican-Germany alliance" and a "protégé" of Cardinal Pacelli. But Steve noticed this professor's Wikipedia entry identifies her as a Communist. That scared him off from relying on her work. When we finally discussed the matter, however, we agreed that her personal viewpoints were immaterial. We were not trying to resolve issues by deciding which historians were most widely respected or politically correct. Leads to original documents and actual evidence were welcome from all sources.

The case of Bishop Hudal is a perfect example of the difference between relying on respected experts and going to the original sources. Three historians who are highly respected among their peers have described Hudal as being out of favor at the Vatican in the mid-1930s, or working at cross-purposes with Cardinal Pacelli, or free-lancing out of selfish ambition. But none of their works mention any of the articles in the *Roman Observer* and *Catholic Civilization* promoting Hudal as a favored spokesman on German issues in 1934 and 1935.

15. What to Do With the Evidence?

We had two different reactions as Steve described how much evidence so many historians had overlooked. His attitude was lawyerly, detached, bemused. He spoke of substandard performance by members of a profession. Historians had missed a lot of tricks. Diane, on the other hand, was not thinking in terms of card games. This material was looking increasingly important for understanding the Holocaust. Her reaction was outrage.

This was not the only difference in our reactions. Steve had one way of moving forward from this point, Diane had another. In June of 2011 he emailed Ronald Rychlak a summary of what we had found about the swastika blessing since his talk with Father Gumpel. He included his translation of the article Diane found in the Library of Congress, proving the photograph depicted a real and deliberate ceremony. He did not have an email address for Father Gumpel, but he knew Professor Rychlak was in close contact with the Jesuit priest. Months passed with no response.

During the summer, talking to a local parish priest, Steve got the idea to send the same material to our Archbishop. Cardinal Sean O'Malley of Boston is well-connected in the Vatican. The local priest gave Steve the email address for getting materials to the Cardinal. Again, he received no response.

So we agreed to Diane's idea and published more material online. What we published in October 2011 did not include the articles from the *Roman Observer* and *Catholic Civilization* in 1934 and 1935. Diane wanted to pursue another idea before we published that portion. This idea was to go to Germany and see what was there. Several of our past disagreements had been resolved by finding more evidence and reflecting together over original documents. Why not go to Munich, the birthplace of the Nazi Party, and see what can be found in its archives, museums and libraries?

16. A Nun Enters the Story

Steve did not need much persuading. He had wonderful memories of Munich. At age 17 he went there to play soccer with an American team against German boys. Four years later, as a Marine 2nd Lieutenant on leave, he spent two weeks immersed in German, mostly in Bavaria.

He never thought of the Nazi era on those trips, and no one in Germany mentioned it. Bavarians were exceptionally friendly to an American who spoke German. Even traveling alone, Steve repeatedly found himself seated with others in restaurants and having delightful conversations. Now he could show Diane Munich, together with his favorite tourist spot, Neuschwanstein, the fairy tale castle of Bavaria's "mad king," Ludwig II.

Diane had a special interest she wanted to pursue as well. She was intrigued by the only female who appeared in the histories and biographies we read. That was Josefina Lehnert, a Bavarian woman better known by the name she took as a nun, Sister Pascalina.

Pascalina began working as a housekeeper for Eugenio Pacelli in the Vatican Nunciature in Munich around 1918. She worked for him until his death in 1958, becoming also something of a personal secretary. In Rome she managed other nuns in his service, and is therefore sometimes called "Mother Pascalina." Various sources said Pascalina and Pacelli first met in the Swiss town of Rorschach. Looking it up on a map, Rorschach turned out to be near an especially picturesque part of Bavaria.

Rorschach has a beautiful location on the shore of Lake Constance, across the lake from the southwestern extremity of the German State of Bavaria. The train route from Munich goes first to the medieval Bavarian town of Lindau, on an island in Lake Constance connected by a railroad bridge, then through a short stretch of Austria, and then across the Swiss border to Rorschach. The place where Sister Pascalina was stationed as a nun was "Stella Maris" in Rorschach. A recent biographer of Eugenio Pacelli describes Stella Maris as a retreat house for convalescent priests, a "tranquil Swiss refuge," run by the Holy Cross of Menzingen order of nuns. From 1918 through the 1930s, Pacelli took his annual vacation at Stella Maris, typically for about a month, sometimes longer. Pascalina returned regularly to her sister nuns at Stella Maris while he vacationed there.

With this background from our reading, we expected an attractive resort on Lake Constance. Arriving at the Rorschach train station, however, we found that we needed to walk ten minutes or so inland and uphill to get to Stella Maris. Rather than a resort near the lake, it was a former girls' school, which had indeed been run by Pascalina's order.

We had read multiple sources stating that Stella Maris hosted vacationing priests, but vacationing at a girls' school wasn't a concept we had encountered before. There was nothing else noteworthy in the neighborhood except a former Benedictine monastery and boys' school. Down the hill was a parish church. We walked the neighborhood for half an hour praying the Rosary and visited the church. Then we returned to the totally charming town of Lindau and had a wonderful dinner at Valentin Restaurant on our 29th wedding anniversary.

On our way back to Munich the next day, we had the best possible visit to Neuschwanstein. A light snow fell during our walk up the mile-long carriage road from the bus stop to the castle. Riding the train back to Munich through the beautiful snow-covered Bavarian countryside, we felt refreshed and ready to head to the archives.

17. Consulting Experts in Archives

Munich's Institute for Contemporary History treated us graciously. The Director of the Institute arranged for an experienced archivist to spend several hours with us. After looking at our copy of the swastika blessing photo, the archivist went out from his office and returned with a bound volume of *Der Sturmer* containing each issue of 1935.

As we discussed the pages leading up to the swastika blessing in issue number 29 of that year, we marveled together at the impact of *Der Sturmer's* propaganda. We had all regarded it as just a scurrilous rag, but as we inspected it together, there was no denying its power as cleverly crafted propaganda. Coming to the photo, on page 5 of issue number 29, we found it remarkably vivid compared to our microfilm copy. In any *Sturmer* display case in July 1935, that photo would easily make an impression.

Paging further through the *Sturmer* for 1935, we found a special edition for the Nazi Party Congress of 1935. The theme throughout the special edition's two dozen pages was the Jewish-Communist world conspiracy. The fact that Joseph Stalin, a non-Jew, was the absolute dictator of the Soviet Union and the directing force of international Communism did not spoil the *Sturmer's* propaganda effort in the slightest.

The special edition featured a photo of Stalin with the caption: "The non-Jew Stalin: Comes from Georgia. He is not the dictator of the Soviet Union. He is, just like Lenin, an instrument in the hand of the Jews. The daughter of the Jew Kaganovich is his wife." On the same page, *Der Sturmer* placed a photograph of Stalin's henchman Lazar Kaganovich, with this caption: "The Jew Kaganovich: The real dictator of the Soviet Union."

We appreciated the archivist's openness about his family's history in the Nazi era. Steve shared his experience translating German General Erwin Rommel's book on infantry tactics, *Infanterie Greift An*. He found the book in the library of his alma mater, Yale University, while visiting in 1975, and used it to design infantry training exercises for his Marine unit. The archivist was familiar with the book and its usage by the military services of various countries. It turns out there are several English translations other than the one Steve created privately for use by 3rd Battalion, 6th Marines in 1976 under the title "Infantry in the Attack."

The next day we went, without pre-arrangements, to the Munich Archdiocesan Archive. It is located along Pacelli Street, in the midst of a high fashion shopping district, a block or so away from Cardinal Faulhaber Street. The Archive building used to be a convent. The frescoes on its pink ceiling present an odd mix of pagan and Catholic symbology.

When we showed the swastika blessing photo to an Archive staff member and explained our research interests, she summoned an archivist. The archivist kindly guided us through the approximately hundred-page index of the *Nachlass Faulhaber*. Meaning "Faulhaber Estate" or "Faulhaber Papers," this collection included many files potentially relevant to our inquiry. As the Archive's staff retrieved folders for us on such topics as "Flaggenfrage" or Flag Question, "Der Sturmer" and "Bishop Hudal," Steve got a broad overview of the contents of the Cardinal-Archbishop of Munich's file system. Meanwhile Diane, with no knowledge of German, prayed for insight about what to focus on. Finding a file related to "Pascalina" in the index, she requested it.

Cardinal Faulhaber's files contained important information going beyond anything we had gleaned from history books or historians. The contents of the Flag Question file showed there was a high level Church-State struggle over the swastika. In early 1934, the Nazi regime began to pressure churches to hoist the swastika flag along with the German tricolor on designated "patriotic days." These included the anniversary of Hitler coming to power on January 30, 1933 and Hitler's birthday in April. Along with other Bishops, Cardinal Faulhaber resisted, but his arguments appeared to be legalistic ones that carried no weight with the Nazis. The Cardinal's file contained a Prussian State law of 1929 providing that "for religious associations there is no obligation to display flags" on national memorial days. The passage was underlined by the Cardinal's distinctively broad marking pencil.

Nazi authorities responded in deferential terms of address that appeared to be a velvet glove around an iron fist. In the file was a letter of March 6, 1934 from a Bavarian official to the rector of the Munich Cathedral:

I have the honor to convey to Your Reverence the astonishment of Herr State Minister that on the occasion of the last flag display days (especially the political officials' oath-taking day) the churches displayed the church colors or the white-blue [Bavarian] colors without displaying the symbol of the new Germany, the swastika flag. This circumstance has occasioned very disagreeable scenes that, in consideration of the preservation of public order and security, may not recur.

Cardinal Faulhaber's files reflected the progression of this struggle further into 1934. The file showed two Bishops agreeing to the display of swastika flags, in Freiburg and Rottenburg. The Diocese of Mainz, by contrast, informed the Cardinal they were seeking the intervention of Nuncio Orsenigo and German Vice Chancellor Papen, to overcome Nazi regime pressure to display the swastika. A historian at the Holocaust Memorial Museum had pointed us to evidence of Nuncio Orsenigo's unavailing intervention, and we had seen historian Guenter Lewy's description of this struggle.

The documents in Cardinal Faulhaber's file highlighted the pressure that all German Bishops faced in 1934 on the "flag question." Under these circumstances, for an Archbishop at a high profile Eucharistic Congress to take the unprecedented step of blessing a swastika flag, and be photographed doing it, was not so much stepping on the toes of his brother German Bishops as cutting them off at the knees.

In his "*Der Sturmer*" folder, Cardinal Faulhaber had clippings of issues that embarrassed, caricatured, or attacked the Catholic Church. The swastika blessing issue might well have fit into that category, but it was not in the folder.

Steve only had time to glance quickly at three folders pertaining to Bishop Hudal. There was an invitation to Hudal's consecration as Bishop by Cardinal Pacelli in Rome in mid-1933. There was also a published sermon that Hudal sent to Faulhaber in late 1934. The title of the sermon jumped off the page: "The Fuhrer-ness [*Führertum*] of the Catholic Priesthood."

18. Sister Pascalina Is a Player

Meanwhile Diane found something in Cardinal Faulhaber's "Pascalina" file that she could understand. It was a copy of a receipt in English to a group of nuns in Clyde, Missouri for a sum of $4,075 "duly credited to my account with the 'Istituto per le Opere di Religione' in Vatican City for the purpose that is well known to you." It was signed by Sister Pascalina. The Istituto per le Opere di Religione, or Institute for the Works of Religion, is the official name of the Vatican Bank.

But what was the unstated purpose? What was a housekeeper doing sending receipts for American money? And what was this document doing in Cardinal Faulhaber's files in Munich?

Absorbed in the Flag Question file, Steve resisted Diane's increasing persistence. When he finally looked at the German and Italian documents in the Pascalina file, a story emerged that completely distracted Steve from what he had come to research. In 1947, Vatican "Sostituto," or Deputy Secretary of State, Giovanni Battista Montini, who later became Pope Paul VI (1963-1978), sent Cardinal Faulhaber a $3000 cash donation from a convent of German nuns in Missouri. Regulations of the Allied Occupation authorities in Germany, summarized in a memo in the Cardinal's file, prohibited Germans from using American dollars. They could neither use dollar bills nor foreign dollar-denominated bank accounts.

So Cardinal Faulhaber had to send the money back to Rome. He explained the situation in a letter to Archbishop Montini, who wrote back saying he had deposited the $3000 into Cardinal Faulhaber's account in the Vatican Bank.

In subsequent documents showing further donations from the American convent, several aspects stood out. First, it was no longer Cardinal Faulhaber's account but Sister Pascalina's that was used as the conduit for dollars from Missouri to Munich via Rome. That way the Cardinal perhaps avoided violating the Allies' currency regulations. Second, Pascalina appeared far more a real player than a mere functionary. This would be astonishing for any female in the Vatican, let alone one whose job description was housekeeper or secretary. She actually had Cardinal Spellman, well known to be the most powerful American Churchman at the time, asking *her* where he should direct donations. Third, the order of nuns in Missouri turned out to be one that Diane knew quite well.

At some point in the 1960s, some of the German nuns of the Benedictine Convent of Perpetual Adoration moved from their mother house in Clyde, Missouri to a large convent with an adjoining Byzantine basilica north of Chicago, next to Our Lady of the Lake Seminary in Mundelein, Illinois. Starting in 4th grade, Diane went with her family several times a week from their suburban Chicago home to the beautiful basilica to pray. They became friends with the nuns, who took the unusual step of inviting them inside the cloister for meals and celebrations. Diane's favorite nun was an elderly German sister, who went by the religious name of Clotsindas. Sister Clotsindas went frequently with Diane and her family to one of the early Catholic charismatic prayer meetings at nearby Carmel High School.

As Diane filled Steve in on these facts, he was feeling hopelessly distracted from his research into the mid-1930s documents in the other Faulhaber Estate files. Our visit to the Munich Archdiocese Archive led to far more original documents than we expected. We had copies of a few pages from the Pascalina file, plus a handful from the Hudal and Flag Question files. But there was much more we did not have time to copy.

We returned from Munich by way of London. That gave us a good opportunity to discuss our adventures, and our findings, with some of Steve's British relatives. We appreciated their generous hospitality, and even more their willingness to be sounding boards. We needed time to reflect on what we had found, and we needed intellectually curious people to help us do that.

19. Guillotines in Munich

As we talked with friends and relatives in England and then America, the most inspiring subject was one of Diane's random finds in Munich. She was struck by one large, imposing governmental building near the central train station, the "Justizpalast" or Palace of Justice. Looking it up online, she found that its major claim to fame was the treason trial of siblings Sophie and Hans Scholl, along with several other university students and a professor, in the middle of World War II.

The crime of the "White Rose Group" was distribution of anti-Nazi leaflets. Sophie and Hans were caught distributing some of the leaflets at the University of Munich, where they were students, ages 21 and 24 years respectively. They were tried at the "Palace of Justice" four days later and were guillotined the same day.

Before leaving Munich, we had visited the memorial to the Scholls and the White Rose Group. The memorial consists of the room in the Justice Palace where their trial was held. The room is sparsely furnished with a vase of fresh flowers on a large table and photos of the White Rose members on the wall. There are copies of six German leaflets they mimeographed and distributed in Munich and other cities before they were caught in February 1943. Oddly, for a German tourist attraction, the room contained no translations into English or any other language. But then again, no tourists arrived during the hour we spent there.

In several 21st century German polls about "Unsere Besten" – our greatest Germans – Sophie and Hans Scholl rank among the top ten. They are right up with Bach, Goethe, Bismarck, Adenauer, Luther, Marx and Einstein. Among younger Germans they come out first, bar none.

We had not heard of them, and we wondered why. We had taught our children about other Christian martyrs to Nazism. We learned all we could about St. Maximilian Kolbe, the Polish priest who volunteered to take the place of a randomly condemned husband and father in the starvation bunker at Auschwitz. We read books by and about Dietrich Bonhoeffer, the Lutheran pastor in the Confessing Church who was killed in a concentration camp at Hitler's order shortly before the end of the War.

We told our children about the "Lion of Münster," Bishop Clemens von Galen, who spoke out denouncing the Nazis' euthanasia campaign against the handicapped, bringing it to a halt for at least some time. And with Steve's interest in Rommel, he did not neglect to tell them the great German general was implicated in the 1944 plot to assassinate Hitler and lost his life for it.

The Scholls have received more attention in America since 2005. That year the German film *Sophie Scholl: The Final Days* garnered an Oscar nomination for best foreign film. Based on actual transcripts of the SS interrogations and the trial, the film shows Sophie's character under the relentless pressure of Nazi authorities. Equally oppressive for her was the popular mindset that viewed any criticism of Hitler or the Nazi regime as an unthinkable violation of patriotic duty.

A powerful introduction to the White Rose Group can also be found in their own words. Here are excerpts from four of the leaflets we picked up in German at the Justice Palace, starting with the first paragraph of the earliest one:

> Nothing is more unworthy of a cultured people than to allow themselves, without resisting, to be "governed" by an irresponsible ruling clique that is given over to dark propensities. Is it not the case that every honorable German today is ashamed of his government, and who among us can imagine the measure of shame that will come upon ourselves and our children if the veil is once removed from our eyes and the most horrible crimes that exceed all measure come into the light of day? (White Rose leaflet no. 1)

> …since the conquering of Poland <u>three hundred thousand</u> Jews in that country have been murdered in the most bestial manner. Here we see the most frightful crime against human dignity, a crime to which there is nothing in all of human history to compare… (White Rose leaflet no. 2; underlining in the original)

> Our "State" today is a dictatorship of evil. "We have known that for a long time," I hear you interject, "and we did not need to have this brought up yet again here." But, I ask you, if you know that, why are you not astir, why do you put up with this dictator robbing you, step by step, openly or secretly, of your rights in one domain after another, until one day nothing, but absolutely and actually nothing will remain except a mechanized State machinery commanded by criminals and degenerates. (White Rose leaflet no. 3)

> Is there, I ask you, you who are a Christian, is there in this struggle over

the preservation of your highest values, a hesitation, an interplay with intrigues, a putting off of a decision in the hope that someone else will take up arms in order to defend you? Has not God himself given you the strength and courage to fight? We must attack evil where it is at its most powerful, and it is at its most powerful in the power of Hitler. (White Rose leaflet no. 4)

These words, and others equally powerful in the leaflets, drove Nazi authorities to such a fury that they denied the Scholls and their fellow defendant Christoph Probst the normal interval between conviction and execution.

Why had we not heard of these martyrs and their message in American Catholic circles? The White Rose leaflets exemplify a Christian defense of human dignity, drawing upon the best of the German literary, philosophical and cultural tradition, in words consistent with Catholic doctrine. Sophie and Hans Scholl were Protestant believers in Jesus who were comfortable working with Catholics. A key influence in their decision to resist the Nazis came when they read a talk by Bishop von Galen. And White Rose member Christoph Probst, 24-year-old father of three, became a Catholic, assisted by a priest, shortly before his execution.

20. New Experts: Engineers and Entrepreneurs

Now that we were home, Steve took a closer look at the diplomatic notes between the Vatican and the German Government during the "flag question" struggle of early 1934. He read back over the German Government's protest note of March that year, and the Vatican's response. The Nazi regime's protest "Promemoria" targeted precisely the sort of technical and legalistic defenses that Cardinal Faulhaber's file contained:

> That the decision whether to display the symbols of nationalist Germany on church buildings is mostly framed as an issue of rights rather than joyful participation in the fulfillment of a duty seen by the people as a patriotic matter of course, shows a deplorable lack of sympathy, with consequences that are not the fault of the government or the people.

Cardinal Pacelli's reply two months later backed up the German Bishops, but left room for negotiation:

> The Promemoria maintains that the scruples of the Bishops against the hoisting of the swastika flag on the churches should be seen as "a deplorable lack of sympathy" with the new reality of the nation. Anyone familiar with the many un-Christian or even anti-Christian meanings that often have been and are being given to this symbol by National Socialists, will be able to understand that the Bishops' scruples were and are justified. To see in this any kind of hostile attitude toward the state is false. Beginning on the day when the swastika is no longer connected by its partisan champions with meanings and missions whose anti-Christian tendency offends the faithful, the resistance based on religious considerations will diminish of its own accord.

This official statement of Vatican policy concerning the swastika, just four months before the swastika blessing ceremony, raised as many questions as it answered. Yes, it demonstrated Vatican support for the German Bishops' resistance to the swastika. But was that support negotiable, based on whether the Nazis desisted from conduct offensive to Catholics?

While we continued to discuss what we had found in Germany, people at one of Steve's client companies asked him to give a lunch hour presentation about our project. Steve prepared a powerpoint show with pictures of the trip together with some of the evidence from 1934 and 1935, in order to get a focus-group reaction. He included articles from the *Roman Observer* and *Catholic Civilization*, overlaid with translations.

Diane attended, and we provided the group with a sushi feast for lunch. Half the company showed up, about 20 people all told. The group included equal numbers of those trained in engineering and those trained in business or accounting. Typical for a Boston area start-up, there were bright young people, and older ones, with a variety of advanced degrees. There was also a considerable range of religious and ethnic backgrounds, some having grown up as far away as South America and Russia.

Steve kept strictly to 45 minutes for the presentation, to leave time for questions. He showed the *Roman Observer's* coverage of Hitler's ceremonial review of 200,000 Nazis. He also shared a video clip from the infamous Nazi propaganda film *Triumph of the Will*. The film's documentary footage from the 1934 Nazi Party Congress depicted the exact ceremony described favorably on the front page of the Vatican's newspaper. Steve showed the two Vatican-supervised promotions of the Jewish-Communist conspiracy theory in 1935, the one from August directed to Argentina, and the one in September on the day of the Nuremberg Laws. Diane encouraged the group to consider how holding authorities accountable, or failing to, affects the weak and the powerless, based on her conviction that God is good.

As the one hour point approached, in the midst of a lively question and answer session, Steve announced there was time for one more question. "I have a lot more questions, and we can take more time," responded the CEO. That led to a pivotal experience. An extended time of probing and insightful questions ensued. Several people tag-teamed with questions along these lines: This is really evil; how do you explain it? What precedents are there? Where did the Jewish-Communist conspiracy propaganda come from? What is the earlier history? Can you connect the dots?

Steve did his best to answer, but he did not have full or satisfactory answers to these questions. The best explanation that came to mind, which he expressed to the group, was the proven utility of antisemitic propaganda for winning over secularized masses to support Catholic political movements. This had occurred in Austria and France at the end of the 19th century and beginning of the 20th. His explanation was only a hypothesis. We both knew we had a lot more work to do.

In the two years since our visit to the Holocaust Memorial Museum, we had consulted with dozens of historians, experts in the field. But the focus group session was different. Historians reacted to our findings in the context of mainstream historiography. They recognized that the swastika blessing ceremony did not fit into any of the pre-existing historical models. We had spoken with historians of many different perspectives. This was a case of facts not fitting anyone's paradigm.

But now we were dealing with a focus group that was not expert in the paradigms and conventions of historians. The group was unburdened by the taboos of that profession, which we had also encountered. The group engaged directly with the evidence and asked pertinent questions. The documents raised issues that related to their present-day moral concerns. By the time the question and answer session ended, we had used up two and a half hours of company time. No one seemed to regret that, least of all the CEO.

We reflected a good deal in the days that followed. How could we understand the evil we were looking at from the mid-1930s? What were its origins and causes? The Jewish-Communist conspiracy theory was something we could understand coming from the mouth of Goebbels. But coming from influential Catholic publications, under the supervisory authority of a Cardinal Secretary of State who is up for sainthood?

What were the precedents, the antecedents, the rationale for top level people in the Catholic Church becoming complicit in such propaganda? Surely Pope Pius XI and Cardinal Pacelli were aware in the 1930s that international Soviet Communism was under the complete control of a non-Jewish dictator named Stalin? Pacelli had been Pius XI's lead negotiator with the Soviet Union over a period of years in the 1920s, trying unsuccessfully to reach some sort of agreement with the Communist regime.

Other questions equally called for answers: What was the impact on Catholics in Germany, especially in Bavaria? What was the degree of harm caused by authoritative Catholic endorsement of this conspiracy theory? Especially in light of the theory's inherent implausibility at the time, what effect did *authority* have in adding credibility to such propaganda?

We knew we had only scratched the surface in Munich. Steve worked hard to get fully caught up on his legal work, knowing that a return trip to Germany was in the offing.

21. Our Family Gets on Board

Massachusetts is unusual for having a school vacation week in February, coinciding with the Presidents' Day national holiday. Diane took advantage of that week to arrange an almost full-family research trip. One of our sons, who knows German and had contributed helpful insights to our work, flew in from his ex-pat workplace in Seoul, Korea. Another son, who had studied German and helped with our earliest research, flew to Munich on his way from Marine Intelligence Officer School to his duty station on Okinawa. Our oldest daughter, an excellent photographer who had edited some of our previous work along with her husband, came with him from Oregon. Our four youngest children, who helped by commenting on some of our early drafts, took a couple days off from school in addition to their vacation week.

Our first destination in Germany was a place most of the family had seen a decade earlier. Berchtesgaden is a picturesque town surrounded by mountains in the southeast corner of Bavaria. Close to Salzburg, Austria, it long served as a rural retreat for the Catholic royal family of Bavaria, the Wittelsbachs.

Munich's famous Hofbräuhaus has a branch brewery and beer hall in Berchtesgaden. That makes sense in a royal resort town, since "Hof" means royal court, and Hofbräu was the royal brewery. The atmosphere of the town is touristy, with hotels, spas and restaurants, and shop windows displaying lederhosen and dirndl dresses. The Hofbrauhaus was fully booked for dinner, hours in advance, so we went to a new hotel in the town center. With its sumptuously appointed interior, the hotel's atmosphere is best captured by our daughter's comment at dinner: "Can't you just imagine James Bond walking in here!"

Seventy and eighty years ago, agents of a different type frequented Berchtesgaden. The town, or more precisely the slopes of the Obersalzberg mountain overlooking it, became the second seat of the German Government after Hitler came to power. Hitler's vacation house on the Obersalzberg became a place for important meetings. On Hitler's 50th birthday, his lieutenants presented him with the "Eagle's Nest" as a gift. Seen from the town below as a small building perched atop the Obersalzberg, the Eagle's Nest was accessed by a gilded elevator in a shaft through the interior of the mountain.

Our main destination was the "Documentation Center," a museum of Nazi history created by Munich's Institute for Contemporary History, near the former site of Hitler's vacation house. It did not yet exist in 2003, when we chose a chalet on the Obersalzberg for a short stay. At the time it was the only vacation rental Steve could find in the southern part of Germany that would accommodate ten people. Now we found that the Documentation Center was just a short distance up the road from where we had stayed that year.

We had no idea in 2003 that the mountain was honeycombed with passages and large rooms built by the Nazis. Everyone was fascinated to tour the underground network, accessible from the Documentation Center's exhibits, leading into the heart of the mountain. It was a veritable underground Nazi town.

From the extensive exhibits in the Center, we learned that Hitler started coming to the Obersalzberg in the early 1920s. Writer-editor Dietrich Eckart, something of a mentor to Hitler, owned a vacation house there before Hitler did. It was eerie to imagine Hitler and the Nazis turning this charming and very Catholic place into their own domain. But then Hitler and Eckart were both nominally Catholic. The Center treated the early years of the Nazi Party in great detail. The extensive displays about causative factors and stages of development did not discuss any Catholic influence in the Nazi Party's early history.

At our B&B in Berchtesgaden, we found an opportunity to discuss the Nazi era with two young men who invited us to join them and our older children for beers. Their take on the Nazi era, as Austrian Catholics, was that the Church did many bad things that are best not remembered and not discussed. The friendly owner of the B&B, listening to our conversation, treated us to a free round of schnapps.

After a train ride to Munich, we set up base in a family-owned hotel, half a mile from the central train station and three blocks from the large outdoor venue of the annual Oktoberfest. After a typically hearty Bavarian breakfast, Steve began his research work by heading to the Archdiocesan Archive with one of our sons. Diane started everyone else off with a tour of some highlights of Munich. At the Archive, Steve and our son did a thorough review of the Faulhaber Estate index, requested every file of potential interest, and asked for copies of many documents from the files.

A fuller picture of Bishop Hudal's role in the mid-1930s emerged from a close examination of Cardinal Faulhaber's Hudal files. First, it appeared that

Bishop Hudal had a regular practice of sending his books to German Bishops. He did this by instructing his publisher to send copies as the books came off the press. Second, there was tension between Hudal and the German Bishops from Hudal's early days as Rector of the "Anima," a German-language religious institute in Rome. Hudal and the Bishops differed over issues of pastoral care for Germans in Rome in the 1920s. One of Cardinal Faulhaber's letters to Hudal speaks of conflicts and avoidance of "civil war" over these issues. Third, it was clear that Hudal was indeed an Austrian, not a German. This was apparent in how he referred to himself, and how others referred to him and the long tradition of Austrians heading the Anima in Rome.

Another fact we did not find in any histories emerged from later documents in Cardinal Faulhaber's Hudal files: The German-speaking Cardinals, gathered in Rome in February 1946, unanimously expected Hudal to be removed from his position as Rector of the Anima. Pope Pius XII kept him in that position for an additional six years.

Cardinal Faulhaber's "Pascalina" file, dated entirely after World War II, contained more surprises upon closer inspection. A series of letters disclosed a sequence of efforts to procure printing paper for the Catholic Church in Germany. The German Bishops' effort to secure approval from the Allies for paper to print catechisms met with failure. Negotiations with Soviet representatives in Berlin to purchase paper in bulk from Russia, while promising at first, likewise came up short.

The solution came from none other than Sister Pascalina, in May 1948. Her correspondence with Cardinal Faulhaber reflected shipments from Rome of more than 90 rolls of paper, for printing, weighing a total of 30 tons. She supervised the loading of six rail cars to take the paper to Germany, presumably under diplomatic seal, to supply the Church's needs for paper in Bavaria, Cologne, and other parts of the country.

Pascalina's powerful role in Pope Pius XII's Vatican is mentioned by some historians, but such claims have been disputed. Her personal interactions with Cardinal Faulhaber, in the course of meeting his post-War financial and printing needs, were worthy of note. This excerpt is illustrative:

As I returned home late yesterday evening [to the Vatican from Castel Gandolfo, the papal summer palace], I found Your Eminence's very kind letter... Eminence, can you remember the terrace where we stood and looked out over the garden with the glorious oak trees and I said to Your Eminence that this would be our kingdom? I had below me the sea, on which the setting sun was just then reflected, and if I looked straight ahead, there was Grotta with its church that I so love. [Grottaferrata is near Castel Gandolfo and is where Bishop Hudal lived after leaving the Anima] – Eminence, why did you never tell me the dire needs of your churches when you were here? I would not have rested until I had taken care of at least three or four of which you speak… Just yesterday I gave His Holiness a reminder – there wasn't much time – and he said immediately: of course Eminence comes first, whenever money comes in. And it is coming in, for today Eminence Spellman asked me where it should be sent. I replied immediately: to the Holy Father.

While this passage dates from 1948, it raises questions about prior years. From 1918 to 1925, Sister Pascalina worked in the Vatican Nunciature in Munich. Cardinal Faulhaber is widely reported to have spent ample time with Nuncio Pacelli during those years. How significant a role did Pascalina play in the earlier years?

As Steve and our son were finishing up their second day of work in the Munich Archdiocese Archive, the friendly and helpful archivist from our January visit emerged for the first time in this visit. But this time his tone was not friendly. What are you doing? I thought you were only researching about a photograph. Now you are looking at all sorts of files… Steve answered and explained very slowly, minding all the complexities of German grammar: I need to look at a broad range of files to know what is important for our research. Eventually the archivist went away, but his tone was no friendlier at the end than at the beginning.

Outside it was Fasching. That is Munich's Mardi Gras, and the streets were full of revelers. While Steve was researching, other family members came upon a group at an outdoor stage singing "Sweet Caroline." It was fun to connect with a Bavarian crowd through the Neil Diamond song that Boston Red Sox fans sing at Fenway Park during every game.

The Bavarian State Library also proved to be a treasure trove. As a monarchy that valued literature as well as art and music, Bavaria long made a point of collecting and preserving, meticulously, every issue of all the many hundreds of newspapers and magazines published in the kingdom. During the Second World War, Bavarians removed their library collections as well as their art treasures from Munich once they realized the city would be bombed.

The Munich Archdiocesan weekly newspaper was in the collection. Steve found a book with citations to it that looked important. Every other possibly significant Bavarian publication was available too. There was just one problem. The bound volumes were in storage and had to be requested three days in advance. All he could do was learn how to make such requests remotely, online, and hope for a future opportunity to get back to the Library.

But the reference librarian showed Steve a few Munich newspapers that were available on microfilm in the reading room. There was time to look at several months of Munich's largest circulation newspaper, the *Münchner Neueste Nachrichten*, or "Munich Latest News."

Steve started with the period following Armistice Day, the end of World War One on November 11, 1918. He was surprised to find enthusiastic support on the paper's front page, week after week, for democratic self-government. Rather than expressing resentment for the Allies' insistence on removal of the German Kaiser and the King of Bavaria, as a pre-condition for an armistice, Munich's largest paper championed America's democracy and constitution as a model. It was only one sample out of the Library's vast collection. But it *was* the most widely read newspaper of the day in Bavaria.

Were the people of Munich generally predisposed to Nazism in 1919? Or not? What were the major influences upon them in the years after their defeat in World War One?

22. Berlin: Pinning Down the Flag Issue

For our two nights in Berlin, we stayed on Karl Marx Boulevard in former East Berlin. The Airbnb.com website made it possible to reserve what once must have been a Communist apparatchik's large and comfortable apartment. In the quarter century since the Berlin Wall fell, the neighborhood has become a mix of reasonably priced restaurants, pubs and small shops.

Steve's first research destination was the Political Archive of the German Foreign Office. Held by the victorious Allies for many years, this large collection of documents, including files of German embassies like the one in Buenos Aires in 1934, now resides in a sprawling building in central Berlin. The cordial Archive staff quickly retrieved the files of the German Embassy to Argentina for the 1920s and 1930s, as well as Ambassador Edmund von Thermann's personnel file and files of the longtime German Ambassador to the Vatican, Diego von Bergen.

The German Argentine Embassy files contained a curious anomaly. The file for 1934 had voluminous materials up to the summer of that year, but none at all for September and October, the months of the swastika blessing and Eucharistic Congress, and very little from August through December. Typically meticulous German record-keeping resumed in early 1935. There was no explanation for the record-keeping gap.

Before the gap, however, there was a bonanza of information in July 1934. Controversies arose earlier in the year, on German national flag display days, when German ex-pats in Argentina tried to display swastika flags. Argentina had a law restricting flag displays. Only the Argentine flag and national flags of countries in friendly relations with Argentina were allowed. In mid-July 1934, the government of the Province of Buenos Aires issued an instruction to police, prohibiting all displays of swastika flags. The decree made national news in a big way.

Preserved in a set of envelopes inside the Embassy file for 1934 were clippings of articles from many newspapers in Buenos Aires and the other cities of Argentina. The articles said the swastika flag was prohibited because it was a political party flag, not the flag of a country in friendly relations with Argentina. A few of the articles reflected the German Ambassador's argument in favor of allowing the swastika, namely that Germany had two national flags, the tricolor and the swastika.

A particularly eloquent article in a Buenos Aires newspaper showed full awareness of recent developments in Germany and the brutal nature of Hitler's regime:

"The Flags of Hatred Can No Longer Fly Under the Skies of Our Liberty"

The Nazi flag, the same one whose shadow fell on those assassinated on June 30th, and whose folds drowned the protests of the victims of Hitler's savagery, can no longer be hoisted under the skies of Buenos Aires. The swastika cross, the symbol of racial persecution, can no longer be caressed by the breezes of a nation whose Magna Carta [the Argentine constitution] offers a home to all the people of the world who want to live here.

Our trip to Berlin occurred more than a year after Father Gumpel questioned the likely extent of Copello's knowledge in far-off Argentina of events in Germany and the full implications of the swastika. The Embassy's stash of newspaper clippings now turned that question on its head. What Argentine, seeing Archbishop Copello bless a swastika, would *not* know it was the Nazi Party flag?

But how many Argentines actually witnessed this Catholic authority associating himself with the swastika? Beyond those in St. Ignatius Church at the ceremony on September 30, 1934, it was hard to say. Diane's research at the Library of Congress found just a small article on an inside page of one newspaper. Apparently the event did not get much publicity in Argentina.

We came away from Berlin with an ample set of photographs of pages from the German Embassy file. Our daughter and her husband were responsible for that. They carefully photographed each of the hundred or so pages Steve marked as he rapidly scanned through the worn but well-kept files.

23. Ember in the Ashes at the Bavarian Library

Back at home, contemplating the as-yet untapped trove of the Bavarian State Library, Steve consulted a book called *Catholicism and the Roots of Nazism*, written by American historian Derek Hastings and published by Oxford University Press in 2010. Despite the title, this work was favorably reviewed by Catholics whom Steve respected. It contained many citations to original sources in Munich.

As he placed advance orders for bound volumes of Bavarian newspapers, Steve read through a unique part of Professor Hastings' book. More than any German author has done, Hastings documented the Catholic element of the early Nazi Party in Munich. Other roots of the Nazi Party have been amply described by many writers: the German nationalist reaction against the Versailles Treaty, the antisemitism and neo-pagan revival of old Nordic and Germanic culture that characterized the *Völkisch* movement, and the antisemitic Thule Society of Munich.

Hastings' contribution was to document the Catholic currents in Munich that also flowed into the Nazi Party. These included Franz Schrönghamer-Heimdal, whose antisemitic rantings led him to deny the Jewishness of Jesus. They also included Hitler's mentor Dietrich Eckart, who likewise denied central elements of Catholic faith even while proclaiming his Catholic identity to his Bavarian Catholic readership.

Professor Hastings' book also referenced an appearance of the Jewish-Communist conspiracy theory, together with an endorsement of *The Protocols of the Elders of Zion*, in the weekly newspaper of the Munich Archdiocese. So, before flying back to Munich, we ordered up copies of Schronghamer-Heimdal, Eckart, and the *Münchener Katholische Kirchenzeitung,* or "Munich Catholic Church Newspaper," for 1919 and 1920.

Our favorite family hotel was ready with a warm welcome, and the requested volumes were waiting for us in the impressively well-ordered system of the Bavarian State Library. The two individual Catholic authors did indeed spout Jewish-Communist conspiracy theory in Munich in the second half of 1919 and early 1920. But there was nothing to indicate authority or influence in their works. They were both early Nazis, members of a tiny group at the time, which could only attract a few dozen people to its meetings. Started in 1919 under the name "German Workers Party," the predecessor to the Nazi Party existed on the fringe of Bavarian nationalism and antisemitism.

The *Munich Catholic Church Newspaper*, by contrast, exuded authority. When the Archbishop of Munich had an important message for his people, it appeared in this weekly paper. When the Archbishop laid down rules for confession, communion, marriages, funerals, and baptisms, they appeared in this paper with explicit force and impact.

Issues of the *Munich Catholic Church Newspaper* during 1919 contained several antisemitic articles, but none about Jewish-Communist conspiracy. They focused on Jewish-*Masonic* conspiracy and Jewish domineering through finance, antisemitic themes that played a major role in the growth of Austrian and French antisemitic movements in the late 19th and early 20th centuries.

Even though the Russian Revolution of 1917 gave an opportunity for antisemites to blame Communism on Judaism, based on the Jewish ethnicity of some Bolshevik leaders, the Munich Archdiocesan weekly did not start to promote Jewish-Communist conspiracy theory until more than two years after that Revolution. In December 1918, when the *Munich Catholic Church Newspaper* took stock of certain good developments at the end of the war's horrors, developments in Russia headed the list of blessings, not horrors. The destruction of Russian Czarism, "which was always hostile to the Roman Catholic Church," was the "punishment" for the "enormous guilt" of splitting off from Rome in 1054. Even in 1919, when Munich experienced a tumultuous month of Communist revolutionary government, the Jewish-Communist conspiracy theory did not surface in the pages of the Archdiocesan weekly.

That trend changed abruptly in April 1920. On April 11th, Catholics looking at their Archdiocese's weekly newspaper found an article entitled "Jewish Imperialism." The article looked highly authoritative. It said the "very respected" Paris journal *La Documentation Catholique* had published an "official American report" on the Russian Revolution. The report "established" that Jewish bankers in America and Europe financed the Russian Bolsheviks, and that all but one of the 30 top leaders of Bolshevism were Jews. Their purpose was Jewish domination over the Christians of Germany and the whole world. This purpose, the article said, "unites Jewish capitalists and communists." The article told readers where they could purchase a new German translation of *The Protocols of the Elders of Zion*. Soviet Communism, readers were led to understand, fulfilled the "Jewish Imperialism" plot set forth in the *Protocols*.

As Diane read Steve's quick translation, the article had the feel of a still-glowing ember of a fire started long ago. But where did that fire originate?

24. French Connection

What was this "very respected" *La Documentation Catholique*? Did it really publish an official American report? Respect for anything French was a rare commodity in Germany after World War I. The French were the driving force at the Paris Peace Confernce of 1919, producing a Versailles Treaty with exceedingly harsh terms for Germany. German hopes for moderate peace terms along the lines of American President Woodrow Wilson's "Fourteen Points" were quickly dashed. France and Britain insisted on keeping a blockade on Germany, forcing the country to choose in mid-1919 between the Versailles Treaty on the one hand, or starvation and military occupation on the other.

A quick search online revealed that *La Documentation Catholique* still exists today. It publishes documents from the Vatican, the French Catholic Church, and other Church authorities from around the world. Its name means *Catholic Documentation*, which is a good description of its content. But a search of the Harvard Library catalog showed it is not among their collections.

As we looked online from our Munich hotel, we had only eight hours remaining until our scheduled departure by train. Steve had found bargain tickets for a high-speed train from Munich to Paris, and for the Chunnel train from Paris to London. Our train left Munich at the crack of dawn. The schedule included a six-hour layover in Paris, which we intended to use to look up an obscure item at the French National Library. Perhaps *Catholic Documentation* might also be found there.

Arriving on the north side of central Paris at the Gare de l'Est, we hopped into a cab and asked to go to the French National Library, on the south side of the Seine River. Half an hour later, we found ourselves at the privileges office in the ultra-modern National Library. That is, if "ultra-modern" is the right term for a cavernous concrete structure, mostly underground, with glass walls looking out onto a garden of wild untended vegetation.

We had to explain our research purposes in French to a staff member whose job was to decide whether our purposes merited the privilege of access to the Library's collections. We were happy when we passed the test. With a few quick strokes at his keyboard, the French gentleman informed us that *Catholic Documentation* was in the Library's collection. Fortunately it was available on microfilm and could be ready for us in less than an hour. We were soon dividing up the work, one taking the 1920 reel and the other the 1919 reel. Diane made the find.

The March 6, 1920 issue displayed the article title and précis on the first page: "Are the Jews the Principal Factors of World Bolshevism?" The three-page article inside was a detailed work of masterful propaganda. With precise details and an air of investigative authority, the article described prominent Jewish bankers financing the Russian Revolution and partnering with Trotsky.

A list of 30 Russian Bolshevik leaders identified the nationality of each. One of them, Lenin, was identified as "Russian." All the others were identified as "Jew." The article, purporting throughout to be an official American report, said capitalist and proletarian Jews alike were united to take over Germany and other countries in a ruthless drive for world domination. A governing body within this immense threat was the "Jewish Kehillah." Like the Spanish name "El Kahal" of 1935, "Kehillah" was derived from the Hebrew word for assembly or congregation.

The article manifested a special resentment toward the Zionist effort, supported by the Allies, to re-establish a Jewish homeland in Palestine: "Even though the Jews, during all the war, did nothing to fill the ranks of soldiers in the different countries, they still obtained the formal recognition of a Jewish State in Palestine."

The article opened and closed with quotations from the *Protocols*. These were dated to 1897, a tactic of antisemites who wanted people to believe the *Protocols* were minutes of meetings at the first International Zionist Congress, which took place that year.

The slur about Jews shirking military service was another antisemitic propaganda tactic. Antisemites were equally capable, when it served their purposes, of claiming that Jews *controlled* the military forces of World War One. In April 1920, for instance, the *Munich Catholic Church Newspaper* said the Austrian Army was "thoroughly infected by Jewry."

The *Catholic Documentation* article drew special authority and credibility by purporting to be an official report of "Les Services Américains." That name, "The American Services," was a real puzzler for Steve. He thought he knew the name of virtually every U.S. Government agency from his time in Washington. He was especially familiar with intelligence agencies. He had researched the history of the American intelligence community while drafting judicial opinions about the CIA and NSA as a law clerk to Judge Malcolm Wilkey on the U.S. Court of Appeals in Washington, DC. He continued to read widely in the field. But he had never heard of any agency called the "American Services."

We certainly felt we were making progress in tracking down the antecedents, and connecting the dots, with respect to the Jewish-Communist conspiracy theory. There was obviously more work to do, but we decided to be thankful for what we had found so quickly, and enjoy Paris. After a cab ride to a sidewalk café along the Boulevard St. Germain, we walked to the nearby Geographic Society to follow up a historical curiosity there concerning St. Thérèse of Lisieux. Then it was a pleasant walk under sunny skies to the Seine, along the Louvre, north through bustling streets, and finally to the Gare du Nord for the train to London.

25. Hitler Piggybacks

After a visit with our English relatives, we were back home wondering: What has been written about these articles from the *Munich Catholic Church Newspaper* and *Catholic Documentation*? They appeared at an important time in history. The Nazi Party was re-launched in Munich, with Hitler now in a prominent role, on February 24, 1920. Its tiny discussion-group meetings of 1919 became boisterous gatherings of hundreds and thousands in 1920.

Antisemitism was the Nazi Party's stock in trade from the outset. The Nazis' potential audience in Bavaria was overwhelmingly Catholic. Did the Nazi movement, as it grew in Munich, draw aid and comfort from the "Jewish Imperialism" article in the Archdiocesan weekly paper?

The Harvard Library seemed to have all the resources needed to answer these questions, with many books on the history of the Nazi Party. Upon close inspection, however, none of them dealt with the development of the Jewish-Communist conspiracy theory in authoritative Catholic publications. That duplicated Steve's experience when he tried to find any historian who mentioned the Vatican's promotion of the same conspiracy theory in 1935.

The only historian who mentioned the April 11, 1920 "Jewish Imperialism" article was Derick Hastings. Until his work appeared in 2010, the article was completely overlooked. In addition to English language works, Steve examined half a dozen of the leading German language histories of the early Nazi movement in Munich. None of them mentioned anything about the *Munich Catholic Church Newspaper*.

As for the *Catholic Documentation* article, again we found only one author who mentioned it. Léon Poliakov, in his multi-volume *History of Anti-Semitism*, touches upon it briefly. He says this article was the first instance of a journal in Western Europe publishing an excerpt of the *Protocols* and affirming their authenticity. That alone signaled the historical importance of the article. Yet everyone else seemed to ignore it.

Once again, original documents proved the key for gaining further understanding. The Harvard Library had microfilm copies of the *Völkischer Beobachter*, or "Volkisch Observer." Owned by the Nazi Party from late 1920 on, this Munich paper reflected Nazi and similar *Völkisch* views throughout 1920. The term "Volkisch" has no English equivalent. It denoted a racist movement that exalted the German *Volk* and its historic character. There were many *Volkisch* groups in Germany. A key common denominator was the antisemitic postulate that Jewish people were not part of the *Volk*. The Harvard Library also had a large volume of Hitler's collected writings and speeches in German. These original documentary sources contained multiple shocks.

On April 22, 1920, the *Volkisch Observer* devoted its entire front page to *The Protocols of the Elders of Zion*. In the three months before the Archdiocesan weekly paper endorsed the *Protocols*, the *Volkisch Observer* had paid virtually no attention to them. Steve found one small notice for the *Protocols* in the paid advertising section in January. He found no other items in the *Volkisch Observer* promoting the *Protocols*, or reviewing them, or even mentioning them.

He found a historical work stating that a pre-publication copy of the *Protocols* was sent to the *Volkisch Observer* in late 1919. That fact and the paid advertisement show the *Volkisch Observer* was aware of the *Protocols* for months before April 1920. Yet it did nothing to promote them during those months except one small ad.

What changed on April 22, 1920? Quite simply, the most authoritative Catholic publication in Bavaria, under the auspices of the Archbishop of Munich, had endorsed the *Protocols* eleven days earlier. A piece of vile hate propaganda too extreme for a Nazi-oriented antisemitic paper to promote at the risk of its own credibility, gained a Catholic seal of approval. The *Volkisch Observer* could now gush over the *Protocols*, leveraging their new-found credibility:

> We can only keep expressing our astonishment that this book that appeared in 1919 has not yet been distributed in millions of copies to the entire German *Volk*, that today there are still German-*Volkisch*-minded men and women who have not yet gotten it into their hands. We therefore wish to call attention to this book with utmost emphasis, because in fact there is no book that so reveals the spirit of Jewry.

Four days later, on April 26th, the *Volkisch Observer* published the "Jewish Imperialism" article verbatim, lifted straight out of the *Munich Catholic Church Newspaper* from April 11th. This was, of course, an act of plagiarism. Bavaria had a well-developed set of laws protecting copyright. Violations by newspapers were promptly punished by penalties that included publication bans. The only way the *Volkisch Observer* could get away with such flagrant plagiarism was if it had permission, or at least tacit approval, from the Archdiocese of Munich.

By April 29th, the Nazi-oriented paper was so fully charged up against the supposed Jewish-Communist conspiracy that it published an open call for vengeance on Jews in general in Bavaria. This vicious piece started with two quotations from the *Protocols* purporting to show the murderous scheming of all Jews. The author accused Munich's Jewish community of collective guilt for not singling out the Communists in their midst. This piece, unlike the plagiarism three days before, drew a 10-day publication ban. The Munich police chief who imposed the ban, Ernst Pöhner, was a notorious antisemite. But this open incitement to violence was too much even for him to tolerate.

What about Hitler? Was there any difference in his rhetoric before and after the "Jewish Imperialism" article? The collection of Hitler's writings and speeches told the tale. Before April 1920, Hitler did not posit an international Jewish-Communist conspiracy. He did not claim Jews were controlling Russian Bolshevism. He did not equate Judaism and Communism. He did indeed say that German revolutionary leaders Luxemburg, Levien and Leviné were Jews. But in the same breath he called Gentiles like Matthias Erzberger and Karl Liebknecht Jews, making his attacks openly ridiculous rather than remotely credible.

Hitler's early broad-brush accusations against Jews related to capitalism, not Communism. From fall 1919 through mid-April 1920, Hitler's attacks focused predominantly on accusations of Jewish control of finance and stock markets. Consistent with other evidence of Hitler's Socialist leanings in this early period, he spoke in mid-April 1920 of the possibility of reaching an understanding between Germany and Russia, saying it was only the Jewish press preventing such a rapprochement.

Hitler's tune changed soon after the "Jewish Imperialism" article appeared. On April 27, 1920, Hitler invoked the international Jewish-Bolshevik conspiracy theory for the first time in any of his reported speeches or writings. "Who," he railed, has brought about economic disaster in Russia? "Only the Jew."

The equating of Communism with Judaism quickly became a staple of Hitler's speeches. In June he said Bolshevism "is all an affair of the Jews, for it expresses their faith." In July he said "Marxism has completely wrecked Soviet Russia, and there rules the Jew." In August he claimed that 430 of the top 478 Soviet officials were Jews. Hitler biographer Ian Kershaw observes that by the early 1920s, "Jew" was synonymous with Bolshevik, Communist, and Marxism in Hitler's mind. That was not the case before the Archdiocesan paper gave instant credibility to a massive lie.

26. Jewish-Communist Conspiracy Theory and the Holocaust

The third week of April is another school vacation week in Massachusetts. The week begins with Patriots Day, a daybreak re-enactment of the "Shot Heard 'Round the World" at the Village Green in Lexington, a Red Sox game begun before noon at Fenway Park, and the Boston Marathon finishing nearby at Copley Square. We missed those events in 2012, as we took a week at the beach. During the week we reflected on the evidence we had found. In the middle of the week, as Diane's birthday approached, she said what she wanted for her birthday present: a trip to Israel.

Through the years we had seen many advertisements for trips to the Holy Land. They were in Diocesan papers, brochures and posters in parishes, and online. They always looked attractive, but we never took the plunge. Now we did. Diane found a bargain airfare to Tel Aviv via Amsterdam, with only a few tickets remaining, and we jumped on the opportunity.

We arrived at our hotel in the tree-lined Jerusalem neighborhood of Rechavia at 5:00 a.m on a cool morning in late April. The hotel stored our luggage, and we had enough energy to walk and explore. It was a mile to the walled Old City. We had the place virtually to ourselves. At early dawn we heard prayers as we passed by the Tomb of King David. The ramparts walk along the parapets offered splendid views of neighborhoods spread out over the surrounding hills.

As the sun rose, we walked toward it, through the Kidron Valley, past olive groves near large cemeteries, alongside the sign-posted Garden of Gethsemane, and up to the crest of the Mount of Olives. The reward for our efforts was a glorious view of the sunbathed white stone walls of the Old City and the golden Dome of the Rock, the mosque on the former site of the Temple.

Hungry by now for breakfast, we walked back along the city walls until we saw a hotel. We asked a clerk at the front desk about breakfast. Masaryk's is the best place, was his reply.

Masaryk Restaurant in the "German Colony" neighborhood of Jerusalem recalled for us the origins of our long inquiry. Thomas Masaryk served as President of Czechoslovakia for that country's first 17 years of existence. His name is honored by a street as well as a restaurant in Jerusalem, on account of the respect he showed the Jewish people. Among the new countries created by the Allies out of the Austro-Hungarian, German and Russian Empires after World War One, Czechoslovakia stood out for its stable democracy, economic vitality, and freedoms for ethnic and religious minorities. Masaryk Restaurant served a delicious Israeli breakfast to this foot-weary and jet-lagged American couple.

During our three days in Jerusalem, we visited the sites memorializing Jesus' passion, death and resurrection. We also visited Yad Vashem. Yad Vashem is three miles west of Rechavia, beyond the Israeli Knesset, or parliament building, on a broad hill named for Theodor Herzl, the founder of the Zionist movement. Yad Vashem is a profound monument that is better experienced than described. Diane experienced a sense of peace on the hillside of trees planted in memory of the victims.

From the standpoint of our research, several aspects of the extensive exhibits were especially relevant. There is an exhibit in the Holocaust History Museum about Christian antisemitism leading to the Holocaust. The exhibit focuses on the tragic history of Christian antisemitic teaching and conduct through the centuries. It does not try to assign responsibility to teachings and actions of particular Christian authorities during the 20th century.

Another display contains an explanatory plaque about Pope Pius XII. It identifies the historical controversy over allegations of silence and inaction in the face of the Holocaust. The display refrains from passing judgment. It says the matter is subject to ongoing evaluation by historians. We did not know it at the time, but this plaque was the focus of considerable negotiation between the Vatican and Yad Vashem. The plaque was changed somewhat during 2012 as a result of those negotiations.

At three points in the Museum, we noticed the Jewish-Communist conspiracy theory playing a role as the Holocaust developed. The first point was in early 1939, when Hitler proclaimed that if war came to Europe it would mean the annihilation of Jewry in Europe. His words equated Jewry both with international finance and with international Bolshevism. We were well aware that this inherent contradiction, equating Judaism with the two opposite poles of capitalism and Communism, gained credibility from an authoritative source on April 11, 1920 in Munich. Hitler was still embracing that same propaganda theme 19 years later, as he contemplated the mass murder of Europe's Jews.

The second point in the displays was from October 1941. Yad Vashem showed Hitler's proclamation to the German troops that month on the Eastern Front. Hitler informed German soldiers that what they were encountering in Russia was the "result of nearly 25 years of Jewish rule." Bolshevism and the worst form of capitalism, he said, were basically the same. "And the standard-bearers of these systems are, in both cases, the same: Jews and only Jews."

The third point was in November 1941. A plaque bore an excerpt from German General von Manstein's Order of the Day for November 20, 1941 on the Eastern Front: "Since June 22 the German nation is in the midst of a life and death struggle ... The Jewish-Bolshevik system must be eradicated once and for all."

Nazi Germany's invasion of the Soviet Union on June 22, 1941 marked the start of systematic mass murder of Jews. Special SS killing units set about murdering Jewish civilians behind the advancing German lines. Hitler explained Germany's invasion as self-defense against an enemy that threatened to destroy all of Western Civilization.

Hitler's and Manstein's words explained to the German Army at the time, and to us today, why Nazi Germany diverted military, logistic, and security assets away from a race against time with the Russian winter and the Red Army. Hitler used those assets, instead, to kill hundreds of thousands of Jewish civilians. It was "self-defense" against Jewish-Bolshevism. The Jewish-Communist conspiracy theory, in short, was a central factor at the outset of the Holocaust.

27. Meeting Experts at Yad Vashem

Following our two-hour self-guided tour through the Holocaust History Museum, Diane walked downhill to Yad Vashem's Valley of the Communities. It is an unforgettable memorial, built of huge blocks of engraved stone, to the destroyed Jewish communities of each city and town across Europe. Diane was shaken to the core from the moment she realized the first town name she was looking at was Czestochowa. It is the site of an important medieval shrine to Mary, the Mother of Jesus.

Steve, meanwhile, walked over from the Holocaust History Museum to the Yad Vashem Library and Archive. At the front desk, he asked if he could talk to a reference librarian about research he was doing. In short order, a courteous and professional Yad Vashem staff member appeared and introduced herself.

Leah Teichtal quickly grasped Steve's description of the photograph and its mid-1930s context in Argentina and Germany, and picked up her phone. Soon two historians arrived. They listened attentively to the historical context of the swastika blessing photo in 1934 Argentina, 1935 Germany, and later 1935 when Copello became a Cardinal in Rome. Steve did not mention the Vatican-published and Vatican-supervised articles from 1934 and 1935, or any of the materials from 1920.

The historians were inclined to disbelieve that the Archbishop would deliberately bless a swastika. As they raised various alternative interpretations of the photo, Steve told what Diane found in the Library of Congress: the Buenos Aires newspaper article, describing the swastika blessing ceremony, on the first reel of microfilm she examined there, on the first day's issue on that reel, in small print on page 12, after starting her research with a prayer to find whatever was important.

"Her prayer was answered," was the response. There was no other substantive response. "You're the expert; you know more than we do about this; we have nothing to add."

But Ms. Teichtal added something that proved quite valuable. She provided contact information for a person at a research institute in Israel who might know something about these issues.

The research institute was called Moreshet. That name sounded familiar. It was the name of the prophet Micah's hometown. Whether or not the old location corresponds with the new, Moreshet today appears on the map near the expressway exit leading to Nazareth.

We already had reservations in Nazareth for the last two nights of our trip. But after two days of touring Mt. Carmel, Haifa, Nazareth, Cana, Tiberias, Sea of Galilee, Jordan River, and Mt. Tabor, we still had no response to the email we sent to the Institute's director at Moreshet. So we decided to try our luck by just dropping in, on our way from Nazareth to the airport in Tel Aviv.

Driving up to the entrance, alongside a kibbutz, we found ourselves talking successively to a gatekeeper, a gatehouse attendant, a retired teacher who drove us into the grounds of the Institute, a young man who gave us a tour of the Institute's historical exhibits, and a young woman administrator. The experience was personally delightful and historically educational.

We learned that the Institute ran programs for Arab and Jewish young people to learn each other's culture and the values of peaceful coexistence. We also learned about the history of Jewish fighters against the Nazis in the Warsaw Ghetto and elsewhere in Eastern Europe. They were the exception, of course. The overwhelming number of Jews offered no resistance. The historical record thus gives further testimony against the insidious proposition that European Jewry posed a threat to Germany and "Western Civilization."

At the end of our visit, the administrator called the person Ms. Teichtal had recommended, Dr. Graciela Ben-Dror. She was no longer at the Institute, but she informed the administrator she was aware of the photograph. That was an intriguing surprise. Of the dozens of historians we talked to in the United States and Germany, none of them knew of the swastika blessing photograph. But we were quickly running out of time to catch our return flight from Tel Aviv. And Dr. Ben-Dror, on such short notice, was not able to talk to us on the phone.

28. The Man Who Knew the Most

By pointing us to Moreshet and Dr. Ben-Dror, Yad Vashem indirectly led us to another historian. He was originally from New York City, and lived on the same kibbutz he moved to six decades ago. As we read through the journal he edited, the *Moreshet Journal for the Study of the Holocaust and Antisemitism*, and his own writing, we knew we had to meet Dr. Ariel Hurwitz.

The title of his book *Jews Without Power* contrasted completely with accusations of all-powerful Judaism threatening imminently to take over the world. Hurwitz's book documents the story of Jewish leaders trying every path they could find, to help European Jews escape persecution and death during the Nazi era. The governments of the leading nations of the world, including the United States, failed them.

We found there was a book by Hurwitz's wife, Cipora, as well. *Forbidden Strawberries* proved to be an inexpressibly moving account by a child survivor of the Holocaust in Poland. We decided to go meet Dr. Hurwitz as soon as Steve could take a break from his work.

In planning this trip, we chose a bed and breakfast in Caesarea that we found online. We had seen signs to Caesarea on our impromptu visit to Moreshet the month before. We knew the name well from the Book of Acts. It was where a Roman military officer and his friends proved, in the presence of St. Peter, that non-Jews could receive gifts of the Holy Spirit. It is also the site of Israel's only 18-hole golf course.

Within hours of meeting Diane and hearing of her work for victims, the owner of the bed and breakfast said there was someone Diane had to meet. Soon the two of them were off having lunch with the owner's friend nearby at Neve Michael Children's Village. This place turned out to be a wonderful model of how to care for the most vulnerable and disadvantaged children.

While Diane was enjoying her tour, Steve got the documents ready on his laptop to show Dr. Hurwitz. He included items from 1920 about Jewish-Communist conspiracy as well as items from the mid-1930s. Driving down Israel's north-south expressway the next morning, we turned off into the northern part of the Negev desert. As we approached the kibbutz, we marveled at the beautifully cultivated fields growing on rolling terrain. To Steve it looked like Lancaster County, Pennsylvania, where he grew up: the Garden Spot, but in the middle of a desert.

We spent the better part of a day with Dr. Hurwitz, at his home. He was kind, hospitable, and better informed on the relevant subject matter than anyone we had encountered before. With each piece of evidence, we were able to discuss how it compared to the current state of historiography on the Holocaust and Nazi era. While most of the evidence we had compiled was not previously known to historians, it was important to have confirmation of that fact from a highly credible source.

In some matters of obscure detail, Dr. Hurwitz was able to correct and clarify. For instance, the 1920 Jewish-Bolshevik propaganda pieces misspelled the name of the "Bolshevik-Kehillah" Rabbi, Judah Magnes. More significantly, they slanderously misrepresented his views and his character. Judah Magnes was highly respected by his contemporaries, far from a "Bolshevik," and instrumental in founding the Hebrew University in Jerusalem.

The two of us approached this meeting with two different perspectives. For Steve, it was a meeting with an expert. He had the same attitude as when he finds the most knowledgeable expert in a complex litigation case. For Diane, it was a meeting with a member of the people that her own people had contributed to demonizing, and worse. Having read Cipora Hurwitz's book, we were fully aware of the results of that demonization in the Catholic culture of Poland. Diane felt trepidation, not exhilaration, going into the meeting. Her mood was all the more somber knowing that Cipora Hurwitz, who survived the Holocaust as a child, had passed away not long before.

Diane's trepidation melted away during our time together. Dr. Hurwitz invited us to the kibbutz café. One of the kibbutzim told us over lunch about drip irrigation, explaining the local agricultural marvel. Dr. Hurwitz showed us the barn where he had milked cows during two decades of his life.

As we finished, Dr. Hurwitz offered Diane a ride in his electric golf-style cart to our parked car. Steve walked along. At the car, as Diane gave Dr. Hurwitz a hug, he said, "Now we're friends." Reconciliation is possible. It was far more than a meeting with an expert.

29. The Vatican Honors the Swastika

Dr. Ben-Dror told us what she knew about the swastika blessing photograph on a Skype call between Boston and Israel. She proved, indeed, to be the first person we encountered who knew about a swastika flag photo from the International Eucharistic Congress of 1934 in Buenos Aires. But it was a different photograph, which we had not seen or heard of before.

Dr. Ben-Dror explained that the photograph was on the cover of her book, not the English version, but only the Spanish one. The Harvard Library had the Spanish edition, but Steve had ignored it in favor of the English translation next to it on the shelf. On the paperback cover of *Católicos, Nazis y Judios*, encased inside a hard cover added by the Harvard Library, was a picture of a giant white cross with several flags in front of it. The cross was familiar to us from other photographs of the 1934 Eucharistic Congress.

The most readily identifiable flag in the picture was the swastika flag. It was held on a pole by a flag-bearer, who stood amidst several other flag-bearers with flags on their poles. Dr. Ben-Dror had no information about the context or provenance of the photograph, and her book did not mention the photo except to feature it on the cover.

The explanation of the photograph surfaced later in the summer of 2012, when Steve looked back over Diane's images of *La Prensa* from the Library of Congress. She had copied more pages than he thought relevant at the time.

Now he looked more carefully. On page 9 of *La Prensa* for October 15, 1934, he noticed a heading in the middle of a full-page article: "Flags and Pendants of the Foreign Delegations Surrounded the Christian Altar."

This section of the article described the culminating ceremony of the Eucharistic Congress. The ceremony took place at the central point of the Eucharistic Congress, around the giant cross with an altar on one side of it.

The "flags and pendants" around the altar were an honor guard of flags from six countries. The article described the flag bearers in the honor guard ascending the steps of the platform. Then the article named the six flags: the Vatican flag, multiple Argentine flags, the French, British, and American flags, and the German flag "with the cross of the National Socialist regime."

Photographs in the two-volume *Official Proceedings* of the International Eucharistic Congress show the steps ascending the platform on the altar-side of the large cross. As the swastika flag ascended to the platform, it was visible to the immense crowd stretching out from the cross and altar. The culminating ceremony consisted of a Pontifical Mass, a sermon by Cardinal Pacelli, and an address to the crowd by Pope Pius XI from Rome. The Pope's address reached the crowd over loudspeakers, by way of a radio connection personally architected by wireless inventor Guglielmo Marconi.

The celebrant of the Pontifical Mass was Cardinal Pacelli. The Official Proceedings of the Eucharistic Congress describe the event in detail, including the text of Pacelli's sermon in Spanish, and the words of Pope Pius XI by trans-Atlantic radio in Latin. Thus the swastika was displayed and honored in Cardinal Pacelli's presence, during a Mass at which both he and the Pope spoke. The flag that was blessed by an Archbishop before hundreds inside a church became visible two weeks later to hundreds of thousands.

What impression did this make on citizens of a country where governmental authorities had *banned* the public display of the swastika just three months before? None of the Argentine newspapers we reviewed discussed this issue. None of the papers carried a photo of the swastika display at the Pontifical Mass, just as none of them published a photo of the swastika blessing two weeks before.

La Prensa, the only paper we found to mention the swastika display at all, used tactful terminology. It referred to "cruz," meaning cross, rather than swastika, in its October 15th article. In its article on the swastika blessing ceremony, it used an indirect Spanish term for swastika, "cruz gamada." By contrast, Argentine newspapers in summer 1934, describing the prohibition of swastika displays, used the direct Spanish equivalent for swastika: "svástika."

On October 14, 1934, a million people heard the voices of Pope Pius XI and Cardinal Pacelli broadcast to a crowd facing the altar and cross next to the swastika flag. What impact did that scene have upon the future course of Argentina? The act was compounded by Cardinal Pacelli's public outreach to the Nazi-SS German Ambassador, by the Vatican-supervised promotion of *El Kahal* and *Oro* the next year, and by German propaganda subsidies to the daily Catholic paper of Buenos Aires in the years that followed. High level Catholic authorities, in these ways, contributed to Argentina's "Década Infame." How much responsibility do Pope Pius XI, Cardinal Pacelli and Cardinal Copello bear for Argentina's transformation from a welcoming place for Jews before the 1930s, to a welcoming place for Nazis after that decade? That question has been overlooked in English-language histories. It can no longer be avoided.

30. Taking Stock of the Evidence

For almost three years, we had been looking into the swastika blessing ceremony on the understanding that Cardinal Pacelli was *not* present. He could not possibly have been, since he was at sea on his way to Buenos Aires on the day the ceremony occurred. Now it turned out he *was* present, but at a different ceremony that was even more significant. Documentary evidence now showed Cardinal Pacelli's involvement in a promotional act for the symbol of Nazism, in front of a crowd of a million or more.

No historian we talked to had considered any possibility as serious as this. The most bizarre facts, out of synch with any historian's paradigm, were aligning into their own consistent pattern: Cardinal Pacelli with the swastika flag, Cardinal Pacelli with the German SS Officer-Ambassador, Vatican promotions of pro-Nazi Bishop Hudal proclaiming Germany's "mission," favorable articles on Hitler personally and the Nazi Party Congress of 1934, the exchange of visits between Hitler and the Vatican Nuncio in Berlin. All these elements in the second half of 1934 carried the same pro-Nazi message, all within several weeks of each other.

The pattern in 1935 was equally striking. The impression of official approval for the symbol of Nazi ideology, conveyed by the photograph in *Der Sturmer*, was consistent with other actions in the weeks that followed. The Vatican effectively blessed the most militant aspect of Nazi ideology during that period, the Jewish-Communist conspiracy theory. Elevating the swastika-blessing Archbishop to Cardinal later in the year was the capstone to the pattern.

A closer look at some individual elements of the pattern revealed them to be even more sinister than they appeared on the surface. The September 28, 1934 *Roman Observer* article about Hudal's speech and Germany's "mission" turned out to be more than a straightforward report of a speech. Steve found a detailed summary of Hudal's speech in the annual proceedings of the German Catholic academic group that sponsored it. The concept of a "mission for Germany" did not appear in the summary.

Hudal's speech was about historical matters decades and centuries in the past. The only present-day aspects were Hudal quoting Hitler on the need to preserve German cultural values of the past, Hudal denouncing the Versailles Treaty, Hudal hoping for the "rebirth" of Germany, and Hudal saying the fate of Germany is the fate of Europe. To judge from the summary, Nazi

Germany's "mission" to be a "trusted bulwark against Bolshevism" was added by the Vatican.

The *Volkisch Observer* printed the full text of Goebbels' speech about "Jewish Communism," the one reported on the front page of the *Roman Observer* on the day of the Nuremberg Laws. The Vatican newspaper's reporting of the speech was generally accurate, but one key element of its account was not in the text of the speech. Goebbels' speech did not contain the statement that Germany and its leader are carrying out a mission for which all the nations of the world should be grateful. Goebbels did use the term "mission" to describe the Nazi death-struggle against Jewish Bolshevism. But the imperative of worldwide *gratitude* for Germany's mission against Jewish-Bolshevism under Hitler was added by the Vatican.

Another article in the Vatican newspaper came into sharper focus in light of the other evidence. On August 4, 1934, two days after Hitler usurped absolute power in Germany upon the death of President Hindenburg, the *Roman Observer* featured a front page article, purportedly from Paris, on the implications of Hitler's new absolute power. The article said: "No one could now prevent Hitler from completely carrying out the famous program of February 23, 1920."

The Nazi Party's 25-point program, announced in the great hall of the Hofbrauhaus on February 24, 1920 by Hitler, contained nothing against Communism, but point after point against Judaism.

Whether the Vatican simply reprinted this article from a French source, or added material of its own, in either event the impact appeared ominous in light of the pattern we saw emerging. Particularly ominous were these lines in the article: "A decisive struggle is beginning for a total renewal... The original idea of National Socialism, proclaimed at the outset of the movement, will enter into a decisive phase of realization."

The overall pattern of 1934-1935 raised the previously unthinkable possibility that the Vatican honored the swastika not despite its meaning, but because of it. Trying to understand, we looked closer at what Bishop Hudal wrote and said in the second half of 1934. Hudal's memoirs mention the weeks-long trip he took to Germany in late summer 1934 to learn what he could about early Nazi ideology. Hudal's new book in December 1934, highly praised by the *Roman Observer*, expressed a desire that two flags wave over the whole country of Germany: the "banner of the nation" and the "flag of the kingdom of Christ."

Pope Pius XI proclaimed in a 1925 encyclical that the Roman Catholic Church is the kingdom of Christ on earth. The Vatican's flag was blessed together with the swastika by Archbishop Copello. The two flags then appeared in the select honor guard two weeks later. Consistent with such symbolism, the Vatican's newspaper lauded Hudal's book for demonstrating the "congruence and harmony, rather than division and irreconcilability, between the German race and the Catholic Church."

The proclamation of a "mission" for Nazi Germany had a menacing ring for anyone familiar with Hitler's 1925 book *Mein Kampf*. In it, Hitler said he chose the swastika to symbolize the mission of the Nazi Party. Then he described that mission in these words:

> the mission of the struggle for the victory of the Aryan man, and, by the same token, the victory of the idea of creative work, which as such always has been and always will be antisemitic.

The German language has several words for "mission": *Sendung* and *Aufgabe*, which are Germanic in origin, and *Mission*, a word that German shares with the Latin-based languages of French, Italian and English. Hitler used the word *Mission* repeatedly in *Mein Kampf*.

Cardinal Pacelli, in the passage about the swastika in his diplomatic note of May 14, 1934, focused on meaning and mission. His complaint was that the swastika was being used by the Nazis for anti-Christian "meanings and missions." His note was in German, and the word he used was *Mission*.

By the end of 1934, moreover, the German Bishops came into line with Bishop Hudal's message that Catholics had a religious obligation to support the Nazi regime. In the lead-up to a crucial referendum in the Saar region, German Bishops' conferences proclaimed that Catholics were obligated to stand up for the "greatness" of Germany.

The Saar was detached from Germany by the Versailles Treaty, with a proviso that after 15 years the people of the Saar would vote to determine its future. Goebbels declared his appreciation for the Bishops' statements in the Nazi Party newspaper shortly before the largely Catholic Saar population voted overwhelmingly to rejoin Germany. By contrast, German Bishops, just five months earlier, had recognized that telling German Catholics how to vote in a referendum placed undue pressure on the consciences of Catholics.

By September 15, 1935, Hitler and the Nazi regime brought the swastika into explicit alignment with a mission that was *not* anti-Christian. The first Nuremberg Law made the swastika the national flag of Germany. The other two Nuremberg Laws stripped Jewish Germans of their citizenship and outlawed marriage and sexual relations between Jews and non-Jews in Germany. When he announced the Nuremberg Laws on September 15th, Hitler's deputy Hermann Göring declared the swastika to be "the anti-Jewish symbol of the world."

The swastika was thenceforth in full public alignment with Nazi Germany's *antisemitic mission.* For those who equated Bolshevism and Judaism, Germany's "mission" to be a "trusted bulwark against Bolshevism" was indistinguishable from the Nazis' original antisemitic mission.

We were now looking at the serious possibility that the impression of authoritative Catholic Church approval for the swastika, created in July 1935 by the photograph in *Der Sturmer*, was an integral part of a broader pattern. Did the Vatican give the photograph to Streicher or the Nazi regime? There were only a limited number of suspects who had the power to accomplish the necessary steps: arranging to have the photograph taken; preventing others from taking and publishing a similar photograph; and getting the photo to *Der Sturmer*.

The Argentine Foreign Minister, who was present at the swastika blessing ceremony, had the power but not the disposition. Carlos Saavedra Lamas was an active peace-maker in the mid-1930s who won the Nobel Peace Prize for his efforts. German Ambassador Thermann had the disposition, but neither his Foreign Office nor his SS chain of command led to Streicher. And if Thermann did the deed, it is hard to understand the ten-month gap between the photographing of the ceremony and the publication of the photograph. We did not have direct evidence to conclude who had transmitted the photo. But the overall pattern of all the evidence from 1934 and 1935, now that we knew the Vatican deliberately honored the swastika at the Eucharistic Congress, left us stunned.

We resolved to do three things. First, try to understand all we could about the Vatican's relationship with the Jewish-Communist conspiracy theory over time. What, if anything, did the Vatican's newspaper say about "Jewish-Communism" in 1920, in the years leading up to 1935, and in the subsequent years leading up to the Holocaust?

Second, try to understand what happened in Bavaria. When the *Munich Catholic Church Newspaper* promoted the *Protocols* and Jewish-Communist propaganda in spring 1920, and Hitler and the young Nazi Party echoed and amplified those themes, was that a one-time occurrence or part of a larger pattern? What were the dynamics between Catholic authority in Munich and Nazi Party activity in the years following 1920? In short, we would research the antecedents and connect the dots to the extent possible, just as Steve's engineer and entrepreneur clients had challenged us to do.

Third, we resolved to make it possible for the general public to access the relevant source materials, the first-hand evidence concerning these issues. The issues and evidence are understandable to anyone, not just historians. They present matters of universal moral concern.

Members of any profession find it difficult to discard long-accepted conventional paradigms when new evidence surfaces to contradict them. Sometimes those with fewer pre-conceptions are better able to handle the evidence. For historians and general readers alike, documentary evidence is crucial for understanding.

After much experimentation with formats, we decided to construct Diane's idea: a timeline of events and documents, with links to the documents in English translation, and links from there to the original documents. For the large majority of documents, copyright had expired. That means they are in the public domain and fully available for online presentation. For those still protected by copyright, excerpts can be presented, within the limits of the legal doctrine of "fair use."

31. Conspiracy Theory: How Central to the Holocaust?

As a preliminary question, to make sure we were not over-estimating the significance of what we found at Yad Vashem, we examined what historians have said about the impact of the Jewish-Communist conspiracy theory as a causative factor of the Holocaust. We found important historical works saying it was a significant factor, and no works denying its significance.

An especially helpful source was American historian Jeffrey Herf's recent book *The Jewish Enemy: Nazi Propaganda During World War II and the Holocaust*. Professor Herf identifies "Jewish Bolshevism" and antisemitic conspiracy theory as the central public explanation the Nazis used to justify the invasion of Russia and the mass murder of Jews.

Herf describes a directive to the German press from Goebbels' Propaganda Ministry on June 25, 1941, three days after Germany invaded Russia. It directed the press to portray the invasion as the united effort of "all European peoples against Bolshevism." Further, the "treasonous cooperation of Jewish plutocracy with the Bolsheviks should always be mentioned."

British historian Norman Cohn's *Warrant for Genocide* devotes a chapter to the role of the Jewish-Communist conspiracy myth in Nazi propaganda. The chapter begins: "The Protocols and the myth of the Jewish world-conspiracy were exploited in Nazi propaganda at every stage, from the first emergence of the party in the early 1920s to the collapse of the Third Reich in 1945."

We turned also to original documents. Steve examined microfilm reels of the Nazi Party's newspaper, the *Volkisch Observer*, at Harvard. He looked at June 1941, the month Nazi Germany invaded the Soviet Union and began the mass murder of Jews. Sure enough, there was the full text of Hitler's proclamation to the German *Volk* on the day of the invasion. The Jewish-Communist conspiracy theory was a centerpiece of the proclamation. These were Hitler's words:

> Never has the German *Volk* harbored hostile feelings toward the peoples of Russia. It is only the Jewish-Bolshevik powers-that-be who for more than two decades have endeavored from Moscow to put not only Germany but all of Europe to the torch. Germany has never tried to take the National Socialist ideology to Russia, rather the Jewish-Bolshevik rulers in Moscow have continually undertaken to impose their rule upon

us and the other European peoples, and not only ideologically, but above all by military might...

For Germans in the *Einsatzgruppen*, the SS-directed task forces that started mass-murdering Jews in mid-1941 behind the advancing German front lines in Russia, and for every other German on the Eastern Front or the home front, these were powerful words. Anyone hearing such propaganda and believing it could well conclude that killing Jews was a matter of self-defense.

Germans were "defending" against an enemy supposedly bent on destroying Germany, Catholicism, Christianity, and all of Western Civilization. That enemy was Jews in general, all Jews, a continuing threat spanning decades and generations. Infants and the elderly were all part of the ongoing threat. Hitler said in 1935 that if the Nuremberg Laws proved insufficient to defend Germany against the threat of Jewish-Communism, then further measures would be taken. The rationale of self-defense against the Jewish-Communist conspiracy remained a constant through the next ten years.

Of course it was all a massive lie. Not only was Soviet Communism under the absolute dictatorship of the antisemitic Stalin. It was also the case that Stalin did not undertake military initiatives against European countries from the time he gained power in the mid-1920s until 1939. He adopted the policy of "Socialism in One Country," namely Russia, as an explicit renunciation of Lenin's prioritizing worldwide Communist revolution. In 1939, when Stalin invaded Poland, he did it as an *ally* of Nazi Germany, under the "Hitler-Stalin Pact." To present the Soviet Union as a *Jewish threat* to the survival of Western Civilization, in the 1930s, was contrary to all fact.

The lie, as we already saw, was promoted around the world. *El Kahal* expressed the lie in Argentina in 1935 as strongly as any Nazi ever did: "Death to the Jew" means "Long Live the Fatherland." From 7,000 miles away, *Catholic Civilization* promoted the book that contained the lie.

But we still did not know why the Vatican would allow or cause *Catholic Civilization* to promote this lie in 1935. Nor did we know why the Vatican would promote the lie in its own newspaper. Further, why would the Munich Archbishop allow his Diocesan newspaper to publish the lie in 1920? Our next step took us back to the antecedents of the articles in *Catholic Documentation* and the *Munich Catholic Church Newspaper*, with their claim to be based on an official report of the American Services.

32. National Archives: US, Britain and France

Steve puzzled during summer 2012 over what "the American Services" could be. He was inclined to believe it was simply a made-up name. If so, it was a cleverly chosen name. Had *Catholic Documentation* attributed the article to the U.S. State Department or U.S. Army Intelligence, a simple contact to those agencies could have quickly exposed the fraud. But where does one turn to contact the American Services?

Electronic searches for "American Services" amply confirmed Steve's suspicion that there was no such agency. But the search results included a book containing the phrase "American Services." *Wall Street and the Bolshevik Revolution*, by Anthony Sutton of the Hoover Institution at Stanford University, cited U.S. State Department documents related to an American Services report on Judaism and Bolshevism. An appendix in the book contained additional State Department documents showing Jewish Russians asking Jewish Americans for financial support in 1917. A family trip to Lancaster over the Fourth of July holiday gave us an opportunity to look up the State Department documents at the National Archives two hours away.

The documented reality in 1917 through 1919 contrasted sharply with the distortions and conspiracy theories that surfaced in France and Bavaria in 1920. The documents helped explain the genesis of the later propaganda, as they showed the State Department examining in 1919 the exact same package of "Jewish-Communism" lies that appeared in the March 1920 *Catholic Documentation* article.

The earliest relevant U.S. State Department files were an exchange of cables in spring 1917 between Russia and the United States. In April 1917, one month after a democratic revolution overthrew the Czar and established a short-lived republic in Russia, and three weeks after the U.S. entered World War One, a telegram from leading Jewish figures in Russia requested help from Jacob Schiff and other prominent Jewish Americans to arrange financing for the new republic.

Far from supporting Bolshevism, Schiff, along with other leading Jewish Americans, including Supreme Court Justice Louis Brandeis, were considering financial support for a *democratic* government allied with the United States. But first they consulted the U.S. State Department. Secretary of State Robert Lansing waved them off. He told them to support the American war bond effort instead. Then the U.S. could loan money to allies such as Russia at low interest rates.

Whether or not Russia's democratic government received loans from the U.S. Government in a timely manner, that government fell in November 1917 to Lenin and the Bolsheviks. The decisive factor in Lenin's victory was not Jews. It was the German Government. Germany transported Lenin from exile in Switzerland to Finland. From there he went to St. Petersburg, the Russian capital. Germany did this precisely in order to topple Russian democracy and take Germany's most populous enemy country out of the war. Germans and others after the war who claimed "the Jews" were responsible for Russian Bolshevism typically did not mention this salient fact.

By 1919, State Department documents showed, the facts of 1917 had been twisted into a detailed conspiracy theory about Jacob Schiff and other Jewish financiers supporting Bolshevism, encapsulated in a five-page draft article. Lenin, in this finely spun tale, was the only non-Jew among 30 Bolshevik leaders. "Jewish Communism" was out to destroy Christian civilization and take over the world. The effort to bring this conspiracy theory into the public square involved some historically prominent and colorful figures.

The lead figure in America peddling the draft article was a Czarist Russian émigré named Boris Brasol. A leading figure in Europe pushing the same "Bolshevism and Judaism" article was Prince Yusupov. Yusupov was the husband of the Russian Czar's niece, and he was one of the men who assassinated Rasputin in St. Petersburg in 1916.

By October 1919, the Bolshevism and Judaism article came into the hands of Sir Basil Thomson, who had the distinction of heading British domestic and foreign intelligence, MI-5 and MI-6, simultaneously. Sir Basil brought the article to the U.S. Embassy in London and asked the Americans to confirm or disprove rumors that the Bolsheviks were receiving money from wealthy American Jews. A State Department investigation ended with Secretary of State Lansing cabling London to say the article had "no special validity." He advised that it would be "most unwise" to let it be published.

The State Department files at the National Archives contain the five-page text of "Bolshevism and Judaism." It is identical to the article that appeared five months later in France. What *Catholic Documentation* published on March 6, 1920 was a French translation of the English original that the State Department had investigated and quashed. One of the State Department documents indicated the London Embassy had put the document into "cold storage." Somehow it got out.

The State Department documents raised some unsettling questions. The documents recognized that the Jewish-Bolshevism article, with its claim to be an "American Services" report, was obviously a fraud. If officials all the way up to Secretary Lansing were aware of the real facts from 1917 about Schiff, Brandeis, and the others, did the State Department do anything to defend their reputation against these fraudulent smears? The Department was aware that the "Bolshevism and Judaism" article had been shared with French intelligence agents, and the U.S. had friendly relations with its World War One ally. As the Jewish-Communist conspiracy theory and the *Protocols* spread through Europe and the United States during 1920, the U.S. State Department had the ability to expose this propaganda as a gross distortion of verifiable facts, facts that thoroughly exculpated the accused parties.

One oddity from the State Department files may prove to be a useful lead when historians look into this sordid affair. The State Department determined that the author of "Bolshevism and Judaism," Russian emigré Boris Brasol, was employed by the War Trade Board. The Legal Adviser of the War Trade Board during World War One was Secretary of State Lansing's nephew, John Foster Dulles, who himself became Secretary of State in the 1950s. Brasol tried throughout 1919 to get his article and the *Protocols* published, but had no success in the U.S. during that year. How much did Lansing and Dulles know about his efforts?

Furthermore, how did the article get to the French Catholic publication, and why did its editors feel free to publish such inflammatory propaganda? Competent fact-checking could ascertain there was no such agency as "the official American Services." We only had a brief time to look at a few issues of *Catholic Documentation* at the French National Library, so we were not yet in a good position to assess its overall character.

The new-found credibility of "Jewish-Bolshevism" and the *Protocols* in 1920 had international consequences. The *Protocols of the Elders of Zion* were published in multiple countries in the western world after March-April 1920. Industrialist Henry Ford published the *Protocols* in serialized form in his *Dearborn Independent* newspaper, beginning in May 1920. The *Protocols* appeared in book form, courtesy of two American publishers in 1920, one of them a long-established publishing house in Boston, the other a new publisher in New York. Within another year they were published in France, Italy, and Poland.

33. Rosh Pina Means "Cornerstone"

We were hardly back home from the National Archives when Diane pressed forward with her desire to show our four youngest children Israel. Steve was too busy with legal work to agree to the trip, with a deadline for a major project fast approaching. Somehow this did not dim Diane's enthusiasm. When the client for the major project granted Steve a two-week extension, Steve returned home and started looking up airfares to Tel Aviv. The combination that worked best was two of us leaving on Saturday, with the other four following the next day.

Steve and the oldest of our teenage daughters went first, with a seven-hour stopover in Paris. That gave them time to visit the neighborhood where friends had invited us to stay in 2000 on our way to World Youth Day in Rome. Rue Vavin, a walk through the Luxembourg Gardens a block away, breakfast at a café on the nearby Boulevard Montparnasse, and Mass at Notre Dame. It was a beautiful father-daughter morning.

After a good night's sleep in Rehavia, and a solid Israeli breakfast, Steve took up the challenge of showing our daughter the sites of the Old City at a brisk pace. She had only a few days in Israel before returning early, so this was her chance: Jaffa Gate, narrow streets lined with small shops, Church of the Holy Sepulcher, Lutheran Church of the Savior, Way of the Cross, a view of the Dome of the Rock from a narrow overarched street guarded by an Israeli soldier, Muslim Quarter, and finally back through the Jewish Quarter.

Meanwhile, Diane had a shorter layover at Charles de Gaulle Airport with our three youngest daughters. She was aware it was the 70th anniversary of the Velodrome roundup. The rounding up of Jewish Parisians by French police, for the Nazis and their extermination camps, is memorialized in *Sarah's Key*, as well as works of history, mostly in French.

In order to get ready to pick up the main party at Ben Gurion Airport, Steve rented a minivan next door to the King David Hotel in Jerusalem. On the way to the airport, Steve had enough time to give our daughter a tour of the Holocaust History Museum at Yad Vashem.

It was for this family trip that Airbnb made the biggest difference. Shortly before heading to the Boston airport, we found a three-bedroom townhouse overlooking the Sea of Galilee. The view in the online photo looked spectacular, and the reality did not disappoint. We arrived around midnight, everyone exhausted but happy. On the way from Ben Gurion

Airport, we had stopped at our favorite restaurant in Nazareth. Tishreen made everyone feel instantly at home with Arab hospitality and wonderful food.

After dinner we paid a visit to Mary's Well, just a block away. With so much of Biblical Israel destroyed through the centuries, it is often difficult to know what place designations are authentic. Mary's Well was the only water source in Nazareth through many, many centuries. So we could be reasonably confident it was the water source for Mary as well as Joseph, Jesus, and their fellow residents in the small town of Nazareth. Today Nazareth is the largest Arab city in Israel, with a Muslim majority and a Christian minority.

We awoke in our townhouse to see the huge fiery ball of the sun sitting on top of the Golan Heights. Walking out onto the back patio, we took in the view we had seen online. The Sea of Galilee lies in a deep depression from the surrounding terrain. Slopes rise up nearly 1,000 feet from the lake. We had breakfast while we took in the entire lake at a glance.

The town of Rosh Pina sits on hilly terrain a couple thousand feet higher still, about five miles from the northwest part of the lake. Rosh Pina was a perfect base for exploring the Galilee region. We split our time in Galilee between the old and the new. From Biblical times, Jesus' adult hometown of Capernaum lay just a few miles below us, with the hillside of the Beatitudes along the way, and the ancient ruins of Tiberias further south, in the middle of a large modern city.

We happened upon the 2000-year-old Galilee boat, exhibited at a museum alongside the kibbutz whose members found it, preserved in the mud, when the Galilee waters receded during a drought 30 years ago. We were glad for the air conditioning of the Galilee boat museum on a day that broke 40 degrees Celsius, well above 100 Fahrenheit, along the Galilee shores.

Two other ways of beating the July heat wave were appreciated by all. One was a lovely beach and swimming club along the Sea of Galilee in Tiberias. The other was a walk in a park and forest preserve near the Lebanon border. We walked alongside headwaters of the Jordan River called the Nahal Snir, and then hiked right in them for much of the way.

Steve made a discovery at Rosh Pina that later proved relevant to our research. Driving to the supermarket in town, he overshot the mark and noticed a memorial as he turned around. Alongside a small park and old stone buildings converted to restaurants, there was a plaque describing the local Jewish settlement in Rosh Pina during the First Aliyah ("going up," or returning, to Israel) in the 1880s. Members of the Rothschild family, often demonized in the antisemitic propaganda we had encountered, generously supported a settlement by Jews from Russia and Romania. When Steve looked into the history of the settlement, he found a description of Jewish settlers and Arab farmers coexisting peacefully through many years.

How was this possible? Was this an exception to the longstanding bitter animosity between the Arab population of Palestine and the Jews who returned in increasing numbers beginning in the late 19th century? Not necessarily. A Jewish population resided in Palestine throughout the centuries, including Tiberias and Safed in Galilee. A pogrom against the Jews of Safed in 1834 was the exception.

Coexistence was much more the rule, through the time of World War One. Jews and Arabs alike were ruled by the Ottoman Turks, who held Palestine from the 1500s until their defeat by the British Army in 1917 and 1918. The "Sherif of Mecca" who allied with Lawrence of Arabia and the British Army, and whose son became the most prominent leader among the Arabs of the Middle East, was an enemy of the Turks, not of the Jews.

Arab farmers in Palestine lived under an additional type of domination both before and after 1918. Most of the land was owned by absentee landlords, and the customary rental terms were harsh. There was no inherent economic conflict between Arab tenant farmers in Palestine and Jewish immigrants who provided enhanced markets for farmers' produce, together with improved farming and irrigation methods, drainage of swamps, ending of malaria, improvement of sanitation, widespread electrification, etc. Our time at Rosh Pina was a window into these realities of the past. The name Rosh Pina, incidentally, was chosen by the settlers of the First Aliyah from the Psalm about the stone rejected by the builders. Rosh Pina, in Hebrew, means "cornerstone."

After our three days in Galilee, we spent a week in a Tel Aviv apartment near the intersection of Dizengoff and Ben Yehuda, in the midst of the Tel Aviv café scene, three blocks from the beach. It proved to be a perfect base for exploring other parts of Israel while enjoying the comforts of home in the heart of a vibrant modern city. We made full use of the beach on days that alternated with day trips to Jerusalem, Caesarea and Masada. Our day trip to Caesarea took in the Roman Aqueduct, the ruins of the Crusader fortress, and the open area that includes the Roman hippodrome and the foundations of the governor's palace where St. Paul was held prisoner until being transported to Rome for his appeal to the Emperor. Our lunch nearby at Neve Michael, with an opportunity for our daughters to meet some of the children, was a wonderful treat.

34. Rome Annihilating Jews

Our day trip to Masada was memorable. Masada is an impregnable fortress and palace built by Herod the Great (70s B.C. to 4 B.C.) on top of a mesa. The steep walls of the mesa rise a thousand feet above the plain near the Dead Sea. Today a gondola takes visitors from a museum at the base to the remains of Herod's buildings on top.

We arrived in the morning to tour the top area first and then the air-conditioned museum during the hottest part of a scorching July day. Two aspects were especially surprising. First, we knew that Masada was the place where the Roman Empire defeated the last remnant of the Jewish rebellion of the early A.D. 70s, after first destroying Jerusalem. But we did not know that Rome committed an entire legion, ten thousand troops or more, to an effort that took the better part of a year.

Most of our information about Rome's destruction of Jerusalem and siege of Masada comes from a Jewish-Roman historian of the time, Flavius Josephus. A Jewish rebellion in the year 66 A.D. prompted the Roman Empire to send a large army to Israel, which the Romans called Palestine. After subduing Galilee and other areas, the Romans laid siege to Jerusalem. When the Jews' defense eventually collapsed, Rome demolished the entire city, including its walls and the Temple. Approximately a million Jews perished, with the rest reduced to slavery or exile.

The only free Jews remaining in Palestine were several hundred who took refuge atop Masada. To destroy them, Rome undertook the immense logistical challenge of sustaining a large force in the desert, remote from any established supply lines. As the months-long construction of the siege ramp approached the curtain wall along the edge of the mesa top, the Jews in Masada made a suicide pact. Josephus tells the story of their final hours, based on the testimony of two women who hid and chose slavery over death.

The second aspect of Masada that especially surprised us was the Byzantine church at the center of the mesa top. It reminded us of the Byzantine church next to the Roman amphitheater near Dr. Hurwitz's kibbutz. A plaque explained that this church was built for the hermits who lived on top of Masada around the 600s. Hermits were a tradition that began with St. Anthony in the Egyptian desert a few hundred years earlier. But we didn't know that hermits built beautiful Byzantine churches with fine mosaic floors.

35. Connecting the Dots:
"Jewish-Communism" 1920-1938

Back home in Boston, we set about connecting dots, from 1920 to 1935 and beyond. What were the Vatican antecedents, if any, to the promotion of the Jewish-Communist conspiracy theory that we found in 1935? Were the Catholic promotions of that conspiracy theory in 1920, in France and Bavaria, consistent or inconsistent with Vatican policy at that earlier time? The process of research, translating, and online presentation of evidence took more than a year. Works by historians helped identify some individual elements. Original sources identified even more. Specific questions about Catholic-Nazi interaction in the early 1920s took us back again to Munich, in March 2013. This chapter and the next tell what we found.

During the first nine months of 1920, the Vatican's newspaper focused in great detail, dozens of times, on the threat of Russian Communism. But none of the articles said Communism was Jewish, or directed by Jews, or part of a worldwide Jewish conspiracy. We found no indication that the Vatican newspaper was promoting Jewish-Bolshevik conspiracy theory during the three-year period from the Russian Revolution to October 1920.

That month, however, witnessed an abrupt change. A front-page article in the *Roman Observer* proclaimed the "Jewish Peril." The article presented "the Jews" directing the Russian Revolution in order to "become the masters of Russia and the world at one blow." Introducing its readers to the *Protocols of the Elders of Zion* and their blueprint for Jewish world domination, the Vatican newspaper presented the view that "the Jewish Bolsheviks have carried out almost to the letter in Russia this program announced in the *Protocols*."

Catholic Civilization followed suit over the next two months, publishing a three-part series of bloodcurdling narratives about atrocities by "Jewish Bolsheviks" in the Ukraine. In fact, from 1918 to 1920, tens of thousands of Jewish civilians in the Ukraine had been murdered by a combination of Ukrainian nationalist forces, the anti-Communist White Russian army, and the Polish military. This grisly precursor to the Holocaust received no coverage in the *Roman Observer*. While Ukraine and eastern Poland were a repeated focus of many articles, nothing we could find in the *Roman Observer* gave any hint that these places had become killing fields for Jews. On the contrary, some articles contained words of praise for the leaders of the three murderous military forces.

Half a dozen *Roman Observer* articles during 1921 repeated key propaganda themes, equating Judaism and Bolshevism, citing the *Protocols* as a blueprint for the Jewish people to become "masters of the world," and blaming disturbances in Palestine on Bolshevik Jewish immigrants.

In 1922, *Catholic Civilization* took these propaganda themes to a new level. First, a vehement article against Zionism in July accused Jewish immigrants of bringing "the most extreme Bolshevik Communism" to Palestine. Then, in October, the Vatican-supervised journal published "World Revolution and the Jews." With all the appearance of a detailed scholarly study, this article cited names and statistics to show that Jews controlled the governing councils at every level in the Soviet Union. Of the 545 upper level Soviet officials, the article informed its readers, 447 were Jews.

The 447 figure had a familiar ring. We looked back at the swastika blessing photograph in *Der Sturmer*. The "Who Governs Russia?" article to the right of the photo proclaimed that 447 of the approximately 550 upper level officials in the "Soviet paradise" were Jews. For more than three years we had regarded that claim as utterly ridiculous. And so it was.

Little did we suspect that the most influential scholarly journal in the Catholic world had endorsed the same statistical assertion 13 years earlier. The only change *Der Sturmer* made was to round 545 up to 550, or "rund 550" as the Nazi paper expressed it in German. *Der Sturmer* attributed this statistic not to *Catholic Civilization*, but to a Belgian journal whose title we have not been able to find in any library or online reference.

Catholic Civilization's outrageous claim of overwhelming Jewish predominance in the Soviet Government stood uncorrected by the Vatican, so far as we can determine, from 1922 to 1935 and after. The reality, in contrast to the ongoing lie, was that Russia was governed during those years by a non-Jewish dictator, Lenin, followed by another non-Jewish dictator, Stalin.

The actual percentage of Jews among Russian Communists was far less than a majority. The most detailed studies we have found place the proportion at various levels ranging from single digits to 20%, at various points during the period from the Russian Revolution to the early 1920s. The percentage became even lower under Stalin from the mid-1920s on.

Comparative percentages, however, do not suffice for a full understanding of the iniquity of the lie. Jewish Communists in Russia in the 1920s and 1930s were Jewish in much the same way that prominent Catholic Communists in Latin America during the 20th century were Catholic: nominally. While their parents and perhaps some of their early childhood formation may have been Jewish or Catholic, as the case may be, they had grown up to be ideologically opposed to all religion.

Just as it would be absurd and bigoted to say that Latin American Communism is "Catholic" because the Castro brothers and Che Guevara were Catholic, so it was absurd to say in the 1920s or 1930s that Soviet Communism was "Jewish." The full iniquity of this smear, as presented by the Vatican and the Munich Archdiocese, is that it converted self-evident rubbish into a proposition to be believed on the basis of Catholic authority.

We did not find Jewish-Communist conspiracy theory in the *Roman Observer* or *Catholic Civilization* after 1922, until six years later. In May of 1928, *Catholic Civilization* wrote an article explaining a recent Vatican decree. The decree had two parts that were confusing in combination. One part condemned antisemitism. The other part dissolved the "Friends of Israel," the foremost Catholic international association seeking to combat antisemitism.

Father Hubert Wolf has described internal memoranda in the Vatican Archives that explain the inconsistency: The first part was intended to protect the Vatican from accusations that in dissolving the Friends of Israel, it was motivated by antisemitism.

For our inquiry, the most significant aspect of the *Catholic Civilization* article was that it accused Jews of dominating both international finance and the Russian Revolution, in the course of "plotting their world hegemony." Self-defense against this international Jewish-Communist-capitalist conspiracy, evidently, was consistent with, rather than contrary to, the Vatican's condemnation of antisemitism.

Six years later, in October and November 1934, *Catholic Civilization* ran its two-part series on "'The Jewish Question' and National Socialist Antisemitism." Part One affirmed "the existence and the seriousness of the 'Jewish peril.'" Part Two stated that Bolshevism "was in great part a creation of Judaism." The two-part article's major complaint about Nazi antisemitism was that it attacked Popes and Catholicism, not just Judaism.

The Vatican newspaper's endorsement of the Jewish-Communist conspiracy theory on September 15, 1935 was the first such instance we found in that paper after 1921. We did not examine all issues. Another instance appeared on November 13, 1936, the day the Vatican newspaper published a brief notice about the latest book by Bishop Hudal. *The Foundations of National Socialism* was a thick tome, presented personally by Papen to Hitler in pre-publication form in June 1936. It proposed an alliance between Nazism and Catholicism, provided that several points of Nazi ideology were modified. The Nazi struggle against Jewish-Communism was not one of the points that needed modification, as this passage made clear:

> As Christians and Catholics, we have not the slightest reason to defend that Jewry which, after the World War, seized hold of the leadership of the worker masses under the banner of Marxism, and misused that leadership richly enough for their own selfish ends …

On November 13, 1936, the *Roman Observer* said of this book:

> From various quarters we have been asked if the recent publication of the book "The Foundations of National Socialism" … was done with the prior agreement of the Holy See, since this rumor has spread. Our information requires us to respond in the negative …

On the same page, the Vatican newspaper reported that Communist agitation in Hungary had "Jewish characteristics," as "in recent months all Communist agitation has been done by Jews."

In March 1937, Pope Pius XI's famous German-language encyclical *Mit Brennender Sorge*, or "With Burning Anxiety," was read aloud from German pulpits. The Pope denounced Germany's violations of the 1933 Concordat and promotions of neo-pagan ideology. But two passages toward the end of the encyclical reinforced, rather than reversed, earlier ominous messages.

First, in a passage directed to German youth, the Pope encouraged efforts to build a "true *Volksgemeinschaft.*" That term was a staple of Nazi ideology. It meant community and solidarity among the German *Volk*, in a racially-defined community that excluded Jews.

Second, in the third to last paragraph of the encyclical, the Pope invoked the concept of Germany's mission. He expressed hope that the wayward members of the German people would return to religion. Then the German *Volk* would be seen "preparing itself, in struggle [*Kampf*] against the deniers and destroyers of the Christian West, in harmony with all well-intentioned other peoples, to fulfill the calling that the plans of the Eternal assign to it."

For unknown reasons, the translation of this paragraph of the encyclical on the Vatican website is a paraphrase that leaves out half the words of the original.

On September 6, 1938, Pope Pius XI told Belgian pilgrims in a private audience that antisemitism is "inadmissible," for "we are all spiritually semites." These words have been cited by historians, and by the Vatican document *We Remember: A Reflection on the Shoah* [Holocaust], to show Pius XI's opposition to Nazi antisemitism. The *Roman Observer's* report about this audience omitted the words about antisemitism, but those words appeared in the Belgian and French press in the days and weeks that followed.

Then, three months later, in December 1938, *Catholic Documentation* in France ran two articles side-by-side. The first reported the Pope's words of September against antisemitism. But the article also reported the Pope saying, at the same audience, "We recognize for everyone the right of self-defense, to take up measures to protect themselves against all who threaten their legitimate interests." For those familiar with the overall pattern, the message was clear: Vatican rejections of antisemitism are consistent, rather than incompatible, with "self-defense" against the international Jewish peril.

As if to emphasize that point, the adjacent article in *Catholic Documentation* presented "The Distribution of the Jewish Population on the Five Continents of the World." The statistics in the article were taken from a German review, *Wirtschaft und Statistik*. The article focused especially on the danger posed by concentrations of Jews in capital cities.

The dots of Jewish-Communist propaganda, in sources published or supervised by the Vatican, connected in a continuous line with consistent messaging from 1920 to 1938. That line was not interrupted by any Vatican renunciation of that propaganda, so far as we can find in original documents and works by historians.

36. The Impact of Newspapers

What influence did the *Roman Observer* and the *Munich Catholic Church Newspaper* have? A long-time official in the Vatican Secretariat of State, who helped supervise the *Roman Observer* under Cardinal Gasparri in the 1920s and Cardinal Pacelli in the 1930s, described what type of influence the Vatican newspaper sought to exert:

> It is not, like so many others, a simple organ of information; it intends to be, and I believe it is, mainly an instrument of formation. It does not simply set out to provide news; it intends to shape ideas. It is not enough for it to report events as they occur; it wants to comment on them to indicate how they should have happened, or not happened. It is not in conversation with its readers only; it talks with the whole world, commenting, discussing, arguing.

These words were written by Giovanni Battista Montini in 1961, when he was Archbishop of Milan. He had been an official in the Vatican Secretariat of State from the 1920s to the 1950s. He became Pope Paul VI in 1963.

We saw ample evidence that key German figures of the 1920s and 1930s recognized the *Roman Observer* as an indicator of Vatican policy. Diego von Bergen, who was Prussia's and then Germany's Ambassador to the Vatican from 1917 to 1943, quoted the *Roman Observer* in reports to the German Foreign Office to show the Vatican's position on issues. Cardinal Faulhaber cited the Vatican paper for the same purpose. He cited it to his fellow Bavarian Bishops, for instance, after the *Roman Observer* stood behind his controversial remarks in August 1922 against the Weimar Republic.

Catholic Civilization exerted a similar influence, because it was known to be reviewed and approved before publication by the Vatican Secretary of State. As described by a long-time member of its staff, the twice-monthly journal was reviewed for conformity with Church doctrine and with "the policies of the Vatican toward nation-states," including the diplomatic "opportuneness" of each article.

We saw repeatedly throughout the 1920s and 1930s that *Catholic Civilization* and the *Roman Observer* took a similar approach on issues. In promoting the Jewish-Communist conspiracy theory in the early 1920s and in 1935, they reinforced each other, confirming to readers the nature of Vatican policy on the subject.

As for the *Munich Catholic Church Newspaper*, it played a decisive role in Bavaria. Many are aware that the Vatican once placed certain books on the "Index of Prohibited Books," which played a lesser role in the 1920s and 1930s than in some earlier periods, and was abolished in the 1960s. Bavarian Catholics, beginning in 1919, experienced particularly stringent *local* Church controls on what they could and could not read.

On December 7, 1919, the Second Sunday of Advent, a new pastoral letter of the Bavarian Bishops was read aloud from every Catholic pulpit in Bavaria. Entitled a "pastoral word of warning against the bad press," the Bishops' message threatened divine judgment upon those who read, or allowed into their homes, published materials contrary to Church teaching or disrespectful toward the Church and its ministers. The Bishops divided the press into white and black, "good press" and "bad press." Those who read the bad press would bring "terrible woe" upon their heads.

The *Munich Catholic Church Newspaper* stood at the summit of the "good press." Its December 7, 1919 issue featured the Bishops' message on the front page. The Archdiocesan paper proceeded to interpret and apply the message. There were three daily newspapers in Munich that could be called "good Catholic press." All other news sources were suspect. The Archdiocesan weekly identified the enemies, exaggerated their numbers, and warned Catholics to shun them: "Nearly three-fourths of German newspapers are in the hands of Jews," not to mention those in the hands of "Freemasons and Social Democrats."

In fact, a scholarly study shows, Jews constituted five percent of the editors of left-wing newspapers in Germany in the 1920s, a grand total of 20 out of 400 editors. But Bavarian Catholics could only learn the facts that refuted the propaganda if they were willing to place their eternal souls at risk by venturing outside the boundaries of the "good press."

The *Munich Catholic Church Newpaper* continued to enjoy its privileged position in Bavaria, not only as good press, but as the definer of good press. Meanwhile, the Bishops' pastoral letter on the "bad press" was read each year from every pulpit on the Second Sunday of Advent. In France, *Catholic Documentation* also enjoyed a favored status. It was published by the "House of the Good Press." The good press was not a coincidental local initiative in the two places. Developing "the good press" was a Vatican initiative, promoted by Cardinal Gasparri, and one of the designated priorities for the Vatican Nuncio in Munich.

The degree of control exercised by the hierarchy over the reading habits and political orientation of Bavarian Catholics in the early 1920s was extreme. Any Catholics who took the initiative to become well-informed about events of the day, and well-versed in scripture and doctrine, ran grave risks if they ventured to make judgments according to their conscience. First, getting information from non-approved media incurred the threat of damnation by the Bishops, even if the information was entirely factual and accurate. Second, making judgments about social and political questions could easily run afoul of the multitude of positions on a wide range of issues taken by the Archdiocesan weekly from 1919 onward.

The pages of the *Munich Catholic Church Newspaper* in 1920 indicate that priests were charged with close supervision over the lives of their people. Among the "Archbishop's Decrees" published in February that year were many rules, including the requirement that Catholics go to Confession and receive Communion during the Easter season. The concluding sentence of this particular rule envisioned priests monitoring who had and had not complied: "Whoever fails to receive Easter Communion and dies without having come to confess this failure, will be shut out from Church burial."

In the universe of Bavarian Catholicism in the early 1920s, if the Cardinal-Archbishop of Munich placed his authority behind the Jewish-Communist conspiracy theory, it was hard to express disagreement. For a Catholic to do so was disobedience. For a Catholic paper to do so risked consignment to the ranks of the "bad press."

The Vatican had issued a statement in 1916 rejecting discrimination against Jews based on their religion. But who could argue with the Archbishop based on that statement, or based on first principles? In the weeks following the "Jewish Imperialism" article of April 1920, we found the "bad press" trying to counter it, but not the "good press." When the Social Democrat newspaper of Munich spoke out in May 1920 against antisemitic propaganda from Christians, it did not dare to call out the *Munich Catholic Church Newspaper* by name. And during the three years following the appearance of "Jewish Imperialism," as far as we can find, Eugenio Pacelli, stationed in Munich as Vatican Nuncio, made no effort to counter it or criticize it in any way.

37. Connecting More Dots: Bavaria 1920-1923

We have already seen how the April 11, 1920 launch of Jewish-Communist conspiracy theory in the Munich Archdiocese was followed by Hitler and the Nazis echoing and amplifying the theme. What happened after that? Our trip to Munich in early 2013 uncovered a number of facts.

First, we learned that Nuncio Pacelli was not in Munich at the time. An issue of the *Bavarian Courier* reported that he returned from Rome on April 12th. Nuncio Pacelli went to Rome in mid-February because of the death of his mother. His role as Nuncio encompassed Vatican-German diplomatic relations and pastoral oversight of the Catholic Church. When an Arch-diocesan newspaper spews powerful hate propaganda, and an extremist political group picks up the theme, that brings into play both parts of a Nuncio's role. So what happened after Pacelli got back to Munich?

On May 2, 1920, the *Munich Catholic Church Newspaper* repeated its April 11th warning that Germany and its Catholics and Christians were in danger of being "reduced to chains by Jewry." This warning, the article explained, was not "Jew-hatred," it was "Christian-defense."

The new article provided Rome's perspective in considerable detail. Jews had rebelled against the Roman Empire in the first century A.D., resulting in the destruction of their nation, the scattering of their people, and centuries of ongoing struggle against Roman Catholic authorities, from Germany to Spain. Echoing the title of the April 11th article, this one authoritatively proclaimed an "eternal war" between "Christian culture and Jewish imperialism."

Incredibly, this article also echoed the *Volkisch Observer's* April 29th accusation of collective guilt against all Munich's Jews for not singling out Communist Jews. Munich's Jews "cover their degenerate ones," the article declaimed. Thus they make it impossible to distinguish good Jews from bad. That accusation was the core of the Nazi-oriented paper's incitement to violence against Munich's Jewish community three days earlier. It was precisely the incitement that prompted the 10-day publishing ban on the *Volkisch Observer*, imposed by the antisemitic Munich police chief. What was too extreme for Ernst Pohner was endorsed for Munich Catholics by their Archdiocesan paper three days later. With the Nazi paper silenced for the moment, the Catholic paper, safe from reproach, picked up the slack.

The extreme concept of violent reprisal against a collectively guilty Jewish community for imperiling Germans, Christians, and Western

Civilization was legitimized for Catholics by calling it "self-defense." The kernel of the most militant Jewish-Bolshevik propaganda that ultimately grew into the Holocaust was encapsulated in the article's title: "Not Jew-Hatred, but Christian-Defense."

The next Sunday, May 9th, Bavarian Catholics glancing at the *Munich Catholic Church Newspaper* found the propaganda campaign against Jews on the front page. Warning that "Jewish rule" will bring to Germany what it brought to Russia, this article proposed the solution: Free yourselves from the "Jewish spirit" of "materialism." Stop Jewish immigration. Root out "the spirit of profiteering." Break off the "fetters" of Jewish tyranny by using "every lawful means" against the Jews.

This prescription was exactly what the Nazi Party had proposed three months before at its heavily attended launch event at Munich's Hofbrauhaus. The 25-point Nazi Program announced on February 24th by Hitler called for combatting the "Jewish-materialistic spirit." The Nazi Program demanded the reversal of Jewish immigration and the enactment of a series of legal measures against Jews. These included stripping Jews of German citizenship, removing them from government positions, stopping their "profiteering," and banning them from ownership and employment in the press.

With authoritative Catholic endorsement in Munich for its antisemitic program and its most potent antisemitic propaganda themes, the Nazi Party enjoyed a solid foundation for growth among an overwhelmingly Catholic population in Bavaria. The historical record contains nothing that shows Nuncio Pacelli counteracting this dynamic over the ensuing three years.

Historians Emma Fattorini and Father Hubert Wolf have written about Pacelli's voluminous Nuncio reports to Rome, which they reviewed at the Vatican Archives. While they describe some negative comments he made about Nazism *after* Hitler's failed "Beer Hall Putsch" in November 1923, they mention no negative comments whatsoever in the period of Nazi growth leading up to the Putsch. Professor Rychlak writes that Pacelli spoke out publicly against the Nazis on at least 40 occasions as Nuncio. But nothing he cites, upon investigation, proves to be an instance of Pacelli speaking against Hitler or Nazism, publicly or privately, before the unsuccessful Putsch discredited Hitler and halted, temporarily, the rise of his movement.

Authoritative Catholic support for central themes of Hitler's movement was not reversed or restrained by Nuncio Pacelli or by his superiors in Rome, during the period that began in spring 1920 and continued for the next three years. And the Vatican's elevation of Archbishop Faulhaber to Cardinal on March 7, 1921 signaled Rome's satisfaction with his exercise of authority.

While one prominent Catholic priest's words against antisemitism in June 1920 were picked up, derisively, in the Nazi Party's newspaper, that was the only such example we found. The most compelling attacks on the antisemitic propaganda campaign in Munich during spring 1920 appeared in a non-Catholic paper, the *Munich Post*. Appealing to the Spirit of Pentecost, this Social Democrat paper accused self-styled Christian political parties of showing not "the slightest trace of a reconciling, active, practical love." The *Post* said they were "systematically poisoning our public life by their antisemitic propaganda," and "paving the way for pogroms against Jews."

A Social Democrat newspaper, however, was the epitome of "bad press." Bavarian Catholics were flirting with eternal damnation if they read materials from such a source, even if the topic was the Holy Spirit and Christian love in practice. But they were on firm ground, according to the highest Church authorities in Bavaria, if they ingested the diet of hatred dished out in their Archdiocesan weekly paper in spring 1920. That diet included Nazi-style race-baiting against blacks in 1921, when the same paper called French-African troops in the Rhineland the "greatest shame for culture of our century and perhaps of all time."

On August 27, 1922, matters took a dramatic turn when Cardinal Faulhaber, speaking to 100,000 German Catholics gathered in Munich, condemned the foundation of the Weimar Republic. The November 1918 Revolution that gave rise to the Weimar Republic, he declared, was "perjury and high treason." With Nuncio Pacelli present, Cardinal Faulhaber attacked the "Jewish press of Berlin" and pronounced what flowed from the 1918 Revolution to be "congenitally tainted" and "branded with the mark of Cain."

Munich's largest circulation newspaper, on microfilm at the Bavarian State Library, revealed the power of this condemnation among Catholics. It reported the young Mayor of Cologne, Konrad Adenauer, who later became Germany's most important political figure after World War II, trying to counter the Cardinal's remarks. Adenauer spoke up tactfully, as the official President of the event, to suggest that German Catholics did not have to agree with the Cardinal's view.

The newspaper described the "consternation" that met Adenauer's remarks, compared to the "jubilant reception" the crowd gave to the Cardinal's words. Some months later Baron von Cramer-Klett, a Bavarian friend of Nuncio Pacelli, wrote a blistering private letter of rebuke to Adenauer for daring to criticize the Cardinal-Archbishop.

The Nazi newspaper in Munich made hay with Cardinal Faulhaber's August 27, 1922 speech. The *Volkisch Observer* congratulated the Cardinal on his antisemitic rhetoric and his rejection of Catholic politicians leading the Weimar Republic, including Chancellor Joseph Wirth. It mocked Matthias Erzberger, Germany's most prominent Catholic politician, who took a public stand against antisemitism in 1920.

Erzberger was assassinated one year and one day before Cardinal Faulhaber's speech. As an architect of the Weimar Republic and Germany's signer of the Armistice on November 11, 1918, three days after the Revolution, Erzberger was a "perjuror" and "traitor" if any German political figure was. The Nazi newspaper article on Faulhaber's speech called Erzberger "Matthias von Biberach." Erzberger, a commoner, never had a "von" in his name. Biberach was where he was buried.

Both before and after Cardinal Faulhaber's speech, Hitler spoke to immense crowds of tens of thousands in Munich, attacking the "Jewish-Bolshevism" of the Weimar Republic, the "November criminals" who founded it, and the "Berlin Jewish press." Less than a month after the Cardinal's speech, Hitler declared the Nazi movement would become "the combat troops for the liberation of our German *Volk*" from Jewish "fetters." A Nazi planning and fund-raising document from October 1922 detailed the Party's objectives of mobilizing militarily and scaling up the *Volkisch Observer* into a daily paper, from a twice-weekly paper.

Fall 1922 saw the Nazi Party rapidly become a paramilitary organization to be reckoned with in Bavaria. With the Archdiocesan newspaper's earlier warnings against Jewish-Bolshevik "fetters" and "Jew republics," combined with the Cardinal-Archbishop's attack on the foundation of the Weimar Republic, Bavarian Catholics were fertile recruiting ground. Hitler's clarion calls against Jewish-Bolshevism received authoritative underpinning when *Catholic Civilization* published its "World Revolution and the Jews" article, with the 447/545 statistic, in October 1922. Mussolini's successful "March on Rome" in late October raised hopes in Bavaria that Hitler would come to power by similar means. Hitler set about building up his "brownshirt" Nazi stormtroops to equal the force of the "blackshirts" of Italian Fascism.

By November 1922, the new momentum of the Nazi movement was so conspicuous that it became a regular feature in the political situation reports by the American Vice Consul in Munich, Robert Murphy. Murphy, a distinguished diplomat who later became U.S. Ambassador to Japan, reported in detail to Washington that month about the "Bavarian Mussolini." Murphy described Hitler's growing movement and its main features: "his campaign against the Jews," his "avowed ultimate aim of becoming dictator," and his "condemnation of the Treaty of Versailles." Continuing to follow Nazi paramilitary growth in 1923, Murphy reported in March how the Nazis "endeavor to prove a united Jewish movement for world hegemony using Soviet Russia as an illustration of the first important step."

A significant aspect of the Nazi military mobilization, beginning in April 1923, was active support by Catholic priests. On April 28th, a Catholic-oriented newspaper in Bavaria, the Miesbach *Anzeiger*, reported that Father Lorenz Pieper, the Secretary of the nationwide People's Association for Catholic Germany, had joined the Nazi Party. Pieper moved to Bavaria from northern Germany at this time and gave pro-Nazi speeches throughout Bavaria in the following months. Such activity by an outside priest could only occur with approval of Bavaria's Catholic Bishops.

The next day, April 29th, the Nazis' newspaper announced a gathering of SA stormtroop units in the Bavarian city of Ingolstadt, with a scheduled talk by the local parish priest. The day after that, the Nazi newspaper's Sunday edition began a regular feature that continued every week until November. It was a lengthy listing of the Sunday Mass times for the Catholic churches of the Munich Archdiocese. This feature, likewise, was possible only with ecclesiastical permission.

During the following months, as Nazi stormtroops held weekend gatherings and paramilitary exercises throughout Bavaria, the *Volkisch Observer* reported Catholic priests holding "field masses," just as they did for regular German Army units during World War One. In some instances, the paper reported blessings of stormtroop flags by priests.

The German Bishops' policies *against* swastika blessings, which Steve had translated three years before, dated back only to 1924 at the earliest. The 1924 Bavarian Bishops' policy was perfectly clear: "The flags of political organizations are to receive no Church blessing." Why were Catholic clergy allowed to bless the most extreme of all political organizations in 1923, at a time when that organization was openly mobilizing to overthrow the Weimar Republic?

By October 1923, the results of Church-supported Nazi paramilitary growth were so threatening that a prominent Catholic politician in Bavaria wrote a pleading letter to Cardinal Faulhaber. Heinrich Held begged the Cardinal to counteract the "enormously great" danger posed by the Nazi movement, as Catholics, especially youth, are attracted by "field masses" and the clergy "allow themselves to be shamelessly exploited as agitators."

One week later, the Chancellor of Germany himself wrote Cardinal Faulhaber. Observing the same threatening developments as Held, Chancellor Stresemann implored the Cardinal to exert his spiritual authority in support of the German nation. Cardinal Faulhaber waited more than three weeks to reply to this urgent appeal. On November 6th he sent a letter refusing the Chancellor's request.

Hitler's bid to enlist Bavarian Catholics to overthrow the Weimar Republic came to a crashing end on November 9, 1923. His "Beer Hall Putsch," initiatiated the night before, collapsed in the face of gunfire from Bavarian soldiers and police near the Odeon Plaza in Munich. Hitler, injured as he fell to the ground during the firefight, managed to escape. But he was captured just days later, brought to trial for treason, and convicted. He received a relatively short sentence, five years, and was released after just one year in prison. His Catholic support largely melted away. Professor Hastings details the many priests who stopped all support of Hitler's movement after the failed Putsch. Those Catholics who remained active in the Nazi Party abandoned any former practice of Catholicism.

38. "Pre-Existing Condition"?

The story of the preceding three chapters has not been told by historians. Derek Hastings mentions more of the individual elements than any other historian we have found. In treating the *Munich Catholic Church Newspaper* articles of April-May 1920, however, he does not describe how the *Volkisch Observer* and Hitler piggybacked on the instant credibility those articles conferred upon the Jewish-Communist conspiracy theory in Catholic Bavaria.

Professor Hastings describes the demotion of the editor of the Archdiocesan paper after the articles of April-May 1920; but that personnel action did nothing to repair the damage that had been done. German historians of the early Nazi movement do not mention the articles or their impact. Hitler's English language biographers ignore the vast bulk of this evidence.

Important inter-relationships of facts can be lost when historians and biographers do not present facts in chronological order. Doing so in a timeline was Diane's idea. Steve resisted that proposal at first, because it seemed so pedestrian, and so inconsistent with good topical writing. Kershaw's engagingly written Hitler biography, for example, mentions Cardinal Faulhaber's August 1922 "perjury and treason" speech. But in the course of writing topically, Kershaw mentions the speech only in connection with topically related events in 1925. That makes it difficult to recognize the pivotal location of the speech in time.

In the common failure of historians and biographers to assess the *personal responsibility* of the Catholic authorities on whose watch the first act of the Nazi horror story developed, there is an oft-repeated theme. It is that Munich and Bavaria were thoroughly antisemitic places. A recent biography of Eugenio Pacelli, published by a division of the Harvard University Press, speaks of the "deep-seated anti-Jewish sentiment" in Munich, where "it was a logical step to view Bolsheviks and Jews as indistinguishable."

This line of analysis is similar to what lawyers know as a "pre-existing condition." If someone smashes into your car and strains your neck, he is personally responsible for your injury. But if you have a documented history of serious, chronic problems with your cervical vertebrae, that is a "pre-existing condition." The other driver's action is not the "proximate cause" of your chronic neck pain, and you will, quite appropriately, be unable to hold him responsible for causing your pain..

In much the same way, if Munich was already a thoroughly antisemitic culture before spring 1920, in such a powerful way that it was natural and commonplace to equate Judaism and Bolshevism, then the articles in April-May 1920 were not so significant. The Archdiocesan newspaper would not, in that event, be a proximate cause of the harms that followed in Bavaria.

A major goal of our March 2013 trip to Munich was to test whether the antisemitic Jewish-Communist conspiracy theory was a pre-existing condition there. We already had reason to question whether extreme antisemitism was a dominant pre-existing condition among politically active Catholics in Germany as a whole. In our trip to Berlin the year before, Steve found microfilm of the Catholic Center Party's flagship newspaper, *Germania*, in the Berlin City Library. He examined the issues for early 1919, when the "Spartacist" uprising was threatening to take over the German Government.

The co-leader of the Spartacists was Rosa Luxemburg, who was a Communist of Jewish ethnicity. Sure enough, the Center Party's newspaper was up in arms over the Spartacist uprising and other Communist threats around Germany. The most prominent feature in the paper, day after day, was an appeal for combat veterans to volunteer in the paramilitary forces opposing the Communists. But these issues of *Germania* did not focus on Jewish Communists, much less posit a worldwide Jewish conspiracy.

Steve also found a book with a preface by the President of Germany, published in 1920. *The German Spirit and Jew-Hatred* was a compilation of survey responses, ranging from a paragraph to a page or two, from hundreds of prominent German professors, politicians, civic leaders, and churchmen. The survey asked what they thought about the recent upsurge of antisemitism in Germany. Almost all the responses denounced antisemitism.

A notable response came from Matthias Erzberger. Erzberger said that he and the entire Reich Government were resolved to combat antisemitic incitement with the full power of the law, as a violation of the Weimar Constitution and the fundamental rights of all Germans. In response to the accusation that Jews were playing a leading role in the German Communist Party, he defended their right to political involvement. He concluded by saying the efforts of the Zionist movement to establish a Jewish State in Palestine had his support and that of the Government.

Erzberger's statement was impressive, but it did not resolve the issue. Erzberger had stature in the German Government, but he was not well regarded in Bavaria. Two Bavarian Bishops provided statements for the book that contrasted sharply with Erzberger. Bishop Baron von Ow-Felldorf of

Passau branded Jews with Bolshevism. Bishop von Henle of Regensburg, while professing to "repudiate Jew-hatred with every fiber of my being," said antisemitism was a reaction to the "dregs" of Judaism.

Before our trip, Steve found references to three books on Bolshevism by Munich authors in 1919 and 1920. One was by Munich's most prominent and prolific Catholic theologian of the time, Father Erhard Schlund. The other two books were both by Fritz Gerlich, the editor of the largest circulation Munich newspaper. All three books were waiting for us when we arrived at the Bavarian State Library. They told quite a story.

Father Schlund's 1919 book on Bolshevism, entitled *Bolschewismus*, contained nothing of Jewish-Communist conspiracy theory and only two passing references to Judaism. Father Schlund took a very different tack from the conspiracy theory. He said Bolshevism was "uniquely explained by the character of the Russian people." He described the two "fathers of contemporary Bolshevism" as Herzen and Bakunin, who were both Gentiles, sons of Russian estate owners.

Schlund identified Lenin, another non-Jew, as "the currently most important man in Russia, who far outranks Trotsky and Chicherin and the others." Remarkably, Father Schlund wrote *after* the short-lived Communist government of April 1919 in Bavaria. His book critiqued that government sharply without focusing on the ethnicity of its leaders.

Fritz Gerlich's 1919 book, *Der Kommunismus in der Praxis*, was a blistering critique of "Communism in Practice," with no mention of Jews. When Gerlich published a second book on Communism in 1920, he felt compelled by escalating antisemitic agitation to address the topic. This is how he approached it:

> Many of our contemporaries nevertheless see these destructive effects of Marxism not as the result of the system of Marxism, but rather as the result of the participation of Jews in its leadership. Even though this view is completely untenable, we must still devote a few words to it here, because the agitation against our Jewish fellow citizens is threatening to become a public danger and to strengthen the elements that would rip apart our people and our government.

Gerlich went on to demolish Jewish-Communism propaganda as a grotesque injustice and a logical absurdity. His words leave no doubt that he considered this smear to be the result of current-day agitation, not historical inevitability.

Gerlich's forthright stance shows that other authorities in Munich, including Archbishop Faulhaber and Nuncio Pacelli, had a choice. They could combat an outrageous propaganda campaign, they could do nothing, or they could promote it. The content of Faulhaber's Archdiocesan newspaper in April, May, November and December 1920 shows which choice he made. As Gerlich's words make clear, Faulhaber and Pacelli had full reason in 1920 to know that the Jewish-Communist propaganda campaign threatened to strengthen the most extreme and dangerous elements in Bavaria.

Steve also looked through the *Munich Catholic Church Newspaper* for 1918 and 1919, as well as Munich's leading Catholic intellectual journal. None of them contained Jewish-Communist conspiracy theory in 1918 or 1919. The Archdiocesan paper presented Jewish-*Masonic* conspiracy theory to its readers in 1919. The paper's articles in 1919 against Bolshevism did not talk about Jews. The intellectual journal ran an article on the *Protocols of the Elders of Zion* in June 1920, *after* the Archdiocesan paper endorsed them.

So what did we find of Jewish-Bolshevik conspiracy theory in Munich that pre-existed the Archdiocesan newspaper's "Jewish Imperialism" article of April 1920? We found five authors in Munich who published Jewish-Bolshevik material in the second half of 1919 and the first three months of 1920. They were Dietrich Eckart, Alfred Rosenberg, Paul Bang, Franz Schronghamer-Heimdal, and one anonymous author.

Eckart and Schronghamer-Heimdal, as mentioned before, were early members of the Nazi Party. Rosenberg was an early Nazi who became the Nazi Party's chief ideologist in 1934. Rosenberg and Eckart were editors of the Nazis' newspaper in the early 1920s. Paul Bang was a Protestant author on the extreme right wing of German politics. The fifth person was an anonymous author of Jewish-Bolshevik propaganda appearing in the *Volkisch Observer* in February 1920.

In other words, before April 1920, Jewish-Bolshevik propaganda in Munich was the province of the extremist fringes of the city. The Nazis had only a handful of followers when 1919 turned into 1920, and no standing in the Catholic Church of Bavaria. Hitler, or whoever advised him, had the perspicacity to refrain from associating himself with a fringe propaganda theme until after it went mainstream in April 1920.

The statements of some historians and the actual evidence turned out to be at opposite poles. What Ventresca presents as deep-seated, logical, and self-evident, was the view of the Nazi extremist fringe of Munich culture in 1919 and early 1920, not the Catholic mainstream. While antisemitic sentiments of various sorts may well have been prevalent in the general population, the poisonous proposition that a Jewish-Communist conspiracy was out to destroy and dominate Christian countries ran contrary to a Munich theologian's book on Bolshevism and was vigorously disputed by the city's most important newspaper editor.

Munich differed in this regard from England. There, a prominent mainstream political figure *did* give a limited endorsement to the Jewish-Bolshevik conspiracy theory before spring 1920. Winston Churchill published an article in February that year arguing that, "with the notable exception of Lenin," the majority of leading figures in Russian Bolshevism were Jewish. Perhaps Churchill, who maintained good contacts in the British intelligence community during the interwar period, was persuaded by the "facts" of the same Jewish-Bolshevism article that Sir Basil Thomson of MI-5 and MI-6 took to the American Embassy.

Whatever his view of the facts, Churchill maintained enough of a moral compass to denounce the idea of collective guilt in his article: "Nothing is more wrong than to deny to an individual, on account of race or origin, his right to be judged on his personal merits and conduct." Churchill expressed hope that two other currents, Zionism and assimilation, would prevail among Jews worldwide, rather than Bolshevism.

When Diane visited Munich's Jewish Museum, she gained a new perspective on the pre-1920 reality of Munich. Under the Wittelsbach monarchy, beginning in the late 1800s, exhibits in the Bavarian National Museum included displays of Judaica with explanations of Jewish feasts and worship customs. The purpose of the exhibits was to memorialize Jews as a respected element of the Bavarian people, exactly opposite to the later Nazi program of eliminating them from the *Volk*. The Jewish Museum today has exhibits modeled on those from the Wittelsbach era.

In another exercise of moral leadership, the Wittelsbachs elevated Jews as well as Protestants into the predominantly Catholic nobility of Bavaria. Whether because of such examples of leadership in Bavaria, or other factors, the Bavarian population was less susceptible to antisemitic political movements than was the German population as a whole. That was demon-strably the case as of 1912. In the last nationwide parliamentary election before World War One, several explicitly antisemitic parties ran candidates for the Reichstag. While ten antisemitic delegates were elected from other parts of Germany in 1912, not a single one was elected from Bavaria.

39. Playing with Fire

Hitler's Beer Hall Putsch can easily be viewed as the folly of a madman accompanied by beer-sotted rowdies. That is the version Diane encountered on a guided tour of Munich in 2013: Hitler and company did not know what they were doing; marching through Munich, they wandered into a narrow street; they were fired upon by police and soldiers, ending their escapade. If only the bullet that killed the Nazi next to Hitler had struck him instead, history would have been different.

Historians who have probed the facts of the Putsch do not take it so lightly. Vice Consul Murphy, to judge from the telegram he sent at midnight during the Putsch, was alarmed. Hitler had a large armed force in Munich on November 8 and 9, 1923, when he staged his Putsch on the fifth anniversary of the "perjury and high treason" German Revolution of 1918. Nazi Party recruiting during 1923 tripled the Party's membership, to more than 50,000. The recruiting campaign was conducted openly for the purpose of over-throwing the Weimar Republic, which the Nazis announced as "Our Mission for 1923" in a banner headline at the beginning of January.

Mussolini's Fascist takeover of Italy in October 1922 was their model. To overthrow the "November criminals," the Nazis built their armed stormtrooper strength from about 1,000 in January to around 4,000 in early March, and more after that. By fall 1923, Hitler was the leader of a large combined paramilitary force of Nazis and other *Volkisch* forces, under the name "Patriotic Fighting League." General Ludendorff, who co-headed the German Army with Hindenburg in World War One, was the League's military commander. From September to early November, the *Volkisch Observer* ran repeated headlines about the imminent overthrow of November Traitors, November Republic, Marxist High Treason, Jewish Decomposition of Germany, and so forth. The Nazis had gotten enough money to make it a daily paper earlier in the year.

When Catholic authorities in Bavaria endorsed Jewish-Communist conspiracy theory, promoted Nazi-program "lawful measures" against Jews, condemned the foundation of the Weimar Republic, allowed a nationally prominent priest to enter and tour Bavaria for months boosting Nazism, and permitted priests to conduct military-type services for Nazi paramilitary forces, they contributed to an immensely combustible situation as of November 8-9, 1923. American Vice Consul Murphy reported to Washington as early as March 1923 that Hitler's growing movement had the potential to spark "a nation-wide conflagration," by heaping upon the Jews "not only the sins of Germany but of the entire world." Nuncio Pacelli, reporting much more frequently to Rome, expressed no opposition or concern about these developments through all of the early 1920s up to November 1923. That is the only conclusion that the current state of the historical record allows. Ronald Rychlak says Pacelli criticized the National Socialists even before they were called "Nazis." The two examples he gives, however, prove the opposite. One example dates from *after* the Putsch. The other example criticizes extremist groups, but not National Socialists.

Catholic authorities in Munich may deserve some credit for acting against the Putsch during the night of November 8-9, 1923, though the historical record is not entirely clear. A history of the Beer Hall Putsch credits Cardinal Faulhaber and the Catholic Church in Bavaria with standing behind the government in opposition to the Putsch. Cardinal Faulhaber did indeed signal a measure of disagreement with Nazi-style antisemitism in a sermon at the Munich Cathedral four days before the Putsch. He denounced those who would deny Jews food and shelter in the winter, and decried "blind hatred against Jews and Catholics." Two days later, in a private letter replying to Chancellor Stresemann, the Cardinal likewise rejected "the hatred that rages blindly against our Israelite fellow citizens."

When Hitler entered Munich's Bürgerbräu Beer Hall around 8:30 p.m. on November 8th, fired a pistol shot into the ceiling and announced the German nationalist revolution, he interrupted a speech by Bavarian Commissar Gustav von Kahr. All the members of the Bavarian governing cabinet, who had invited Kahr in September to serve as de facto dictator of Bavaria, were present at the speech, except one. Three key Bavarian officials, including Kahr, met briefly with Hitler in a side room, then emerged to declare to the large crowd their support for Hitler's Putsch. General Ludendorff arrived to take command of the new German military, under Hitler as the head of the provisional national government of Germany. The stage was set for the March on Berlin that would achieve the same victory for German Fascism that Mussolini had achieved for Italian Fascism.

The lone Bavarian cabinet member not present was Franz Matt. As the "*Kultusminister*," his remit covered religion, education and culture. Very early on the morning of November 9th, well before dawn, posters went up around Munich with Matt's signature. The posters proclaimed that the constitutional government still stood, despite the Hitler-Ludendorff Putsch.

The posters appealed to the bureaucracy, police and army to remain true to the constitutional government, and exhorted Bavarians to "refuse obedience to the Prussian Ludendorff." The posters' stated authority was "Dr. Matt" on behalf of "the entire constitutional ministerial cabinet."

Matt was a reliable Catholic who restored compulsory religious education in the school system soon after taking office in 1920. He worked from that year on, unsuccessfully, to negotiate Bavarian governmental approval for the Bavaria-Vatican Concordat. The Concordat was a high priority for Nuncio Pacelli, and the reason he remained in Munich after being named Nuncio to Berlin in 1920.

Some historians state that Matt was at dinner with Cardinal Faulhaber and Nuncio Pacelli on the evening of November 8th, at the Archbishop's palace in Munich. Many in Munich at the time believed Cardinal Faulhaber dissuaded Commissar von Kahr that night from his initial declared support for the Putsch. Thousands of Munichers who supported the Nazis, especially students, protested in the streets against Cardinal Faulhaber for "betraying" the Putsch. The demonstrations continued for months, into 1924.

Cardinal Faulhaber denied any involvement. Matt denied he was with Faulhaber and Pacelli. The posters had some degree of authoritative Catholic support, as they were prepared during the night of November 8-9 in the offices of the Catholic Women's League in Munich. Other leading members of the main Catholic political party of Bavaria also helped prepare the posters.

In the early afternoon of November 9th, it was only a small group of Munich police and Bavarian soldiers who blocked the path of Hitler and Ludendorff, who were marching at the head of a much larger column of stormtroops, and fired into their ranks. A thousands-strong Bavarian division of the German Army, stationed near Munich, failed to obey orders to oppose the Putsch.

Given the pointblank range of the firefight, it was probably something other than chance that directed no bullets at Hitler. Hitler was as distinctive with his moustache then as he was after. Shooting the leader is the obvious way to stop a rebellion. It is possible that the same considerations that shaped Matt's poster also had an influence on the loyalist force. Just as the poster did not exhort Bavarians to "refuse obedience" to Hitler, so the loyalists did not shoot him.

Is there a possible reason why Catholic authority in Munich on November 8-9, 1923 might *not* want Matt's poster to rally Bavarians against Hitler, or Bavarian soldiers and police to shoot him? Cardinal Faulhaber effectively provided an answer to that question on February 15, 1924. Speaking to a Catholic academic audience at Munich's Löwenbräu Beer Hall, on the eve of Hitler's trial for treason, Faulhaber praised Hitler as a leader who was attuned to the values of the Bavarian people, and called the Nazi movement an "originally pure spring." The Cardinal complained that the "pure spring" had become polluted by anti-Catholic influences.

Was Faulhaber's speech just a momentary tactic to cope with the protests against the Cardinal for his "betrayal" of the Putsch? No. The next year, 1925, the same year Hitler's *Mein Kampf* appeared, Cardinal Faulhaber's praise of Hitler and his originally pure movement also appeared in print. Faulhaber's new book, with a title meaning "The German Sense of Honor and the Catholic Conscience," included the Cardinal's Hitler-friendly and Nazi-friendly words, verbatim, from the year before.

Faulhaber's considered endorsement of the "originally pure spring" of Nazism overshadowed any goodwill the Cardinal showed Jews when he said not to let them starve and freeze, on the eve of the Putsch. The most con-spicuous feature of the original Nazi Party, as we have seen, was militant antisemitism, pursued by "lawful measures." There was no inconsistency between opposing starvation and freezing of Jews, on the one hand, and affirming the "originally pure spring" of Nazi lawful measures, on the other.

An additional feature of Nazism that became prominent by 1923 was armed Fascist thuggery. In 1925, Faulhaber's words praising Hitler and original Nazism appeared in a section of his book welcoming the "Fascistic wave" that was "flowing through the nations." Faulhaber singled out Mussolini for especially high praise.

Then why would Catholic authority in Munich oppose the Putsch? Several possible answers are found in a report from the Bavarian Ambassador to the Vatican, sent on November 9, 1923. Ambassador Ritter zu Groen-esteyn reported, among other things, a concern in the Vatican that a Concordat entered into with a dictator might be repudiated by a later German Government. This, combined with a note from Faulhaber to Pacelli on November 8, 1923, expressing satisfaction with terms for a Vatican-Bavaria Concordat as of that date, provides one of several possible explanations.

German Government authorities had objected that the Weimar Constitution did not allow individual states to enter into foreign treaties. Even a Catholic Chancellor, Joseph Wirth, informed Nuncio Pacelli that a Bavaria-Vatican Concordat was not possible. Bavarian Government authorities and local Bavarian Church interests also blocked Pacelli's proposals for a Concordat from early 1920 through September 1923. But authorities at both levels, Bavarian State and German Reich, faced with the same counter-revolutionary threat that prompted Heinrich Held and Chancellor Stresemann to write Cardinal Faulhaber in October 1923, now agreed to the Concordat. The Concordat proceeded rapidly to conclusion after the Putsch, reaching final form in January 1924. It was signed by the Vatican and the Bavarian Government in March of that year, with the German Government acquiescing.

Cardinal-Archbishop Faulhaber and Nuncio-Archbishop Pacelli played with fire from spring 1920 to November 1923. They were side by side from Faulhaber's August 27, 1922 speech through the months of clergy-supported Nazi mobilization that followed. Faulhaber's praise for the "originally pure" Nazi spring in February 1924 was published a year later, after ample time for reflection and correction by Nuncio Pacelli. This, combined with Faulhaber's praise for Mussolini's Fascism, showed that far from learning a lesson, Faulhaber and Pacelli were open to playing with Nazi fire in the future.

Diane learned another significant fact by taking the guided tour of Munich. The Nazi Party's "Brown House," their national headquarters building, was directly across the street from the Vatican Nunciature in the 1930s. Their proximity was not an unavoidable coincidence. The funds for the Nazis' purchase of the "Barlow Palace," facing the Nunciature palace on Brienner Street, came in large measure from a loyal German Catholic, Fritz Thyssen. Thyssen wrote a book several years later, expressing his regrets for supporting Nazism.

Unlike the rest of Munich's magnificent buildings, the Barlow Palace was not rebuilt after World War II. Neither was the Vatican Nunciature. Today the site of the Brown House is occupied by the new Documentation Center on the History of Nazism, under the auspices of the Institute for Contemporary History. The Center is scheduled to open in April 2015. Facing it is the site of the former Nunciature, which remains an untended empty plot.

40. "Jewish-Communism" and Father Coughlin

In June 2013 we published the evidence from our investigation on the Galebachlaw.com website. We still did not understand *why* the patterns from 1920 to the 1930s developed. But we wanted to put the evidence into the public realm, bring it to the attention of historians, and solicit their reactions. By publishing online and using email to share links to our investigation, we soon gained useful leads.

Professor Mary Ann Glendon of Harvard Law School, a former U.S. Ambassador to the Vatican, kindly brought our investigation to the attention of a friend who has done extensive research on Pope Pius XII. Steve participated in a Harvard Law School seminar co-led by Professor Glendon during fall term 2012, on social and legal issues from a Catholic and Christian perspective. Professor Glendon now informed Steve that Professor Ron Rychlak was looking into the matter of our investigation and would be in touch about it. She did not know we had been in touch before, and we waited for him to contact us.

In late July 2013, Rychlak emailed Steve, saying he had read the entire investigation. He recognized that it raised serious issues, and said he would do further research into the matter. Steve rested content, whether correctly or not, that people in contact with key personnel in the Vatican were now aware of our research.

A historian at the U.S. Holocaust Memorial Museum responded to our newly published investigation by sending a list of related books worth examining. While Steve had read most of them already, two of the books produced important new leads. The first was *Vatican Secret Diplomacy: Joseph P. Hurley and Pope Pius XII*, by a Boston College history professor, Father Charles Gallagher, S.J. That book led us into an additional theater for Jewish-Communist propaganda: the United States of America.

We were not familiar with the details of Father Charles Coughlin's radio broadcasting career. Our research had not touched on him at all. Coughlin was a major issue for Father Joseph P. Hurley when he worked in the Vatican Secretariat of State under Eugenio Pacelli as Cardinal and Pope, in the late 1930s and early 1940s. We were vaguely aware that Coughlin was a demagogue and an antisemite, with a huge radio audience for his weekly broadcasts in the 1930s. We did not know what role, if any, Jewish-Communist conspiracy theory played in his antisemitic demagoguery. As it turned out, this theme did not appear in Father Coughlin's broadcasts for many years. Then it surfaced with a vengeance.

After examining Father Gallagher's book, Steve found a library shelf full of books by and about Coughlin at the Harvard Library. These included collections of his radio broadcasts from their start in the 1920s through his heyday in the 1930s. Incredibly, Father Coughlin launched his radio campaign against the supposed international Jewish-Communist conspiracy right after *Kristallnacht*.

This "Night of Shattered Glass," in November 1938, was a nationwide pogrom against the Jews of Germany. It fulfilled Hitler's words of September 15, 1935. He said if the Nuremberg Laws proved insufficient to defend Germany against the Jewish-Communist conspiracy, further measures would be taken. The measures taken on *Kristallnacht* included the burning of almost every synagogue in Germany, the shattering of the shop and office windows of almost every enterprise owned or operated by Jews, and physical assaults by Nazi stormtroopers and thugs that killed or injured thousands of Jews. Additional tens of thousands were thrown into concentration camps. The Nazi regime then imposed a $400 million fine on the Jews of Germany collectively.

Kristallnacht occurred on the 15th anniversary of Hitler's failed Beer Hall Putsch, and the 20th anniversary of the German Revolution of 1918. A convenient pretext for the event was the assassination of a German diplomat in Paris by a Jewish youth several days before.

For Father Coughlin to choose the aftermath of *Kristallnacht* as the time to launch the Jewish-Communist conspiracy theory on American radio was a breathtaking act. When Coughlin undertook this new phase of his radio demagoguery on November 20, 1938, he had just returned to the air after a hiatus, two weeks before. His regular audience in the 1930s numbered in the millions. Some estimates say 30 million.

Given Father Coughlin's antisemitic reputation today, we were surprised to find that his radio broadcasts before 1937 did *not* contain militant antisemitic material. Rather, they focused largely on Catholic social teaching applied, faithfully or not, to issues of the day. Coughlin railed constantly against financiers and capitalists, often by name, and some of the names were Jewish. Jewish-Communist-capitalist world conspiracy propaganda would have fit seamlessly into his attacks, but for many years it did not.

In mid-1937 Father Coughlin acquired a new Church superior in the person of Edward Aloysius Mooney, the newly appointed Archbishop of

Detroit. Mooney was a veteran of the Vatican Secretariat of State. Cardinal Gasparri made him the Vatican's chief diplomat to India in 1926. Under Cardinal Secretary of State Pacelli in the early 1930s, Mooney became the Vatican's representative in Japan. Returning to the United States in the mid-1930s, Mooney served four years as Bishop of Rochester, New York, before his appointment to Detroit. He quickly became head of the national conference of United States Bishops, known then as the National Catholic Welfare Conference, a position he held from 1935 to 1945.

Archbishop Mooney amply demonstrated his power to control Father Coughlin. When Coughlin attacked President Roosevelt in fall 1937, Mooney publicly rebuked him. But when Coughlin launched his radio campaign against the Jewish-Communist conspiracy, no such rebuke issued from the Archbishop. Coughlin's antisemitic hate propaganda continued for months and years, while American Bishops, prominent Catholics, and American officials tried to get Archbishop Mooney and the Vatican to stop him. Their efforts were unavailing. Finally in 1942, when the United States was at war with Nazi Germany, a U.S. Government threat of criminal prosecution succeeded in shutting Coughlin down.

The centerpiece of Father Coughlin's radio address on November 20, 1938 turned out to be something very familiar to us. It was the March 6, 1920 article from *Catholic Documentation*. To convince his listeners that the Russian Revolution was controlled by Jews, Coughlin read from that article's list of Bolshevik leaders, identifying each of them except Lenin as Jewish.

Then Coughlin brought the lie up to date. Unabashedly citing "the Nazis" as his source, he claimed that in 1935 the central committee of the Russian Communist Party had 59 members, of whom 56 were Jews. The other three, he said, were married to Jews. Coughlin also informed his audience that the "official" *Catholic Documentation* newspaper listed the names of Jewish bankers who financed the Russian Revolution.

What was the role of the Vatican, and its well-connected Archbishop in Detroit, with respect to Father Coughlin's Jewish-Communist conspiracy propaganda? We know several facts that may help start an inquiry into that issue. First, Archbishop Mooney had reason to know of Coughlin's interest in the Jewish-Communist conspiracy theory, before Coughlin launched into this theme in his November 20, 1938 broadcast. On August 8, 1938, Coughlin's weekly newspaper, *Social Justice*, summarized the *Catholic Documentation* article, in a piece signed by Coughlin.

Second, the fraudulent nature of the *Catholic Documentation* article came to light immediately after Coughlin's November 20th broadcast, in what Coughlin's staff described as a "flood" of telegrams and letters to their office. The flood occurred because Coughlin called the *Catholic Documentation* article an official report of an existing agency, the "American Secret Service," rather than the non-existent "American Services" cited in the original 1920 article.

Listeners naturally suspected the report did not originate from the Secret Service. That is the agency charged with protecting the President of the United States. Coughlin responded to their flood of complaints and questions by issuing more falsehoods. The "Secret Service" attribution of the report, *Social Justice* explained, could mean it originated from any military, diplomatic, or security element of the American Government.

Third, the effort to keep the big lie of the 1920 *Catholic Documentation* article alive and influential was international in scope. Coughlin said he got the article from a book published in Ireland. A priest in an Irish missionary order, the Holy Ghost Fathers, packaged an English translation of the article with other antisemitic hate propaganda into a book. The author was Father Denis Fahey. He described the article's publication in France, along with claims that "the Jews have placed obstacles in the way of its publication." Both the 1935 and 1938 editions of Fahey's book bear an imprimatur from the Bishop of Waterford, Ireland.

The Vatican did nothing to counteract the international spread of the Jewish-Communist conspiracy theory, as far as we can find, from 1920 when it surfaced in *Catholic Documentation* through the 1930s when it gained traction in Ireland and America. As we have seen, the Vatican *promoted* the lie at key points in time. Father Coughlin was known to the Vatican before 1938. When Cardinal Pacelli toured the United States for a month in fall 1936, at the height of President Roosevelt's re-election campaign, Coughlin was the constant topic of press inquiries. The *New York Times* and other papers speculated whether Cardinal Pacelli would restrain Coughlin's weekly rants against Roosevelt. Pacelli's silence on the subject made headlines.

Two days after the election, Cardinal Pacelli had lunch with the President at Roosevelt's family estate at Hyde Park, New York. Three days after that, in his weekly Sunday evening radio address, Father Coughlin announced he was going off the air. Coughlin made a point to deny that anyone told him to stop broadcasting. He returned to the air after Vatican Secretariat of State insider Archbishop Mooney was placed in authority over him.

41. Tracing a Common Thread

We pondered over Father Coughlin: How exactly did he come up with the Jewish-Communist conspiracy theory and start broadcasting it in 1938? Why in 1938 rather than before? Then we realized the same question arises with other figures in this story.

The Argentinean author of *El Kahal* said in his introduction that the Russian Revolution was "a current and complete example" of the international Jewish conspiracy to destroy Christian civilization. When did he get that idea? And his hideous statement on the same page, that "death to the Jew" is synonymous with patriotic self-defense: where did he get that idea, and the audacity to put it into a book?

Gustavo Martínez Zuviría, who authored *El Kahal* and *Oro* in 1935 under the pen-name Hugo Wast, was a respected figure in Argentina. From 1905 to 1930, he published 19 novels. His time from 1931 onward was largely occupied by his new position as the director of the Argentine National Library in Buenos Aires. Why did he publish two novels in 1935 incorporating the *Protocols* and Jewish-Communist conspiracy theory?

Martinez Zuviria states in the introduction of *El Kahal* that he had been concerned about the Jewish problem for many years, since his youth. Yet his novels, from 1905 to 1930, do not appear to contain any Jewish-Communist conspiracy theory. Like Coughlin in the 1920s and early 1930s, he regularly dealt with subjects like financiers and radical politicians that offered easy opportunities to inject antisemitic themes. His 1919 novel *Ciudad Turbulenta, Ciudad Alegre*, for example, deals with liberal and radical political figures, as well as Old Testament denunciations of idolatry, and New Testament critiques of Pharisees. Yet that book, written after the Russian Revolution, does not contain Jewish-Bolshevik propaganda, or any other antisemitic material we could find.

The situation is similar with Bishop Alois Hudal. We have seen vicious antisemitic statements from his 1935 and 1936 books, equating Judaism and Communism, and informing Hitler that Catholics have no reason to come to the defense of Jews. He, too, authored books before the 1930s. Steve examined Hudal's books from 1914 and 1922, and a collection of his sermons published in 1933. He found nothing of Jewish-Communist conspiracy theory in Hudal's pre-1930 writings and sermons. Like Martinez Zuviria, Hudal had ample opportunity to reveal his antisemitism, given his subject matter. His

1914 book, *The Religious and Moral Ideas of the Book of Proverbs*, for instance, deals with Jewish subject matter without injecting antisemitism.

What Coughlin, Martinez and Hudal have in common, with respect to the Jewish-Communist conspiracy theory, is that they injected it into their material once they came into close contact with the Vatican Secretariat of State. All three of them had close contact with Cardinal Pacelli. Gustavo Martinez Zuviria served as the President of the Press and Publicity Committee for the International Eucharistic Congress of 1934. Before he came in contact with Cardinal Pacelli, his writing did not contain antisemitic conspiracy theory.

Alois Hudal began working as a consultant to the Vatican in 1930. In June 1933, he was consecrated as a Bishop by Cardinal Pacelli personally. That was a highly unusual honor. Unlike Pope John Paul II, who consecrated more than 300 Bishops, Eugenio Pacelli only consecrated 30, during his time as Cardinal Secretary of State and his time as Pope. Most of those consecrations were for men being sent on Vatican diplomatic missions, or men working in Vatican positions in Rome. One of the consecrations was that of Francis Spellman, who became Pacelli's trusted protégé in America.

Hudal's consecration was unique in having no publicly visible Bishop-specific purpose. He remained in his post as Rector of the "Anima" chapel and residential college in Rome, a position never held by a Bishop before or since. Hudal's association with Pacelli enhanced his credibility in the Church and the world. Before Bishop Hudal began his association with the Vatican and Cardinal Pacelli, he did not publish antisemitic conspiracy theory.

In short, the extreme antisemitism of the Jewish-Communist conspiracy theory was not a "pre-existing condition" of Charles Coughlin, Alois Hudal, or Gustavo Martinez Zuviria, any more than it was of the *Munich Catholic Church Newspaper*. It was a condition, rather, that developed *on Eugenio Pacelli's watch*, first as Nuncio, then as Vatican Secretary of State. The degree of his responsibility for the onset of that condition in each of them can be debated. What is clear beyond all debate is this: As each of these four promoted Jewish-Communist conspiracy theory openly and publicly, over an extended period of time, Eugenio Pacelli did nothing to restrain, rebuke or counteract their ultimately deadly propaganda. On the contrary, he was the responsible supervising authority when *Catholic Civilization* and the *Roman Observer* actively promoted the same propaganda in the 1930s.

A second book on the Holocaust Museum historian's recommended reading list in summer 2013 provided an additional insight into Eugenio Pacelli. Steve had looked before at Emma Fattorini's book about Nuncio Pacelli's early reports to Rome from Munich, based on her research in the Vatican Archives. Now he examined it more closely. On page 116, there was a quote from Nuncio Pacelli's report of April 30, 1919, about the liberation of Munich "dalla durissima tirannia russo-giudaico-rivoluzionaria." This means "from the harshest Russian-Jewish-revolutionary tyranny."

This was the earliest example we had seen, thus far, of a Catholic authority equating "Jewish" with Russian Communism. Nuncio Pacelli's report in 1919 went privately to the Vatican Secretary of State, like all his Nuncio reports. We later found evidence that his private views of Jewish-Communism were in harmony with Cardinal Gasparri and with the future Pope Pius XI. A historian has identified a private statement made in late 1918 by the Secretary of State, Cardinal Gasparri, accusing the Jews of heading revolutionary movements in Russia and Poland. Another historian states that Achille Ratti (Pope Pius XI, 1922-1939), as the Vatican's representative in Poland in December 1918, commissioned a report and forwarded it to Rome, saying that all the Bolshevik leaders except Lenin were Jews.

None of these three instances were public endorsements of Jewish-Communist conspiracy theory. That did not occur from an authoritative Catholic source, so far as we can determine, until March 1920 in France and April 1920 in Munich.

42. Why Did They Do It?

All this leads to a question that troubled us throughout our inquiry: Why? Why did high level Catholic authorities in the Vatican in the 1920s and 1930s promote the Jewish-Communist conspiracy theory and countenance subordinates who did the same? What possible motivation did they have?

Writers have put forward various reasons for Catholic and Christian complicity in the Holocaust. None of them suffice to explain the specific promotions of Jewish-Communist conspiracy theory we have presented here. Daniel Goldhagen in *A Moral Reckoning*, Catholic author James Carroll in *Constantine's Sword*, and Yad Vashem in its Holocaust History Museum displays, point to the centuries-long history of Christian antisemitism. Goldhagen and Carroll point to widespread complicity of Christian clergy, and they find underlying causes in certain passages of New Testament scripture. But the Jewish-Communist conspiracy theory was *not* part of the centuries-long history. And it had nothing to do with scripture.

Our search for *policy-related* motivations for an ultimately deadly lie led us back to Washington in the second half of 2013. Unlike Harvard, the Library of Congress had copies of the *Roman Observer* from the early 1920s. Inserting what we found there into our Timeline of Events and Documents proved to be helpful for understanding.

The first significant pattern noticeable in 1920 was the *Roman Observer* showering attention on Germany and Munich Catholicism right at the time of the April-May 1920 articles in the *Munich Catholic Church Newspaper*. On April 11th, the day "Jewish Imperialism" appeared in the Munich paper, the front page of the Vatican paper contained 17 headlines and news items about Germany. One week later, the *Roman Observer* ran a lead story praising the Catholic press of Bavaria, mentioning the *Munich Catholic Church Newspaper* by name.

On May 6, four days after "Not Jew-Hatred but Christian-Defense" appeared in the Munich Archdiocese, the Vatican paper ran a lead story about that Archdiocese, praising Archbishop Faulhaber and Nuncio Pacelli. The next day, the Vatican printed another lead article in its paper about Munich, this time praising the Bavarian Catholic Press Association, the publisher of the *Munich Catholic Church Newspaper*. No other time period we examined contained so many articles giving attention and praise to Munich Catholicism. Any Italian-literate priest or other Catholic in Munich, wondering if his

Archdiocesan paper had gone off the rails in spring 1920, could learn that the authorities over that paper had enthusiastic support from the Vatican.

An important international conference was underway in the second half of April 1920. Most of the daily issues of the Vatican newspaper in that period covered developments at the "San Remo Conference." San Remo was where the Allied Powers of World War One agreed to give Great Britain a mandate to govern Palestine, previously part of the now-defeated Turkish Ottoman Empire. The stated purpose of the mandate was to establish a Jewish homeland there, in fulfillment of the Balfour Declaration. The *Roman Observer* articles about the conference contained no criticism of the Allies, and no criticism of Zionism. Around the same time, however, the *Munich Catholic Church Newspaper* said that granting the mandate to Britain "interfered directly with the rights of the Pope" and concluded: "It is really the Pope who will yet have the last word in this matter."

Soon after the British Government appointed a Jewish Englishman, Sir Herbert Samuel, as the High Commissioner, or governor, of Palestine, the Vatican paper began to speak with strong criticism. Eight front-page articles in June and July 1920 denounced Zionism, with headlines about a "Systematic Invasion" of Palestine and a "Dangerous Policy" of Britain. The paper raised the specter of Jewish "hegemony" over the Holy Land.

Meanwhile, the *Munich Catholic Church Newspaper* reported on July 25th that Christians and Muslims in the Holy Land had formed a union to "represent their common interests." That paper had good sources. Just five days earlier, the Latin Patriarch of Jerusalem, the highest Roman Catholic authority in Palestine, had called for internationalization of Palestine, to prevent control by Zionists. He claimed to speak for the "unanimous voice" of the entire non-Jewish population of Palestine.

On October 9, 1920, the *Roman Observer* reported the British Government had "entrusted the custody of the Holy Land" to a Jew. The article said the Jews in the Holy Land were calling Sir Herbert Samuel "The Prince of Israel." On October 15th, the Vatican paper ran its detailed promotion of Jewish-Communist conspiracy theory side-by-side with a critical article on Zionism and Palestine, at the top of page one.

The article on Zionism and Palestine equated Jewish immigrants with Bolsheviks, claimed they were seeking to "destroy all the sacred vestiges of the Holy Places," and charged High Commissioner Samuel with giving the Zionists free reign while they "are growing daily in their audacity and insolence." In November, repeating that Jews were calling Samuel "The

Prince of Israel," the Vatican paper said Muslims and Christians in Palestine were becoming increasingly fervent in their opposition to Zionism, because it is "a matter of life and death" for them.

When Winston Churchill visited Palestine in early 1921, in his capacity as British cabinet minister for the colonies, the Vatican paper took him to task for advocating a Jewish "national center" in Palestine. That would be "an ethnical, juridical, and political absurdity," said the *Roman Observer*. Two weeks later a front-page article equated Judaism with Bolshevism, saying its goal is "the triumph of the Jews over the Christians" and "the predominance of the Jewish race in the whole world." When riots against Jews broke out in Palestine in May, the Vatican newspaper blamed the violence on the "Zionist invasion" and "Communist Jews."

In June 1921, Pope Benedict XV spoke out personally against the danger that "the Jews might attain a position of preponderance and privilege in Palestine." He called for governments to pressure the League of Nations to reject the British mandate over Palestine. The *Roman Observer* followed up with five articles on Palestine over the next month, three of them equating Jews with Bolsheviks.

In September 1921, an Arab leader's plea against the Balfour Declaration, on the *Roman Observer's* front page, said that Jewish immigrants to Palestine were "imbued with the spirit of Bolshevism." In October, the paper described an attack by Cardinal Bourne, the highest ranking Catholic in Britain, on the British Government's efforts to establish a Jewish State in Palestine.

From April to July 1922, as the League of Nations deliberated whether to ratify the British mandate for Palestine, the *Roman Observer* ran a series of seven articles headlined "Zionism and Palestine." One of them described a speech in Rome by the visiting Patriarch of Jerusalem. He said Zionism was trying to seize all of Palestine, erect a Zionist kingdom, expel the present inhabitants, and use terrorism to accomplish its goals.

Two days later Cardinal Secretary of State Gasparri sent a diplomatic note to the Council of the League of Nations objecting to the mandate, because it would give the Jews "an absolute preponderance" over the other peoples of Palestine. Gasparri succeeded in getting a postponement of the vote, while the Vatican pressed Catholics and governments to oppose the mandate.

In July 1922, on the eve of the vote, the Vatican paper ran a front page article on "The Jews of Poland," accusing them of Bolshevism and "repellent filthiness." The article said that Polish Zionists wanted to transform Poland into a "colony" of the Jewish State in Palestine. On July 24, 1922, the League of Nations ratified the mandate for Britain to administer Palestine for the purpose of establishing a national home for the Jewish people.

Catholic Civilization weighed in with two attacks on "Jewish-Bolshevism," one shortly before the League of Nations vote, and one three months later. The July 15, 1922 attack came in the course of a long, bitter article against Zionism, whipping up hatred toward "the despised and odious tyranny of the Jew" in Palestine. The October 21, 1922 article was the one with the 447/545 statistics purporting to show complete Jewish control of the Soviet Union. It concluded with a veiled reference to the *Protocols of the Elders of Zion*, saying that "sages" have taken over all of Russia, as "the yoke of another nation, the Jews, has been imposed on the Slavs."

A review of the timeline of events and documents in the early 1920s reveals a distinctive pattern. When the issue at hand was Russian Communism, as it was continuously for the first eight months of 1920, the Vatican did not focus on allegations of Jewish domination of Russia or a Jewish-Bolshevik conspiracy to destroy Christian countries. Even when the Red Army was approaching the gates of Warsaw in summer 1920 and threatening to roll on into other countries, Jewish-Communist propaganda did not appear on the *Roman Observer's* front page.

Only after the danger was past, with the defeat of the Red Army in August 1920 and its retreat into Russia, did the "Jewish Peril" article appear. Equating of Jews and Bolsheviks continued regularly over the next two years, repeatedly in the same context: appeals against Zionism, against a Jewish State in Palestine, and against Jewish "predominance" in the Holy Land.

In short, the deployment of the Jewish-Communist conspiracy theory by the Vatican in 1920-1922 had no connection with facts in Russia or immediate threats from there. It had a consistent connection with policy toward Palestine. Indeed, the Vatican did not deploy the Jewish-Communist tactic in its newspaper until three years after the "Jewish-Bolsheviks" took over Russia. The Jewish-Bolshevik conspiracy theory had actually become *less* plausible by that time, as the non-Jew Lenin consolidated one-man dictatorial rule from 1917 to 1920. Less plausible, that is, unless the theory came to be endorsed by authorities who were believed.

Why would the Vatican place its authority behind this conspiracy theory in late 1920, and 1921, and 1922? We had an idea where to start looking for an answer to that question. It was an account Steve had read by Theodor Herzl, the founder of the Zionist movement, of his meeting with Pope Pius X in 1904.

43. Rome, Jerusalem, and "Replacement Theology"

The modern Zionist movement began with Austro-Hungarian journalist Theodor Herzl's publication of his book *Der Judenstaat*, or "The Jewish State," in 1896. Herzl was born in Budapest in 1860 and studied at the University of Vienna. He witnessed the success of a resurgent antisemitic movement in Austria-Hungary in the late 1800's, threatening to trample Jewish citizens' recently gained civic and economic rights. As a correspondent in Paris, he saw the impact of antisemitic propaganda during the fraudulent treason case against the Jewish French General Staff officer Alfred Dreyfus. Concluding that Jewish efforts to assimilate and gain acceptance in European countries were futile in the face of relentless antisemitism, Herzl proposed the solution of a Jewish State, or at least a restored Jewish homeland in Palestine under the rule of the Ottoman Turks.

Herzl followed up his book with intensive personal lobbying efforts. He gained credibility through his success in meeting with key political and cultural figures across Europe, including Kaiser Wilhelm II of Germany. Traveling to Istanbul to seek a meeting with the Sultan of the Ottoman Empire, he gained high level meetings with the Sultan's subordinates and raised hopes for the eventual success of his project. In 1897 he organized the first World Zionist Congress in Basel, Switzerland. As President of the Congress, he reconvened the convention annually until his death in July 1904.

Around the beginning of 1904, an Italian Count approached Herzl and offered to arrange a meeting with Pope Pius X in Rome. The audience took place on January 25th, which the Catholic Church celebrates as the Feast of the conversion of St. Paul, born Saul of Tarsus. This is what the Pope told Herzl when asked to support the Zionist movement, as recorded in Herzl's diary:

> We cannot give approval to this movement. We cannot prevent the Jews from going to Jerusalem – but we could never sanction it. The soil of Jerusalem, if it was not always sacred, has been sanctified by the life of Jesus Christ. As the head of the Church I cannot tell you anything different. The Jews have not recognized our Lord, therefore we cannot recognize the Jewish people...

Herzl's diary includes some words of the Pope that Herzl said confused him. The words are revealing, however, to anyone familiar with "replacement theology":

He spoke of the Temple at Jerusalem. It had been destroyed forever. Did I suppose that one ought to reconstruct it and perform the sacrificial services there in the ancient way? He also talked about Josephus Flavius and quoted him; but I didn't quite understand that.

We had learned about replacement theology at a retreat some years earlier. The priest who led the retreat described the long-dominant notion in Roman Catholicism that Rome and the Catholic Church had replaced Jerusalem and the Jewish people in the eyes of God. While it was not an immutable dogma, a doctrine defined by a worldwide Church Council or *ex cathedra* by the Pope, this proposition was believed by many authorities in the Catholic Church over a period of many centuries. When replacement theology was finally addressed by a Church Council in 1965, it was rejected. It had never been consistent with scripture.

For Pope St. Pius X in 1904, replacement theology was accepted and believed. The destruction of the Temple was forever, because Jerusalem's replacement by Rome was forever. Pius was not alone in this belief. For like-minded authorities in the Vatican, any effort to re-establish the Jewish nation of Israel and restore Jewish control of Jerusalem was a direct threat to the status and standing of Catholic Rome as the unique focal point of God's favor on earth.

True devotees of replacement theology believed it impossible for the Jews to regain Jerusalem or rebuild the Temple. They knew that Julian the Apostate, Roman Emperor in the 360s A.D., had set about to rebuild the Temple in Jerusalem for the Jews. The prompt failure of the project and death of Julian in battle served for many centuries to confirm their beliefs about that impossibility. But this did not prevent devotees in the Vatican after World War One from doing their part to make sure the impossible would remain impossible.

By October 1920, when we saw the Vatican newspaper start promoting Jewish-Communist conspiracy theory, the impossibility of Jerusalem and Palestine coming under Jewish control was in grave jeopardy. The danger had grown over the preceding three years. On November 2, 1917, the British Government issued the Balfour Declaration, committing His Majesty's

Government to support the establishment of a homeland for the Jewish people in Palestine.

The threat quickly became more than just a piece of paper, as the British Army captured Jerusalem and much of Palestine in November and December that year. At the Allies' Peace Conference in Paris in 1919, the practical realization of Theodor Herzl's dream was a central topic. The Versailles Treaty adopted and incorporated the Balfour Declaration. In April 1920, the Allies met on the Italian Riviera at San Remo and decided to give Britain the mandate to govern Palestine in order to implement the Balfour Declaration. Sir Herbert Samuel's appointment as High Commissioner followed immediately.

On his way to Palestine in June 1920, Samuel stopped in Rome to give assurances to Pope Benedict XV and Cardinal Secretary of State Gasparri. Benedict told Samuel his initial concerns were alleviated by Samuel's public commitments to religious toleration and liberty, and by Samuel's recognition of the interests of the Catholic Church in the Holy Land. Two days after the meeting, however, Cardinal Gasparri told a French diplomat at the Vatican that Samuel was going to Palestine for the sole purpose of supporting Zionism.

Cardinal Gasparri's concerns were reflected in *Roman Observer* articles from June 1920 onward, in highly alarming terms, as we saw in the last chapter. Headlines and content from 1920 to 1922 were well designed to arouse worldwide Catholic opposition to Zionism. References to Jews calling Samuel "The Prince of Israel" played directly into fears that a restored Jewish Kingdom of Israel would overturn the claim of Rome and Catholicism to be the replacement of Jerusalem and Judaism. Equating Jews with Bolsheviks was the strongest possible way to inspire fear and hatred toward the Zionist enterprise. Meanwhile, those who rejoiced in the prospective fulfillment of scriptural prophecies about the restoration of Israel, Jerusalem, and God's chosen people found not a word of encouragement in any of these articles.

An especially troubling aspect of the articles was their description of the role played by the Latin Patriarch of Jerusalem. We had learned, starting with our chance discovery in Rosh Pina, that Jewish immigrant farmers and Arab tenant farmers were not naturally and always enemies.

Now it appeared, beginning as early as July 1920, that Patriarch Barlassina was actively inciting joint Christian-Moslem resistance to British authorities. Barlassina's reported remarks in Rome in 1922, accusing Zionists of using "terrorism" to seize all of Palestine and expel the Arabs, could easily incite violence by people induced to fear for their lives. Articles in *Catholic Civilization* in 1922, as well as earlier articles in the *Roman Observer*, excused Arab violence against Jews in Palestine and blamed the Jews for bringing it upon themselves.

By the mid-1920s, Arab violence and British appeasement ended the foreseeable prospects for a Jewish State arising in Palestine. Sir Herbert Samuel was replaced as High Commissioner in 1925 by a career British military man. With dangers of Jewish "predominance" at low ebb after 1924, the attacks in *Catholic Civilization* on Zionism and Jewish-Communism ceased. Articles in the late 1920s and early 1930s dealt in detail with Communism without mentioning Jews. The 1928 article about the "Friends of Israel," with its reaffirmation of Jewish-Bolshevik conspiracy theory, was the exception during that period. We did not find any indications that Jewish-Bolshevik propaganda appeared in the *Roman Observer* during those years.

In sum, the Jewish-Communist conspiracy propaganda campaign in the early 1920s was a tactic. It had little or nothing to do with truth or fact. It had much to do with preventing Jewish control of the Holy Land.

44. The Vatican and the Treaty of Versailles

Our review of the Vatican-connected press in the years after World War One found additional prominently displayed concerns, centered on the Treaty of Versailles. The Versailles Treaty of 1919 reshaped the map of Europe. Geographically speaking, the Treaty removed 13% of Germany's European territory and all of its overseas colonies. The victorious Allies thoroughly dismantled Germany's defeated partners, the Austro-Hungarian Empire and the Turkish Ottoman Empire. The Allies recreated Poland, reduced Austria and Hungary to small separate nations, and created the totally new countries of Czechoslovakia and Yugoslavia. Politically speaking, the Versailles Treaty confirmed the overthrow of monarchies in the defeated countries and established democracies in their place.

Important aspects of the Paris Peace Conference of 1919, and the Versailles Treaty it produced, grievously offended the Vatican and threatened what it perceived to be its vital interests.

The first offense was foundational. The Allies excluded Pope Benedict XV and his representatives from the Peace Conference. England and France had reached that decision already in 1915, when Italy made it a secret precondition for entering the war on the side of the Allies. The Vatican learned of that agreement during the war and tried to reverse it, but without success.

Why did Italy insist? The Vatican was still trying to get back at least some part of the sovereign jurisdiction it lost with the fall of the Papal States half a century before. Italy had turned the center of the Vatican's jurisdiction, the city of Rome, into the national capital. The struggle between Italy and the Vatican over ultimate control of Rome was known worldwide as the "Roman Question." At Paris in 1919, Italy kept the Roman Question off the negotiating table by denying the Vatican a seat. By contrast, at the Congress of Vienna in 1815, the last European-wide peace conference before Versailles, the Papal States, dissolved by Napoleon in the 1790s, had been restored.

A threat to the Vatican's perceived vital interests emerged near the beginning of the half-year-long Peace Conference. The leader of the Zionist movement, Chaim Weizmann, was welcomed at the Conference, unlike the Pope. On January 3, 1919, Weizmann signed an agreement in Paris with the leader of the Arab delegation to the Peace Conference. Emir Faisal was the same Arab leader who, along with his father, allied with Lawrence of Arabia and the British Army in 1916 for the Arab Revolt against the Ottoman Empire. The Weizmann-Faisal Agreement affirmed the Balfour Declaration. It allowed large-scale Jewish immigration to Palestine along with Arab sovereignty over the vast lands outside Palestine, from Syria to Iraq to Arabia.

Faisal declared the Arabs would welcome the Jews, and the two groups would help each other prosper. Although the agreement became a nullity after a French army drove Faisal out of his chosen Arab capital of Damascus in 1920, it held great promise during the year 1919.

The break-up of the Austrian Empire eliminated a historically Catholic great power. In the countries the Allies formed from that Empire, some Catholic populations were placed at a marked disadvantage. In Yugoslavia the Eastern Orthodox Serbs dominated the central government, at the expense of Catholic populations in the provinces of Croatia and Slovenia.

An even greater perceived offense occurred in Czechoslovakia. The Slovaks in the eastern half of the country were overwhelmingly Catholic, but the more numerous Czechs dominated culturally, economically, and politically.

The Czech-American founder and first president of the country, Thomas Masaryk, opposed the privileged status the Catholic Church had long enjoyed in Austrian domains. Masaryk offended the Vatican by designating a new national holiday in honor of John Hus, a Roman Catholic priest who had been burned at the stake five hundred years before by Catholic authorities. And, as we learned at the restaurant that bears his name in Jerusalem, Masaryk championed equality of rights for Jews.

Separation of Church from State became a widespread initiative in Europe after World War One. A feature of French and Italian government before the war, it now threatened to prevail in Germany and Spain, as well as Czechoslovakia and other nations. Control of education became a major political battleground. In Bavaria, for example, the large majority of government schools were run by the Catholic Church, with the Bishops having ultimate hiring and firing power over teachers and staff. Post-war governments in Bavaria and elsewhere threatened to end such Church control. Pope Pius XI denounced separation of Church and State as "oppression" against the Church, resulting from "the apostasy of society," in a 1933 encyclical directed at Spain.

The overall picture of Europe in the wake of the Versailles Treaty of 1919 was a beleaguered Catholic Church, with the Vatican on the defensive, seemingly losing key battles almost everywhere. It appeared far more likely that the Jews would regain Jerusalem and Israel than that the Vatican would regain sovereignty over Rome. Italian historian Fattorini describes a report from Eugenio Pacelli to Rome in 1919, preserved in the Vatican Archives, referring to the Versailles Treaty as "an international absurdity."

It might seem hard to blame the Jews for Versailles, since the Allied leaders at the conference were overwhelmingly Gentiles. It would appear even harder to blame Jews for the "Roman Question" in Italy, as there were very few Jews in that country. But the Jews had long been blamed for initiatives to separate Church and State, and for the loss of the Papal States, even before there was Russian Communism to blame them for. Indeed it was worldwide indignation of Jews and Gentiles alike, over Pope Pius IX's 1858 kidnapping of a Jewish boy, Edgardo Mortara, that led Austria to withdraw its army upholding Rome's rule in the Papal States. And the Mayor of the Italian capital city of Rome in the years just before World War One was a Jew, Ernesto Nathan. When the front page of the *Munich Catholic Church Newspaper* attacked Jewish world conspiracy on May 9, 1920, it called out Ernesto Nathan by name.

In early 2014, we found two additional windows into the Vatican's perspective on the events of 1919 and 1920 and the way they shaped inter-war Europe. A trip to the Czech Republic gave us an opportunity to take a side trip to Munich and look more closely at the *Munich Catholic Church Newspaper* for 1917 through 1920. What we found in 1917 and 1918 was a paper focused on scripture, religious teaching, local Church events, and pastoral care in the midst of wartime suffering. The lead story of each issue was about the Gospel reading for the week, except when there was a special message from the Archbishop or the Bishops Conference.

From early 1919 onward, however, the Archdiocesan paper took on a much more international and political character, with detailed coverage of Vatican events and international political-cultural issues from a Vatican perspective. With a Vatican Nuncio in town, of course, the Munich paper had excellent sources of information for its new sections called "Ecclesiastical Review," "Vatican Review" and "From World and Church."

During 1919 and 1920, we found ten articles in the Archdiocesan paper on Zionism and Palestine. The earliest, in March 1919, was an article saying it would be "extremely painful for the Holy See if a predominant position in Palestine were conceded to unbelievers." Articles in the second half of 1920 encouraged a worldwide mobilization of Catholics to oppose Zionism. The *Munich Catholic Church Newspaper* took just as strong positions, repeatedly, against separation of Church and State, and against the Versailles Treaty and the exclusion of the Pope from the Peace Conference. The results of the First World War were perceived as so adverse to the Church that the paper called it the "Freemasons' War." In March 1920, an article stated that the Pope had "implicitly condemned" the Versailles Treaty.

But the most frequent denunciations were directed against one specific product of Versailles, the new nation of Czechoslovakia. In a dozen articles in 1919 and 1920, the *Munich Catholic Church Newspaper* railed against Czech authorities, reporting priests forced out of the public schools, outrages against Catholic lay persons, Freemasons dominating the government, threats to the survival of the Church in that country, and John Hus honored as a national hero.

Steve was amazed to find the paper calling Masaryk's wife and daughter Jewish. In fact Masaryk's American wife, Charlotte Garrigue Masaryk, had a solid "WASP" pedigree as a Unitarian, with an ancestor on the Mayflower and a father descended from French Huguenots. There had been nothing surprising about Jan Bata being branded as a Jew by the Nazis. But now Steve was looking at a Catholic paper with close ties to Rome, through its Nuncio in Munich, doing the same thing.

The second window we encountered in early 2014 was *Catholic Documentation*, the first "very respected" Catholic journal to promote Jewish-Communist propaganda. Our stop in Paris two years before had focused on just that one issue of March 6, 1920. Now, finding a complete set of bound volumes within driving distance, at the University of Sherbrooke, Canada, we took a close look at all the issues in 1919 and 1920.

Catholic Documentation began publishing in February 1919. Its first issue focused extensively on the proceedings at the Paris Peace Conference, on the "Holy See and International Politics," and on "The Israelites Stake Their Claim" – to Palestine. Every issue contained documents from the Vatican and other high Catholic authorities.

Catholic Documentation's stance against Zionism was adamant, and it introduced a rough form of Jewish-Bolshevik propaganda as early as August 1919, together with much more propaganda against Jewish-finance. In January 1920 it described a strategy for countering the "Jewish invasion" of Palestine: "create a public opinion against Zionism, in union among Christians and between Christians and Muslims." This article also celebrated Rome's conquering of Jerusalem in A.D. 70.

But we saw the very strongest vitriol, once again, directed against Czechoslovakia. We did not see *Catholic Documentation* calling any of the Masaryks Jews. Instead, they tarred Thomas Masaryk with Marxism and Bolshevism. A lengthy article in November 1920 confidently predicted the early demise of Czechoslovakia. *Catholic Documentation* quoted a Vatican official saying the Slovaks might join Poland or Hungary. Two priests had already started a Slovak autonomy movement, and Catholic Bishops in Czechoslovakia were threatening that the province of Slovakia would secede unless Catholic demands were met. The article called the Allies' peace terms "the Protestant Peace," as they "dismembered Catholic Austria-Hungary," submitted the Slovaks to the Czechs and the Catholic Croats to the Serbs. All of this displayed a "fundamentally anti-Catholic spirit."

While the Zionist "threat" in Palestine was under control from the mid-1920s onward, the other grave offenses, from a Vatican standpoint, continued well into the 1930s. As for Czechoslovakia, far from suffering an imminent demise, it proved to be the longest-lasting of the democracies set up by the Allies, with a robust economy boasting a Depression-era expansion of a major export business, under Jan Bata, into 100 countries.

45. Taking Off the Gloves

In early 2014 we came upon an important new historical work. *The Pope and Mussolini: The Secret History of Pius XI and the Rise of Fascism in Europe*, by David Kertzer, was the first book by any historian that supplied a plausible explanation for the facts we had found. As the title indicates, the book focuses on Pope Pius XI and Fascist Italy. Despite its broader subtitle, the book does not cover Vatican relations with Hitler and Nazi Germany. But the pattern of facts it discloses from Italy, based on extensive research in Italian governmental and other archives, bears eerie similarities to parts of the pattern we found in Germany.

The Pope and Mussolini shows the Vatican providing crucial support to Mussolini from 1922 through the 1930s. Pope Pius XI, first with Cardinal Gasparri, then with Cardinal Pacelli as Vatican Secretary of State, promoted a violent, thuggish, totalitarian movement, whose ideology was opposite to Christian faith, but whose leader carried out important missions for the Vatican.

Mussolini, who started as an anti-Church Socialist, agreed to restore Church privileges, provided increased state subsidies to the clergy, and reversed the separation of Church and State in Italy. In 1929 he concluded the Lateran Accords with the Vatican. Mussolini agreed to give the Pope sovereignty over Vatican City, pay a large sum of money in compensation for the remainder of the lost Papal States, establish Catholicism as the official state religion of Italy, and institute Catholic education in government schools under control of the Bishops. Pius XI praised Mussolini for resolving the "Roman Question" and declared him a man sent by Providence.

Catholic Civilization and the *Roman Observer* played an important role in signaling Vatican support for Mussolini at key times. In October 1922, the month Mussolini came to power, the Vatican directed *Catholic Civilization* to reverse course, stop criticizing the Fascists, and start supporting Mussolini's government. In 1924, with Mussolini's regime on the verge of collapse under the weight of public indignation over the Fascists' murder of their leading opponent in the Italian parliament, Pope Pius XI came to the rescue. *Catholic Civilization* instructed Catholics on their religious obligation to support the governing authorities and not to support the opposition Socialists. At the height of Mussolini's crisis, the *Roman Observer* ran a series of articles, which Steve had already translated for the Timeline, instructing Italian Catholics that "conscience" meant doing what they were told.

Just as we saw in Bavaria in 1923, priests in Italy celebrated Mass and conducted ceremonial services for the Fascists and their uniformed paramilitary formations. The Vatican tolerated Fascist violence, even against priests and Catholic political activists, while its newspaper pretended Mussolini was opposed to the violence, and continued to give him positive coverage. This followed the same pattern we saw in the *Roman Observer* in 1934, when the Vatican refrained from criticizing Hitler for the Night of the Long Knives, instead giving him glowing personal coverage in the months that followed.

The result of the Vatican's embrace of totalitarianism in Italy was the successful undoing of the perceived outrages of preceding decades, and the securing of vital Roman Church interests. Separation of Church and State was completely reversed. Vatican temporal sovereignty was restored. The clergy secured a central role in education. Socialist and Communist parties were crushed. And Italy's invasion of Ethiopia in 1935 made a mockery of another creation of Versailles, the League of Nations.

The "Jewish Question" took longer to address in Italy than in Germany. Mussolini was not antisemitic. Among his many adulterous interests, Mussolini's longest-term lover, before and during the 1920s, was a Jewish woman. Kertzer shows the Vatican newspaper and *Catholic Civilization* promoting the concept of anti-Jewish racial laws in Italy in the months before they were enacted. Upon enactment of Italy's equivalent of the Nuremberg Laws in November 1938, the *Roman Observer* objected only insofar as the new laws infringed upon the Church's control over marriage. And Kertzer cites Mussolini's personal notes of an earlier meeting with Pope Pius XI, in 1932, for a revealing point: Pius plied Mussolini with elements of Jewish-Communist conspiracy theory.

It is striking that overt Catholic clerical support for Fascist paramilitary mobilization in Bavaria occurred in 1923, right after the Vatican decision to support the Fascist movement in Italy. The many references we saw in late 1922 and 1923 to Hitler as the "Bavarian Mussolini" carry a more ominous tone in light of clerical support for both Fascist leaders at the time.

Cardinal Faulhaber's words of August 27, 1922 gave Bavarian Catholics, including clergy, a green light to participate in a Fascist movement openly seeking to overthrow the Weimar Republic. While Faulhaber wrote officially to the Vatican that he had no intent to impugn the Weimar Republic, neither he nor the Vatican made any such disavowal publicly. Cardinal Faulhaber's later praise for Hitler as a leader in 1924 and 1925, and for Nazism as an "originally pure spring," helped preserve a discredited traitor's ability to return as the "German Mussolini" at a later point in time.

When Pius XI and Mussolini concluded the historic Lateran Accords restoring Vatican sovereignty on February 11, 1929, Hitler boasted about the implications for Germany. He gave a speech interpreting the Vatican's action as an endorsement of Fascist totalitarianism and a rejection of Catholic political parties. The same model, Hitler proclaimed, should be pursued in Germany. His speech was the lead story in the *Volkisch Observer*.

Far from spurning Hitler's interpretation, Cardinal Pacelli personally instructed a Catholic Chancellor of Germany to form a coalition with the right-wing elements in the Reichstag, of which the Nazis were by far the largest part, in 1931. Chancellor Heinrich Brüning refused. A year later Pacelli's close associate Fr. Ludwig Kaas, head of the Catholic Center Party, wrote an article for a prestigious German international law journal, effectively agreeing with Hitler's interpretation. Totalitarianism, Kaas wrote, had accomplished wonderful things in Italy, including an agreement with the Church, an example that should serve as a "model" for other countries. Pacelli and Kaas thus demonstrated that Hitler's boast of 1929 was not far off the mark. Kertzer concludes that Cardinal Pacelli was more pro-Fascist than Pope Pius XI. "Cardinal Pacelli remained Mussolini's most powerful ally in the Vatican."

It took only six months from the time Hitler came to power in 1933 until his regime signed a new Concordat with the Vatican. Many historians have written that Concordats are not endorsements of governments, but rather protections for the Church, regardless of the type of government. That is true in theory. But it is not how *Catholic Civilization* explained the Vatican-Germany Concordat two months after its ratification. In an article that was supervised, according to the long-established review procedures, by Cardinal Pacelli and his staff, *Catholic Civilization* wrote of the Concordat that

> with this, hope is established for the future, if the rulers are not lacking in a sense of good faith and integrity, which must be assumed in all honest contracting parties, and much more in the men of the German Government, who are well aware of the terrible "present hour." Nor should one vainly skip by the "great hour" that is passing, for we can truly

call it "a historical and providential hour" for Germany. But why not also add: for Christian Europe and for all the civilized world?

The "historical and providential hour" struck for the Czechoslovakian portion of "Christian Europe" in March 1939. Eugenio Pacelli was crowned Pope Pius XII on the 12th of that month. On March 13th, the leading Catholic priest in the Slovakia provincial government, Monsignor Jozef Tiso, flew to Germany to meet with Hitler. On March 14th, back at the Slovak parliament, Tiso declared Slovakia's secession from Czechoslovakia. Early the next morning, March 15th, Nazi Germany invaded the helpless remainder of the Czech nation.

Historians have noted the failure of the Vatican to condemn Nazi Germany's invasions of Czechoslovakia and Poland in 1939, and France in 1940. Half a century ago, Holocaust survivor and historian Saul Friedländer presented a series of documents from these years in *Pius XII and the Third Reich*. Some of the documents were troubling, but perhaps there was insufficient context to understand them. In April 1939, Germany's Ambassador to the Vatican, Diego von Bergen, cabled Berlin reporting Pope Pius XII's words to a visiting group of Germans: "We have always loved Germany ... and We love it much more now. We rejoice at the greatness of Germany ..."
In June 1940, as French resistance to Hitler's invasion collapsed and Italy declared war on France to mop up the spoils, the Vatican's Nuncio in Berlin, Archbishop Cesare Orsenigo, visited the German Foreign Office. A German official wrote that the Nuncio said he "hoped the Germans would march into Paris by way of Versailles."

46. Ruling from Rome

In reading the *Roman Observer*, *Catholic Civilization* and the *Munich Catholic Church Newspaper* from almost a century ago, we encountered a different tone from mainstream Catholic publications today. Major differences are naturally to be expected in matters where the documents of the Second Vatican Council are widely seen to have reversed previous trends. These include rejection of antisemitism and replacement theology in *Nostra Aetate*, affirmation of human rights as opposed to totalitarianism in *Gaudium et Spes*, and championing of freedom of conscience in *Dignitatis Humanae*.

The difference that surprised us was something else. It was the championing of Rome as a world power. We saw the Pope glorified as the greatest sovereign in the world, as distinct from a voice to be listened to in matters of morality, or the steward of Christian tradition and teaching. One of the clearest examples appeared on the front page of the *Roman Observer* two days after Cardinal Pacelli arrived in Buenos Aires. Under the headline "Grandiose Homage of the Metropolis," the Vatican newspaper broadcast the city's greeting to the Papal Legate, addressing him as if the Pope were present in person: "Your Eminence! I greet in the Pontifical Legate the foremost Sovereign of the World to whose spiritual power all other Sovereigns bow in veneration."

Homage by rulers and countries to the Pope was a constant theme on the front page of the Vatican's newspaper in the 1920s and 1930s. The *Roman Observer* celebrated dozens of occasions when heads of state, governmental delegations, and national pilgrim groups visited the Pope. Time after time, headlines portrayed these visits as "homage" to the Pope. Even the Japanese puppet state of Manchukuo, which was nothing but an egregious Japanese military occupation in northeastern China, merited half the *Roman Observer's* front page, with a large photograph, when it paid homage to Pope Pius XI in 1938.

A passage written by Domenico Tardini, one of Cardinal Pacelli's subordinates in the Vatican Secretariat of State in 1937, proclaimed the concept of Papal worldly sovereignty:

> Rome now has with the Pope a truly universal authority; an authority which, although of a spiritual quality, must necessarily be expressed through an entire organization of external government based and centered here. So it is that, at long last, Rome truly governs the world.

Pope Pius XI, in his long-distance address to the crowd at the Pontifical Mass in Buenos Aires on October 14, 1934, held out the promise of world peace by means of international sovereignty of the Church as the kingdom and empire of Christ:

> And I wish that, together with the victory of the kingdom and the empire that necessarily pertain to our mildest and most loving King, there will be a peaceful triumph in the most noble land of Argentina and ultimately in all parts of the globe; even more, in everyone's intellect and will. In that way, indeed, this poor world that we see so afflicted by the shedding of fraternal blood will be able to experience true lasting peace, free from so many evils and uniquely governed with generosity; the peace of Christ in the kingdom of Christ.

The Europe of 1934 from which Pius XI spoke these words was actually much more peaceful than the following years when Rome exerted its influence. Kertzer shows Cardinal Pacelli and his subordinates Tardini and Pizzardo providing behind-the-scenes support for Italy's invasion of Ethiopia in 1935. And the Vatican openly welcomed Franco's role in the Spanish Civil War, which he initiated in 1936.

The Pope's assertion of imperial governing authority appeared also in his document appointing Cardinal Pacelli as Legate to the Congress. That document, proclaimed in Buenos Aires by Fr. Ludwig Kaas, who had left Germany the previous year and now worked directly for Cardinal Pacelli, exhorted all to "obey completely and with alacrity the laws of the divine kingdom."

Rome governing the world became a reality in the 1920s and 1930s through the application of law, not faith. The new Code of Canon Law, completed in 1917 after more than a decade of work by Pietro Gasparri and Eugenio Pacelli, set forth the governing rules. Concordats made Canon Law the norm, country by country, in place of customs and traditions peculiar to each local part of the Catholic Church, in matters ranging from selection of Bishops to supervision of the Catholic press.

Concordats could also, depending on the disposition of the country's governing authorities, signal a practical alliance for goals and missions set by Rome. That type of relationship was foreshadowed by *Catholic Civilization's* article about the Vatican-Germany Concordat in November 1933.

It was reflected more directly in the September 1934 *Roman Observer* article expressly setting forth Germany's "mission." In Italy, Kertzer documents Pope Pius XI repeatedly giving instructions to Mussolini via a secret intermediary, instructions that Mussolini often, but not always, followed.

Ruling from Rome did not necessarily mean using only loyal Catholics for missions. Mussolini's reputation when he began achieving key objectives for Rome was *anti*-Catholic. Hitler was openly persecuting Catholics in 1934 when the Vatican newspaper stated Germany's mission. The anti-Catholic reputation of Mussolini and Hitler provided an element of plausible deniability to the Vatican, offering a potential for achieving some missions without being held to account publicly. The Timeline contains one example after another from the 1920s and 1930s showing that Vatican policy was not constrained by Catholic teaching. Meanwhile, the Pope's reputation as the keeper of Christian tradition shielded the Vatican from much scrutiny. These factors help explain the long time lag between the acts and their exposure by historians such as Kertzer.

The self-confident assertion of power by authorities in Rome was bolstered by the notion, promoted strongly by Popes in the late 19th and early 20th century, that the Roman Catholic Church was a "perfect society." Indeed, Pope Pius XI presented the Church in a 1925 encyclical as a perfect society and the kingdom of Christ on earth.

A common thread among key figures in this story is their self-identification as avatars of Rome. In Hudal's pre-1930 writings and sermons, for instance, while Steve found nothing of Jewish-Communist conspiracy theory, he found a deep devotion to the heritage of Rome. This passage is typical:

Is there anyone to whom Rome has nothing to say? Even if he knew nothing of its historical greatness and its past, the stones of the Forum and the ancient Christian basilicas would speak to him and initiate him into Roman thought and feeling... On the ancient Roman streets, milestones are still found with the heading: *Pro patria consumor.* For the Fatherland I give my all. Whenever Roman soldiers, tired and sunburned, coming from far away and walking back onto these streets, cast a glance upon these words, they were struck by the words as an exhortation: For the Fatherland, eternal Rome, I offer myself up.

Eugenio Pacelli likewise evinced a strong Roman patriotism that colored the way he spoke of both Judaism and Catholicism. In a speech in 1936 he proclaimed: "Jerusalem and its people are no more the City and the People of God: Rome is the new Zion, and everyone who lives the Roman faith is a Roman." Earlier, when he was ordained a priest in 1899, he expressed his identity succinctly on the ordination cards prepared for the occasion: "Eugenio Pacelli, Roman."

Writers often refer to Eugenio Pacelli's ancestors as Roman nobility. That status was hard-earned, yet vulnerable. Pacelli's grandfather, and his grandfather's brother, started out as commoners in the small town of Onano, far northwest of Rome. Through a relative who was a priest in Rome, the brothers gained trusted positions in the administration of the Papal States.

Eugenio Pacelli's grandfather, Marcantonio, was the number two man in the Vatican's Interior Ministry for the last two decades of the Papal States. He is well known as a key founder of the *Roman Observer*. His position also involved him in the arrest and punishment of those opposing the Pope's temporal rule. When Papal States police took a six-year-old Jewish boy, Edgardo Mortara, from his family home in Bologna in 1858 and brought him to Rome, the Interior Ministry was the office in charge of the Papal States police. Marcantonio and his brother were fixtures in Rome, both living to about 100 years of age. When the Papal States fell to the forces of Italian unification, many Italians felt they had gained a country. But the Pacelli family had lost theirs.

Is the Roman Catholic Church about temporal sovereignty, worldly power, accumulation of wealth, and homage paid by subordinate powers? For both of us, Jesus' words resolve the issue: "My kingdom is not of this world." When Steve became a Catholic at age 29, he professed publicly that he believes all that the Catholic Church teaches to be revealed by God. Church as empire and Pope as emperor are not part of that teaching. Diane's faith has been lifelong, marked by experiences of God's mercy and love, which do not include the sponsorship of a worldly empire.

47. Accountable to No Man

If words and actions such as those documented in the Timeline, and presented in this book, come from leaders of a group one is committed to, what is the right response? For us as Catholics, the question we faced, as the evidence came increasingly into focus over the course of five years, was this: Are we capable of applying the most basic standards of right and wrong when those standards are violated by the highest leaders of our Church? Can we apply moral standards to Catholic leaders whose words and actions became one of the contributing causes to the Holocaust?

If we thought of the Roman Catholic Church as an empire, we might hesitate. But Jesus said, "I am the way and the truth and the life." Why fear the truth?

If the evidence shows that certain persons, over a period of time, used their control of our Church to violate everything that Jesus stood and stands for, that is something for us as Catholics to combat, not cover up. Our way of combatting it is to expose it. Our way of exposing it is to present the evidence for all to see. The main causes of the Holocaust, flowing from Hitler and Nazi Germany, are known to all. Now, with access to original documents, everyone also can assess to what extent the central figures in this story contributed to the causes of those horrors, or not. Our commitment is to maintain the Timeline and add to it as relevant materials come to our attention.

We do not purport to be "experts." Lawyers are familiar with courtroom "battles of experts." When highly credentialed experts are lined up on opposite sides of a case, expressing opposing views, what the jury needs is not more experts. It needs facts. Original documents can break an intractable deadlock among experts, especially when they are documents that were created, produced or supervised by one of the parties in the case.

The most intractable battle of experts we have encountered is the one over Pope Pius XII. One might expect that the work of historians over the course of decades would resolve major issues and narrow the degree of disagreement. That has not occurred. Countless new books continue to appear about Pius XII, the Catholic Church and the Nazi era. The two most recent books illustrate how far key issues are from resolution.

David Kertzer's *The Pope and Mussolini* presents Eugenio Pacelli as "the most powerful ally" in the Vatican for Italy's Fascist dictator in the 1930s.

Kertzer has outstanding academic credentials. When Steve first noticed a book by Kertzer several years ago, he asked a priest about him. The priest was involved for many years in Catholic-Jewish dialogues. "His scholarship is impeccable," was the response. If Kertzer is your expert, you could well conclude that Pacelli is complicit in crimes against humanity.

Robert Ventresca's *Soldier of Christ* takes a measured tone in his biography of Pope Pius XII. As the title suggests, Ventresca presents Pacelli, with human weaknesses and limitations, sincerely trying to represent Christ on earth. He concludes, "there is a strong argument to be made that taken as a whole his reign over the church was consistent with the moral, pastoral, and political leadership expected of the Vicar of Christ." Ventresca is a credentialed historian. His book has a Harvard seal of approval, published by a division of that university's press. If Ventresca is your expert, you could well conclude that Pope Pius XII is a fitting candidate for Catholic sainthood.

So, the result of decades of work by experts, as matters stand today, is that Eugenio Pacelli may be anything from a war criminal at one extreme, to a saint at the other. You can choose your favorite credentialed expert and get whatever answer you want. Or you can look at the facts for yourself.

We do not underestimate the challenges along the path to accountability. Two key steps are repentance and restitution. As to the first, the official 1998 Vatican document on the Holocaust, *We Remember: A Reflection on the Shoah*, acknowledged and expressed profound regret for the complicity of "sons and daughters" of the Roman Catholic Church in the Holocaust. But there was no repentance for the conduct of leaders, only praise. The document praised Pope Pius XI, Pope Pius XII, and Cardinal Faulhaber, for certain of their words against antisemitism and Nazism. Those words are in the Timeline, and readers can assess the overall record of each man.

Perhaps the greatest obstacle is that, as Catholics, we have no institutional memory of procedures for holding a Pope accountable. While few today have heard of it, there is a long tradition holding that "the Pope is accountable to no man." The concept was introduced in the early 500s by Pope Symmachus, who was fighting accusations of corruption. An official Papal document in 1302 entitled *Unam Sanctam* explained why the Pope is accountable only to God, not to man, and why temporal rulers must be subordinated to the Pope. The Lateran Accords made Papal non-accountabililty a continuing reality in the 20th century. Only a sovereign can hope to be non-accountable in this world. The Vatican's concern in the 1920s, reported by the Bavarian

Ambassador, that a treaty with a dictator is vulnerable to being overturned by the people, has not been borne out by the Italian people.

Papal unaccountability, like temporal sovereignty, clashes with facts of the early Church. The first Pope, Peter, was publicly called to account by Paul for hypocrisy, as recorded in the second chapter of the Book of Galatians. Paul had no exalted status at the time, yet he was heard. At some point Paul's example of holding Peter accountable, and Peter's example of receiving correction, passed into desuetude, and the Symmachus tradition took hold.

Historians have sometimes acted in ways that further the cause of *non*-accountability. Lord Acton recognized this phenomenon and described it in the late 19th century. Acton is well known for his dictum that "power tends to corrupt," but his longer passage that contains the dictum is less well known:

> ... I cannot accept your canon that we are to judge Pope and King unlike other men, with a favourable presumption that they did no wrong. If there is any presumption it is the other way, against the holders of power, increasing as the power increases. Historic responsibility has to make up for the want of legal responsibility. Power tends to corrupt, and absolute power corrupts absolutely...

The past decade has seen the rise of a movement within influential circles of the Catholic Church to restore aspects of Catholicism that largely disappeared after the Second Vatican Council (1962-1965). Pope Benedict XVI sparked this movement in 2005 when he said the Council should be interpreted in a spirit of "continuity" rather than "discontinuity" with the past. He said that a hermeneutic, or interpretative principle, of discontinuity "risks ending in a split between the pre-conciliar Church and the post-conciliar Church." If the evidentiary record of the 1920s and 1930s is taken into account, however, a large majority of Catholics, including leaders, might well agree that a split from certain aspects of the pre-conciliar Church is essential to the future of humanity.

The memorialization of historical figures, favorable and unfavorable, shapes the future course of peoples. Lord Acton's famous passage continues with words that apply to any effort to glorify the memory of a powerful person without careful consideration of how he exercised the authority he was given:

> "There is no worse heresy than that the office sanctifies the holder of it."

48. Did Hitler and Pacelli Ever Meet?

Prince Konstantin of Bavaria, a member of the Wittelsbach royal family, wrote that Nuncio Pacelli attended one or more Nazi Party meetings in 1922. In an admiring 1952 biography of Pius XII entitled *Der Papst*, or "The Pope," Prince Konstantin presents a charming human side of Eugenio Pacelli from his days in Bavaria. In doing this, the Prince quotes several amusing reports from the Munich police security detail assigned to the Nuncio. He also quotes this police report:

> Members of the Nazi Party testify, in accord, that Nuncio Pacelli attended Nazi Party meetings two-to-three times, in order to get a personal impression of the Party of Herr Hitler. By documentary evidence, participation in a Nazi Party meeting in the year 1922 could be established.

A German defender of Pope Pius XII cites this passage in a book whose title means *The Pope Who Defied Hitler*. He credits the Prince for being a knowledgeable observer, and he credits Pacelli for taking the measure of Hitler at an early stage. Neither this book nor *Der Papst* copes with the historical significance of Pacelli attending Nazi Party meetings in 1922. That year, as we saw, marked the start of large-scale Nazi paramilitary mobilization, with support from Catholic clergy.

Sister Pascalina, as an octogenarian, told a Boston author that Hitler visited Pacelli one night in 1919 at the Munich Nunciature, and Pacelli gave him money. Pascalina said she answered the door and let Hitler in. She said she eavesdropped on the conversation between Hitler and the Nuncio. According to her, they discussed the need to oppose Communism, and the money was for that purpose. She attributed the Nuncio's liberality with these funds to his naiveté. The impression left by Boston author Paul Murphy, in *La Popessa*, is a generous-hearted Churchman naively helping a down-and-out anti-Communist and his "small, struggling band."

This passage has been seldom cited, and never analyzed in light of the facts presented here. If Pacelli supported Hitler in 1919, it was not because of Hitler's anti-Communism. That came later. Hitler's documented rantings in late 1919 and early 1920 were not against Communists; they were against Jews. Moreover, his first documented antisemitic statement, in September

1919, contains ideas found in *Catholic Civilization* articles, but not found in any of Hitler's earlier writings.

In 1929, his last year in Germany, Nuncio Pacelli wrote a carefully crafted letter to the Vatican's Nuncio in Vienna, describing who Hitler was and denying he ever met the man. Did Vatican Secretariat of State personnel need elementary information about Hitler in 1929, or was he well known to them by then? The Vatican's newspaper covered Hitler as early as 1923, when it described, uncritically, the Nazis' "full mobilization" against Communists and Socialists on May Day in Munich that year.

Is it possible that Pacelli might prepare a document for the historical record to create an impression opposite to the facts? We came upon two instances of that type of misdirection in our research.

The first instance occurred in August 1933, one month after the signing of the Vatican-Germany Concordat. In a private conversation, Cardinal Pacelli told a British diplomat he had agreed to the Concordat only because "a pistol had been pointed at his head." These words, reported by the diplomat to the British Foreign Office, remained private for many years. After they were published in the Documents of British Foreign Policy, historians and defenders of Pope Pius XII began to cite them to show the Concordat was a necessary defensive measure, agreed by the Vatican under great pressure, as a desperate attempt to achieve whatever protection was still possible for German Catholics from Nazi persecution.

The public explanation of the Concordat in *Catholic Civilization* in fall 1933 was directly opposite to Cardinal Pacelli's private words. As we saw, *Catholic Civilization* lauded the Concordat as a "great moment." The article expressly denied that the Concordat's great importance was protection of the Church in Germany. The Church already had Concordats with Bavaria, Prussia and Baden, the article explained. Those three German states contained more than 90% of Germany's Catholic population. The great importance of the Concordat, the article concluded, was in presaging a "historical and providential hour" not only for Germany, but for "Christian Europe and all the civilized world." Oddly, while we have found a multitude of secondary sources citing Pacelli's private words, we have yet to find any citing this important public explanation, which was necessarily reviewed and approved by Pacelli's office before publication.

The second instance occurred around the time of the Saar referendum in January 1935. Cardinal Pacelli had a private meeting with one of the most pre-eminent Catholic political philosophers of the 20th century, Dietrich von Hildebrand. When Pacelli expressed his hope that "the moderate elements in National Socialism gain the upper hand," Hildebrand objected: "It is not a question of moderate or radical – National Socialism is, in its substance, filled with the spirit of antichrist." Cardinal Pacelli responded, "racism and Christianity are absolutely irreconcilable, like fire and water. So there can be no peace, no bridge."

Hildebrand's memoirs indicate he was satisfied with this answer. He must not have known of the *Roman Observer* article the month before, praising Bishop Hudal for demonstrating the harmony, rather than irreconcilability, between the Catholic Church and the "German race." And Hildebrand had no way to know of the letter from Pope Pius XI to Hitler. That letter, a direct Vatican effort to build a bridge to Nazi Germany, incontestably approved by Cardinal Pacelli, was prepared and sent the same month Pacelli met with Hildebrand.

Dietrich von Hildebrand illustrates what was knowable about Nazism from a Catholic perspective in 1934 and 1935. During May 1934, the same month Cardinal Pacelli wrote his diplomatic note with the passage about the swastika, Hildebrand authored a revealing passage of his own. In the weekly newspaper he published in Vienna, exiled from Germany and his teaching position in Munich, Hildebrand wrote:

Without question, our reaction to Nazism is for us Catholics a decisive test of our real relationship to Christ. The response to this horrible heresy reveals in many, who confront the heresy in an unambiguous and stout-hearted manner, a shining heroism and a deep grounding in Christ... And it reveals a religious vacuum in all those who allow themselves to be impressed by the Nazi movement in any way, be it in the form of an apologist's zeal to defend the movement or in a hesitant lukewarmness that looks for the movement's so-called "positive" aspects. The result of this litmus test is not outweighed by going to Mass however fervently, or receiving the sacraments however frequently, or committing to the Church however decisively.

49. The Train Ends at Auschwitz

At Yad Vashem, on a steep hillside between the Holocaust History Museum and the Valley of the Communities, stands a railway boxcar. It is a memorial to those who were crammed into boxcars and taken to the death camps. The markings on the boxcar at Yad Vashem identify its place of origin: Munich. Reflecting on that boxcar, Diane thought of the origin of the Nazi movement, and the final destination of the Nazi train. She suggested we visit Auschwitz before finishing the book.

February 2014 marked our final research trip. We combined our visit to the Bavarian State Library with a train ride through the Czech Republic, and a drive into Poland to Auschwitz. Our time in Munich proved fruitful. In addition to our detailed review of the Munich Archdiocesan paper, we had a chance to examine two books we had only read about second-hand up to then.

The first was Cardinal Faulhaber's 1925 book. In the midst of the section praising Mussolini and Italian Fascism along with Hitler and the "originally pure" Nazi spring, Steve found a passage about *American* Fascism. Faulhaber highlighted the "Legionnaires" as a group compatible with the "Roman Church," unlike the Ku Klux Klan.

We had never seen a historian refer to this passage. "Legionnaires" is the commonly used name for members of the American Legion, a patriotic veterans' organization formed in the U.S. after World War One. Americans would naturally think of Legionnaires fighting *against* Fascism, not for it. Steve was aware, however, that a two-time Congressional Medal of Honor winner, Marine Corps Major General Smedley Butler, was recruited in 1933-1934, unsuccessfully, to lead an American coup d'état. Butler blew the whistle on the ringleaders, including the head of the Massachusetts American Legion and a well-connected member of the Connecticut American Legion. When he read years earlier of the Marine General's exposé of the infamous "Business Plot," and the Congressional investigation about it, Steve never imagined that a Cardinal in Munich previously envisioned the American Legion as a potential Roman-friendly Fascist force in America.

The second book was a recent biography of Sister Pascalina by a historian in Bavaria. The German title, *Gottes Mächtige Dienerin*, means "God's Mighty Maidservant." It is a sympathetic biography based partly on archival materials from Sister Pascalina's "Menzingen" order of nuns, as well as the Pascalina file of the Faulhaber Papers. One item jumped out from the rest. It was a photo postcard sent by Pascalina in Genoa to one of her fellow nuns in Munich, dated November 2, 1934, with these words: "By all the beloved saints, sincere greetings on the last day of the great trip."

Pascalina's memoirs, with a German title meaning "I Was Allowed to Serve Him," described her trip with Cardinal Pacelli in 1936 to America. In her interviews with the Boston author of *La Popessa*, she claimed she was with Pacelli inside the Papal conclave of 1939. Although her memoirs describe the Eucharistic Congress of 1934 as a great triumph, she did not disclose she had been on that trip as well. She asked the nun in Munich to keep that a secret.

Historians have only scratched the surface of Pascalina's role and influence. Cardinal Faulhaber's files show that not just Pascalina, but her Menzingen order of nuns more generally, was important to him in unstated ways. In a 1948 letter to Pascalina he expressed regret that the Mother General of the Menzingen order was unable to visit Munich, and added: "I will be happy if the path from Bavaria to Menzingen becomes open again as it was before the War. As you wrote, I have burned the letter."

Our trip from Munich across the Czech Republic gave us opportunities to stop in Prague and Zlin. A two-day visit to Prague made it easy to understand why Prague attracts more tourists than any other European city except Paris. In the city of Zlin, further eastward, we visited the recently opened Bata museum. We were delighted to see the role of Jan Bata, as well as his older brother Tomas, documented in a first-class series of fascinating displays.

From the city of Ostrava in the northeast corner of the Czech Republic, we rented a Czech Skoda car to drive to Auschwitz. On a dreary weekday in the middle of winter, we joined hundreds of visitors touring the death camp complex. The Polish guide for our group tour gave a detailed, thought-provoking account of the horrors of Auschwitz. We walked through the brick military buildings that became a concentration camp after Germany's conquest of Poland. There we came upon a dungeon that was familiar to us from books about St. Maximilian Kolbe, the "starvation bunker" where he and many others died.

Then we drove to Auschwitz-Birkenau, about a mile away, to see the enormous site the Nazis built to murder more Jews faster than anywhere else. The total killed there exceeded a million. Speed and efficiency, with a train line direct into the Auschwitz-Birkenau killing grounds, were the only way the Nazis succeeded in murdering most of Hungary's Jews in 1944, as Germany's Eastern Front was collapsing. Decisions by the Allies not to bomb the death camp and its rail lines were also fateful. Our time at Auschwitz was a time of reflection and mourning.

What right have we or anyone else to hold accountable those connected to mass murder at Auschwitz or those who contributed less directly, to any extent, to the Holocaust? Every right, because we are human. Each of us can take responsibility for the times we have abused our own authority. We can ask forgiveness of those we have injured. We can work to repair the harm we have caused. When it is a matter of grievous harm done by leaders or members of a group we belong to, we can embrace the demands of accountability.

50. Prologue as Epilogue

Failure by a Pope to acknowledge the truth and admit grave wrongdoing by himself or a predecessor can have major historical consequences. The ability of the *Protocols of the Elders of Zion* to gain traction among Catholics in the 1920s and 1930s was enhanced by precisely such a failure by a Pope. The Pope was Leo XIII, and the time was the late 19th century.

Pope Leo XIII (1878-1903) and his Secretary of State, Cardinal Mariano Rampolla, encouraged the anti-Masonic writings of a French writer named Gabriel Jogand-Pagès. Under the pseudonyms Leo Taxil, Docteur Bataille and Miss Diana Vaughan, Jogand-Pages became an effective popularizer of the predecessor to the Jewish-Communist conspiracy theory, namely the Jewish-Masonic conspiracy theory. His writings were so popular and widespread among French Catholics, they even made their way into a cloistered Carmelite convent. It was the convent of a saint whose statue stands today in many Catholic churches, Thérèse of Lisieux, and she played a startling role in a story involving Jogand-Pages and Pope Leo XIII that came to a head in 1897.

Gabriel Jogand-Pages was born to a devout Catholic family in the south of France. His parents sent him to a Jesuit-run Catholic boarding school at the age of five. He emerged from the school disillusioned with the Catholic clergy and began publishing scandalous stories about priests and Popes, as well as critiques of the Bible. He participated in anti-Catholic movements and joined the Masons.

Shortly after a Papal encyclical against the Masons appeared in 1884, Jogand announced his conversion back to Catholicism. He began writing exposées of all the dastardly aspects of Freemasonry he had supposedly encountered during his time as a Mason. On a visit to Rome, he received encouragement at the Vatican, in personal meetings with Pope Leo XIII and Cardinal State Secretary Rampolla. *Catholic Civilization* heralded the "formidable revelations of Dr. Bataille and of Miss Diana Vaughan," as well as the "terrific explosion of Taxil." Following the lead of *Catholic Civilization*, the Catholic press in France and other countries echoed Jogand's lurid tales about the evils of Masonry. In 1896 the Vatican organized the first International Anti-Masonic Congress in Trent, the site of the 16th century Council of Trent. Jogand-Pages, as "Leo Taxil," gave a keynote address.

The publicity for Jogand's propaganda was powerful enough to make its way into St. Therese's Carmelite convent in Lisieux, France. We had visited, as a family, this convent where Therese passed her short life. Carmelites were strictly cloistered, and Therese never left the confines of her convent after entering it at age 15. Nor did worldly influences enter the cloister. Only spiritual reading was allowed, not newspapers of the day. Yet even Therese and her Carmelite sisters learned about the heroic Catholic convert "Diana Vaughan" and her struggle against the Masons. Therese sent Diana a letter of encouragement, enclosing a photograph of herself dressed as Joan of Arc in a convent skit. She received an acknowledgement from "Diana," who was actually Jogand's secretary, not the escapee from a secret female Masonic order that countless readers of Jogand's books believed her to be.

In 1894, Jogand took his propaganda to a new level by publishing a book under the name Docteur Bataille, disclosing that the entire worldwide Masonic movement was controlled by Jews. "Until now," he wrote, "this question has been hardly touched upon by antisemitic authors." He described the "invasion of Jews everywhere," with secret behind-the-scenes Jewish lodges directing the visible Masonic lodges. The entire operation, according to Docteur Bataille's *The Devil in the 19th Century*, was run by the Jewish-Freemason "Sovereign Patriarchal Council of Hamburg," the ultimate Jewish "Kahal" or "Kehillah."

On Easter Monday 1897, "Leo Taxil" held a press conference in Paris for the occasion of the first-ever appearance of Diana Vaughan, who had reportedly been in hiding to escape Masonic reprisals. Jogand began by telling the packed hall at the Geographic Society on the Boulevard St. Germain how much he enjoyed playing tricks on people, starting with the time he convinced the city of Marseilles that sharks were infesting its waters, and the time he convinced the people of Geneva that the lost city of Atlantis lay beneath their lake. But no hoax gave him so much pleasure as the one he had just succeeded in playing on the Catholic Church for the past dozen years. Docteur Bataille and Diana Vaughan, together with everything about Freemasonry written under their names and the name of Leo Taxil, were one gigantic hoax.

Projected large during the press conference, on a wall of the Geographic Society's main hall, using the latest "limelight" projecting technology, was the photograph of Therese of Lisieux dressed as Joan of Arc. Jogand used the photo to illustrate the enormous success and impact of his hoax. He told the press conference he had met in Rome with Pope Leo XIII and Cardinal

Rampolla, and they had encouraged his work. Jogand also said the Vatican had reason to know his assertions about Masonry were false.

Pope Leo XIII and *Catholic Civilization* took immediate steps to manage the controversy. Leo summoned the Cardinal-Archbishop of Paris to Rome for consultations. *Catholic Civilization* covered the controversy in its next issue, *and* in the one after that.

No one at the time believed Jogand's claim that the young woman displayed by limelight on the wall was a Carmelite nun. Therese of Lisieux learned about the hoax and the display of her photograph. She was devastated by the news. She died less than six months later at the age of 24.

But there was no repentance in the Vatican. Quite the opposite. *Catholic Civilization* condemned Jogand for his act of "moral suicide," while defending what the Vatican-supervised journal had written in support of his message. Crucially, for the future of Jewish-Masonic conspiracy theory among Catholics, the journal included these words: "From the above-mentioned it does not follow that everything Taxil said about Masonry is false, much of it being verifiable as true from genuine sources ..."

As a result, Jewish-Masonic conspiracy theory was later able to enjoy credibility in the Catholic world, rather than ridicule and contempt. When the *Protocols of the Elders of Zion* appeared in translations in Europe and America in 1920, full of Jogand-like Jewish-Masonic conspiracy theory, there was no widespread historical memory of Jogand's hoax. There was no repentance to be remembered, concerning Vatican complicity in promoting Jogand's lies. The Jewish-Masonic conspiracy propaganda of the *Protocols* was not associated with Jogand then, and it has not been since.

Abridged Timeline of Events and Documents

The Complete Timeline is at the Galebach Law Office website:

http://investigation2.galebachlaw.com/itimeline.html

1914

July 28, 1914 World War One begins when Austria-Hungary declares war on Serbia.

Aug. 20, 1914 Pope St. Pius X (1903-1914) dies.

Sept. 3, 1914 Giacomo della Chiesa, Archbishop of Bologna, Italy, becomes Pope Benedict XV (1914-1922).

1915

Apr. 26, 1914 Treaty of London, secret agreement, whereby Italy agrees to enter World War One on the side of Entente Powers France, Britain and Russia against Central Powers Germany, Austria-Hungary and the Turkish Ottoman Empire.

1917

Mar. 8-15, 1917 Revolution in Russia results in a republic, as the Czar abdicates.

Apr. 6, 1917 United States declares war on Germany and enters World War One.

May 29, 1917 Archbishop Eugenio Pacelli is received by King Ludwig III as the new Vatican Nuncio to the German State of Bavaria.

Nov. 2, 1917 Great Britain issues the Balfour Declaration.

Nov. 7, 1917 Lenin, inserted into Russia by the German Government, launches the Bolshevik Revolution.

Dec. 9, 1917 Allied forces under British General Allenby capture Jerusalem.

1918

Mar. 3, 1918 Treaty of Brest-Litovsk ends hostilities between Russia and Germany.

Nov. 7-8, 1918 Revolution in Munich topples the Bavarian monarchy.

Nov. 8-9, 1918 Revolution in Berlin topples the German Reich monarchy, and the monarchs of other German States abdicate.

Nov. 11, 1918 Armistice ending the fighting of World War One is signed by Matthias Erzberger on behalf of the new German Republic, at the instruction of German Army commanders Hindenburg and Ludendorff.

1919

Apr. 6-13, 1919 Soviets-Councils Republic of Bavaria is formed in Munich.

Apr. 29-May 3, 1919 Overthrow of Soviets-Councils Republic; Communists point a gun at Nuncio Pacelli to requisition his automobile; anti-Communists fire machinegun rounds into the Vatican Nunciature in Munich.

May 8-10, 1919 Nuncio Pacelli receives instructions from Vatican to secure Nunciature archives and go to Switzerland.

June 28, 1919 Germany and the Allied Powers sign the Treaty of Versailles.

Aug. 11, 1919 Weimar Republic Constitution is adopted in Germany.

Sept. 12, 1919 Hitler for the first time attends a meeting of the German Workers Party, a small antisemitic group in Munich.

Sept. 16, 1919 First documented antisemitic writing by Hitler, his letter to Gemlich.

1920

Feb. 24, 1920 National Socialist German Workers Party is launched before a large crowd at Munich's Hofbrauhaus; Hitler proclaims the 25-point Nazi Party Program, whose central points are directed against Jews and the Versailles Treaty:

1. We demand the unification of all Germans into a Greater Germany on the basis of the right of self-determination of peoples.

2. We demand equality of rights for the German *Volk* with respect to other nations, and annulment of the peace treaties of Versailles and St. Germain.

3. We demand land and territory (colonies) for the sustenance of our *Volk*, and colonization for our surplus population.

4. Citizens can only be those who are members of the *Volk*. A member of the *Volk* can only be one who is of German blood, without consideration of denomination. Therefore no Jew can be a member of the *Volk*.

5. Whoever is not a citizen shall be able to live in Germany only as a guest, and must be subject to legislation concerning foreigners.

6. The right to decide about leadership and laws of the State may only belong to a citizen. Therefore we demand that all public offices, no matter what kind, whether in the Reich, the states, or the local communities, may be occupied only by citizens. We combat the corrupting parliamentary system of filling positions only according to party affiliations without consideration of character or abilities.

7. We demand that the State be obligated first of all to provide opportunity for livelihood and living for the citizens. If it is not possible to sustain the entire population of the State, then the adherents of foreign nations (non-citizens) are to be expelled from the Reich.

8. All further immigration of non-Germans is to be prevented. We demand that all non-Germans who have immigrated to Germany since August 2, 1914, be forced to leave the Reich immediately…

23. We demand a legal war on verifiable lies and their promulgation by the press. In order to enable the establishment of a German press, we demand that:

a) All writers and employees of newspapers published in the German language must be members of the *Volk*...

24. We demand freedom for all religious denominations in the State, so long as they do not endanger its existence or offend against the morals and ethics of the Germanic race. The Party as such advocates the standpoint of a positive Christianity without binding itself confessionally to a particular denomination. It combats the Jewish-materialistic spirit within and around us and is convinced that a lasting recovery of our *Volk* can only succeed from the inside out on this foundation:

common good before self-interest.

25. For the execution of all this we demand the establishment of a strong central Reich power. Unconditional authority of the central parliament over the entire Reich and all its organizations. The formation of chambers by estates and occupations for implementing, in the individual states of the federation, the framework of laws decreed by the Reich…

The full Nazi program can be found in the Complete Timeline at Feb. 24, 1920.

Mar. 6, 1920 *Catholic Documentation*, no. 57, pp. 326-328:

"The Jews Are the Principal Factors of Worldwide Bolshevism: Note established by the official American Services"

Are the Jews the authors of the Russian Revolution and Bolshevik horrors? The Jews – dreaming of dictating their will to all governments, thanks to the power of gold – do they have an interest in the red wave breaking upon all Europe and even upon the whole world?

… The authenticity of this piece is guaranteed to us; as to the exactitude of the information that it contains, it is such that we can only leave it to the responsibility of the official bureau that authored this note, and we are happy that a public discussion may shed some light on these sanguinary shadows.

"God has given us, his chosen people, the power to spread; and what seems to everyone to be our weakness has been our strength, and has now carried us to the threshold of worldwide domination. There is little that remains to be built on these foundations." (Secret Protocol no. XI of Zion, 1897.)

I. – In February 1916, it was learned for the first time that a revolution was being fomented in Russia. It was discovered that the following persons and firms had been engaged in this destructive work.

1 – Jacob Schiff . . . Jew

2 – Kuhn Loeb and Company . . . Jewish Firm

… There is thus hardly any doubt that the Russian Revolution, which broke out one year after the above information, was launched and fomented by distinctively Jewish influences.

Indeed, in April 1917, Jacob Schiff made a public declaration that it was thanks to his financial support that the Russian Revolution succeeded.

II. – In the spring of 1917, Jacob Schiff began to finance Trotsky (Jew) to conduct a social revolution in Russia; the New York newspaper *Forward*, a Jewish Bolshevik daily gazette, put forth its contribution as well towards the same goal.

III. – In October 1917, the social revolution took place in Russia, thanks to which certain Soviet organizations took control of the Russian people. In these Soviet councils, the following individuals made themselves prominent: [30 names follow; 29 of them are identified as Jews, Lenin is identified as a Russian]

IV. – At the same time, a Jew, Paul Warburg, formerly involved with the "Federal Reserve Board," became noticeable for his active relationships with certain Bolshevik personalities in the United States, which, together with other information, led to the blocking of his re-election to the aforesaid Board.

V. – Among the intimate friends of Jacob Schiff, there is a rabbi, Judah Magnes, a totally intimate friend and devoted agent of Schiff. The rabbi Magnes is a vigorous protagonist of international Judaism, and a Jew named Jacob Billikopf stated one day that Magnes was a prophet. At the beginning of 1917, the so-called Jewish prophet launched the first truly Bolshevik association in that country under the name "Council of the People." The danger of this association only appeared later. On October 24, 1918, Judah Magnes publicly declared that he was a "Bolshevik" and was in complete accord with their doctrine and their ideals.

This declaration was made by Magnes at a meeting of the American Jewish Committee in New York. Jacob Schiff condemned the ideas of Judah Magnes, and he himself, in order to fool public opinion, left the American Jewish Committee. Meanwhile Schiff and Magnes remained in perfect harmony as members of the Executive Committee of the Jewish Kehillah.

VI. – Judah Magnes, financed by Jacob Schiff, is, moreover, in intimate relationship with the worldwide Zionist organization "Poale," of which he is in fact the director. His ultimate goal is to establish the international supremacy of the Jewish workers party. There again is established the link between multi-millionaire Jews and proletarian Jews.

VII. – Several weeks ago, the social revolution broke out in Germany; automatically, a Jewess, Rosa Luxemburg, took over political control, and one of the principal leaders of the international Bolshevik movement is a Jew, M. Haase. At this moment, the social revolution in Germany is developing according to the same Jewish directives as the social revolution in Russia…

The Allies gained a marvelous victory over German militarism. From the ashes of German autocracy is arising a new worldwide autocracy – Jewish imperialism, whose ultimate goal is the establishment of Jewish domination over the world.

Even though the Jews, during all the war, did nothing to fill the ranks of soldiers in the different countries, they still obtained the formal recognition of a Jewish State in Palestine. The Jews have equally succeeded in forming a Jewish Republic in Germany and in Austria-Hungary; these are the first steps toward the future worldwide domination by the Jews, but this is not their last effort.

International Jewry feverishly gathers its strength, spreading its poisonous doctrines, realizing enormous sums of money (a few weeks ago they realized almost instantaneously in the United States a billion dollars, ostensibly to establish schools and chorales in Palestine and expended enormous sums for their propaganda).

Christianity remains silent, inactive, passive and inert. Who among Christian men of state will dare to hear the prophetic words of international Judaism? Who among them has ever taken account that the Jews think exactly what they say, and here is what they say:

"We must force the Goy Government to support by its action the vast plan that we have conceived and which now approaches its triumphal goal, probably thanks to public opinion, which we have secretly organized to help what is called 'the Royal Secret' of the press, which, apart from a few negligible exceptions, is already in our hands. In short, to sum up our system of subverting the Goy Government in Europe, we will show our power to some among them by assassination and terror, and if they think it possible to resist us, we will make them reply to the American, Chinese or Japanese cannons." (Secret Protocols of Zion, no. VIII, 1897.)

A full translation of this article is in the Complete Timeline at March 6, 1920.

Apr. 11, 1920 *Munich Catholic Church Newspaper*, no. 15, page 107:

"Jewish Imperialism"

The very respected Paris journal "La Documentation Catholique," issue no. 57, has published an official American report on the Russian Revolution, whose authenticity is well-attested. According to this report, the Jews Jacob Schiff and Max Breitung, as well as the "House" of Kuhn, Loeb & Co., "took an interest" in the Revolution early in 1916. One year later the Czar's empire collapsed. The American "observers" knew about it! Early in 1917 Schiff entered into a partnership with the Jew Trotsky Bronstein. In a similar way the Jewish millionaires and the Jewish proletariat banded together in Sweden and Germany. The report names individuals and firms. The Revolution succeeded. Jacob Schiff boasted publicly about his instrumental role. Before people could realize it, the Jews were seated throughout the Soviet councils of the Revolution. The report counts, for example, thirty leaders with their Russian "noms de guerre" and their Jewish family names, for instance Trotsky = Bronstein, Zinovieff = Apfelbaum, Kameneff = Rosenfeld, Bogdanoff = Silberstein, Maklakowsky = Rosenblum etc. Among Schiff's confidantes is a Rabbi Judah

Magnes, a prophet of Judaism, and, as his distant friends maintain, one of the first "Bolsheviks" on American soil, and at the same time a leader of white-and-blue Zionism. The Rabbi's ideal is Jewish world domination, an ideal that unites Jewish capitalists and communists. Especially interesting is the report's establishing that the firm Kuhn, Loeb & Co., for which Jacob Schiff serves as a director, stood and stands in association with the "Westphalia-Rhine Syndicate" in Germany, with Lazare Frères in Paris, with the Gunsburg Bank in Petersburg-Tokyo-Paris, with the firm Speyer & Co. in London-New York-Frankfurt and with the Nya Bank in Stockholm. All these institutions "take an interest in" Bolshevism! – No wonder that "Documentation Catholique," which also is familiar with and cites to the "Protocols of the Elders of Zion" (German translation available from Beek's Auf Vorposten Publishing House in Charlottenburg), exclaims: "From the ashes of German autocracy a new world power raises its head, Jewish Imperialism, whose purpose and goal is Jewish world domination." The Jews have universally avoided military service in order to finally refashion the Christian peoples of Germany and Austria-Hungary into Jew republics. That would be the first step toward the future domination of the world.

May 2, 1920 *Munich Catholic Church Newspaper*, no. 18, pages 125-126:

"Not Jew-Hatred but Christian-Defense!"

What position did Christ take on the Jewish question? He must have taken a position. For the Jewish question is the most burning and decisive, and frankly the most distressing, question of the present time. It will be the fundamental question of the future and of the end times. It is not only a national, but also an international problem, a world question that concerns all peoples. No, more! Not only a world question of political and economic life, but a worldview question, a question of spiritual warfare. For at the deepest level it is about an eternal war between earth and heaven, between Christian culture and Jewish imperialism.

This is a distressing question! For we fully recognize that among the Jews are a great number of noble people, true Israelites in whom there is nothing false; yet where is the name or the group, where is the party, where is the protest, by which the spirits can be distinguished? We would gladly greet them as friends; yet they keep silent. They reject all our complaints. They cover their degenerate ones with their power, their money, their press, their names. So it does not become possible to distinguish Jew from Jew…

… For wherever Jews rise up, where they attain to power, influence and wealth, they prove themselves to be oppressors of peoples and persecutors of Christianity. For them it is all about the realization of all those illusory hopes for the Kingdom of God, on account of which they rejected and crucified the Savior. For them the Kingdom of God is really nothing else but the world domination of Israel and its religion. For the sake of this hope the Jewish people undertook powerful revolutions against the Roman Empire, which finally ended with the complete destruction of their national greatness and the scattering of the Children of Israel throughout the whole world. The bloody war was followed by secret and open struggle with economic means and weapons of the mind. The Jews sought first of all to tear apart young Christianity with heresies. Evidence of that is found in so-called Gnosticism. At the same time, however, they stepped up at every opportunity to agitate for persecution of Christians. Jew-hatred was already at work in the court of Emperor Nero and occasioned the first persecution of Christians. Jew-hatred vengefully built the pyre for the martyr bishop Polycarp. Jews were the favorites and counselors of the apostate Emperor Julian, who wanted to rebuild the temple at Jerusalem to please them and to defy God. Jews conspired with the Persians against the Christian Emperor in Constantinople. In short, wherever a conspiracy is at work against the Christian State, Jews stand at the very least as helpers in the background. That was so in the past; that is so in the present. More about this next time!

A full translation of this article is in the Complete Timeline at May 2, 1920.

May 9, 1920 *Munich Catholic Church Newspaper*, front page, no. 19, pp. 131-132:

"Where Stands the Adversary?"

At the assembly in Lvov, a young Jewish rabbi cried out:

"The time will come when the Christians will wish to become Jews; but the Jewish people will push them away with contempt. The main enemy of the Jews is the Catholic Church. That is why we have planted the spirit of dependency and disunity in this tree. We are the ones who magnified the conflict and disunity among the Christian denominations. First of all we will struggle against the Catholic clergy with the greatest determination. We will smear them with mockery, contempt and scandalous stories about their life, in order to make them despicable to the world. We will take over the schools. And the Church will soon lose its influence if it is made to be poor. Its riches will become the booty of Israel!"

This trumpet call of war from the year 1912 rings in my ear like the shrill battle cry of Lucifer. Now I know from what source those scandal stories flow, those mocking caricatures and rabble-rousing articles against the Pope, Bishops and Priests, against Catholic institutions and sacraments, and whence the smutty flood of newspapers and magazines. Everyone knows of course that a great portion of the press is in the hands of the Jews. I no longer wonder in vain what the origin is of the degradation of our art, the debasement of our fashion, and the undermining of Christian morals. I know who is hiding behind the film "Vow of Chastity" and whose stage it is where the only plays performed are the likes of "Devil's Wives" and "Rectory Farce." The French culture war against the Church was opened by the Jew Gambetta with the slogan, "Clericalism, that's the enemy."

How is it in our schools? Of every ten professors in our universities, six are Jews, authentic, baptized, or related. Bewail to God what a frightful battle has been waged from there against our Christian faith, in the name of science; and now the spirit of Christianity is supposed to be driven from the public schools. There also the Jews are among the leaders. Hardly had Nathan ascended the mayoral seat of Rome [in 1907] with the help of the Freemasons, than he went about removing religious instruction from the public schools. We have seen the same and even worse in Austria, Bohemia and Hungary. What is being planned in Prussia and Germany is known to everyone. The Jew has said: "We will take over the schools." Hasn't he prophesied correctly, if the Church wants to act weak? "The riches of the Church will be the booty of Israel." That is what happened in France. In Germany it will be no different. And whoever wants to know what Jewish rule would bring us, can open his eyes and look at Hungary and Russia. Are these not true persecutions of Christians, in light of what has happened there? And who led them? I'll name only a few names: Bela Kun, Szamuely, Lenin and Trotsky.

In Budapest an insolent Bolshevik dared to drive his auto into the midst of the Corpus Christi procession and mock the Blessed Sacrament with shameful gestures. Who can blame the people if they boxed the blasphemer in the ear? All the signs confirm that we are headed into a new era of persecutions of Christians, and it is Jews who are stoking the fires. But will they have the power to carry out their plans? Jewry dominates the world. World finance is Jewish finance. They dominate commerce, trade, the press, art, politics, the States, the spirits. They have at their disposal more than two powerful armies, Freemasonry and international Social Democracy.

What then is to be done? We must immediately liberate ourselves from Jewry and the Jewish spirit, from materialism and worldliness. We must be completely Christian in thoughts, intentions and conduct. But then we must break off, by every lawful means, the fetters with which Jewry has bound us. Shut the gates to immigration from the East! The countries of the New World keep close watch against foreign immigration, but with us the dam is yielding before the immigration of peoples that oppress us and then force us into migrating. What must we do? We must use lawful means to bring down the tyranny that makes us into Jew-slaves. Christian peoples may not be governed by Jews. "America for the Americans! Asia for the Asians! Africa for the Africans!" resounds today throughout the world. And "Jerusalem for the Jews!" Good, so this also applies: "Germany for the Germans!" And "Christendom for Christianity!" What must we do? We need a new Reformation! Marx, the founder of Socialism, himself a Jew, says: "An organization of society that casts out the exploiters, that removes the possibility of exploiters, has been made impossible by the Jews." Everything must be built anew, all of economic life must be built anew according to Christian concepts, the spirit of profiteering rooted out, the nature of law must once again become German and Christian. And if the enemies are too powerfully many – the Lord says: "Do not fear, little flock. For it has pleased the Father to give you the Kingdom!"

June 23, 1920 Eugenio Pacelli is appointed Vatican Nuncio to the German Reich, but remains based in Munich for the next five years.

Oct. 15, 1920 *Roman Observer* article presenting the Jewish-Communist conspiracy theory and the *Protocols*:

"A Peril"

The foreign press, and especially that of France, has taken up what has been called the Jewish peril...

Opportune Distinctions

La Croix says that the considerable role played by the Jews in the Bolshevik Revolution, of which they were the leaders, the posts that the Jews hold in the political and financial congresses, the relations they have with official personages everywhere for gaining favors, especially with what has been set up in Palestine by the British Government, all of this powerfully attracts attention to the Jewish peril that seems to be overlooked in the face of the alleged German peril...

Jewish Peril

This past June the *Times* spoke to its readers of a book by Sergio Nilus, published in Russian in 1902 and in 1905, a translation of which came to be published in London under the title *Jewish Peril.*

The author reproduced in this book the speeches given by a Jewish personality at the Zionist Congress of Basel in 1897, who espoused the clear religious and social policy of the Israelites. Sergio Nilus spoke of having gotten this document from a woman who had gotten it from a Masonic dignitary.

The reader will judge for himself about these excerpts:

... [four paragraphs of the *Protocols* are reprinted here]

These are so clear that they do not need any commentary.

Is It Possible?

La Croix said it decided to question Abbot Meniglier about this, since he is something of an expert and well informed about Russian matters ...

– Do you believe that the Jews have a plan of revolution that was applied in Russia?

Yes...

– But is it true that the Jews had established themselves enough to direct the Russian Revolution?

I believe that they planned to bring about their dream, that is, to become the masters of Russia and the world at one blow...

– Do you believe, therefore, that the Jews have actually established the reorganizational plan that is attributed to them by the author of *The Jewish Peril*?

Fiction and Reality

I am convinced of that...

– All these reports of Bolshevik horrors, are they not exaggerated?

Certainly not. The fact is that we only know parts of the reality...

A fuller translation of this article, along with the side-by-side article on Zionism and Palestine, is in the Complete Timeline at Oct. 15, 1920.

1921

Apr. 23, 1921 *Roman Observer*, page one:

"Concerning a Masonic Visitor"

… The Jew remains always a Jew, even when he no longer believes in the religion of his fathers, and always, especially in the Masonic Lodges, thinks of nothing but his own interests intimately linked with those of Judaism. The label of his businesses may vary: here they will be called Zionism, elsewhere Bolshevism; but the goal is always the same, the triumph of the Jews over the Christians, the predominance of Jewish race in the whole world, to be attained by whatever agreement, by whatever means…

May 8, 1921 *Roman Observer*, page one:

"Zionism and Palestine: The Genesis of Serious Disorders"

We have already spoken of the recent visit of Sir Churchill in Palestine. But, for an ever better understanding of the situation and a correct evaluation of it, it is useful to add the following report ...

On April 19th, Sir Herbert Samuel, the British High Commissioner, who had gone to Egypt to meet this prominent guest, re-entered Jerusalem together with the English Minister…

The journey was marked by several significant aspects…

It was after these events that the English Minister received the representatives of the indigenous population, or explained to them, in his opinion, that the Balfour Declaration was misunderstood, because it was not contrary to the interests of the population, whose rights were safeguarded in the interest of the well-being and prosperity of the Country (see *Roman Observer* of May 1st).

Of course this pacifying word encountered some prejudiced minds. The intentions of the English Government, so well presented by Sir Churchill, contrasted with the events that took place during the preceding year or so, under the Zionist invasion, which was not sufficiently restrained and controlled to satisfy the basic terms of the Declaration…

As a result there were meetings, protests and demonstrations, in a widespread agitation, which some Bolshevik elements took as the occasion for the most serious rioting and uprisings. This is the genesis of the riots in Jaffa reported on May 2.

In fact, during a Bolshevik demonstration led by Russian Zionists, a real battle broke out between Muslims, Christians and Jews. The police were not able to stop it in time and thereby prevent the bloody aftermath. It was a dreadful day, during which the anger of the population overflowed into the gravest reprisals. Forty dead and many wounded were counted among the population and especially among the Jews.

Also in Jerusalem, similar provocations by Communist Jews erupted in bloody tumults…

But it must be noted that the conflict now assumes an entirely new aspect. First, because the day of bloodshed ended to the disadvantage of the Jews, as it was caused by Semitic immigrants and by Bolshevik fanaticism. It is this poison of violence or rage that gradually, together with the general discontent, produces the most distressing effects.

Indeed, we have already noted that the greater part of the 10,000 Jews who entered Palestine in the past year under the patronage of the *Israelite foyer* came from Galicia and southern Russia. It is clear that numerous revolutionary elements, emissaries of that Russian Communism which is now identified with Judaism, were thus able to penetrate into the Holy Land, taking advantage of all the benefits of the Zionist organization, under whose umbrella they are preparing the revolution…

Whether the population has seen in this a pretext for a Jewish coup to seize power, whether this is a glimpse of another serious facet of the Zionist peril, the fact is that this arose in its turn by taking the Semitic-Bolshevik provocation as an excuse for giving vent to their vendetta…

A fuller translation is in the Complete Timeline.

May 30-31, 1921 *Roman Observer*, page one:

"Concerning a 'Jewish Policy' and a 'Jewish Awakening'" from our correspondent in Paris, April 27

The French press, the exponent of prevalent opinion in our most influential political circles, has for some time been dealing with and denouncing a "Jewish peril" that is not lacking for documentation, not only as to its obvious existence as regards the destiny of the Middle East and Palestine, but also as regards European politics.

The danger here appears so precise and so vast that there is indeed talk of a "Jewish policy" that England would be forming and continuing under pressure from extremely influential Jewish elements...

And here we turn to the famous *Protocols of the Elders*, which would show the Jewish people the path to follow to become masters of the world, and the publication of which arouses all the anger and protests of Israel.

They were declared a fraud, they were held to be true: that has remained among the unsolved questions of literary history...

June 11, 1921 Open letter from a Jewish citizen of Munich to Munich Police Chief Ernst Pöhner:

German-*Volkisch* excesses are, at the moment, the order of the day in Bavaria and especially in Munich ... In recent days, moreover, placards flaunting swastikas were displayed at all the street corners of Munich ... Insofar as these placards made a demand for the exclusion of Jews from eligibility to vote, from the universities and from the press, such frills and phantasies may find their pathological motivation in the heat wave that set in unusually early in Bavaria this summer ... We are not unaware that the Bavarian Ministers of Commerce and Finance, in particular, are well informed of the seriousness and extent of this state of affairs, that the Ministerial Cabinet in recent days took up these matters once again, and that the Bavarian State Secretary of the Interior, Herr Dr. Schweyer, condemns to the utmost these excesses of antisemitic agitation at every opportunity that arises within the parliament and outside it. The leader of the Democratic Party, Dr. Dirr, has also just recently given resolute expression in the Landtag to the alarm of his party over the rabble-rousing character of the placards tolerated by the Directorate of the Munich Police. But the real political leaders of the Bavarian People's Party, Herrs Held, Wohlmuth, Knilling, Giehrl, Stang etc., have until now maintained utter silence in the discussion of these matters, at least in the *Landtag*.

Source: *Berliner Tageblatt* [Berlin Daily News], June 11, 1921, reprinted in Hans Lamm, ed., *Von Juden in München* [From Jews in Munich] (1958), pp. 306-309.

June 18, 1921 *Roman Observer*, page one:

"Zionism and Palestine: New Disturbances" – from our special correspondent in Paris, June 15

It is reported from Cairo that the Egyptian press is publishing news of new disturbances in Palestine, provoked by the state of mind created among the indigenous Christian and Moslem population against Zionism, and exacerbated after the recent events that showed the evident sympathy of the supreme civil authorities for the Jews, combined with the uprising of Bolshevik Jews this past May.

July 4-5, 1921 *Roman Observer*, page one:

"Zionism and Palestine" – from our correspondent in Paris, July 2

While the Commission of Indigenous Delegates moves toward Europe to express directly to Governments …

To all this is added the ever more serious threat of Bolshevism that the indigenous residents consider an epidemic imported by the Zionist immigrants ...

Moussa Kazaiur Hosalny, President of the Anti-Zionist Executive Committee, has taken the occasion to say in recent days: We have continually warned the governments of the Allies of the fact that the Jewish immigrants are introducing and popularizing in Palestine the principles of Bolshevism ... Therefore we call for the stopping of immigration.

Aug. 21, 1921 *Munich Catholic Church Newspaper*, no. 34, p.213, on the "Black Shame":

From World and Church: The "German Emergency League against the Black Shame" has now published the first issue of its propaganda monthly, "The Shame on the Rhine." In eloquent and impressive words, it is shown therein how Europeans are endangered by the most frightful tropical diseases of all sorts through the occupation of European districts by colored soldiers, how white women and girls are infected

- 159 -

with tropical syphilis and other serious venereal diseases, how white children are extremely endangered in their moral upbringing by the quartering of colored soldiers in homes of the citizenry, finally how the occupied districts are being mulatto-ized, and thereby conditions are being created whose consequences for the spiritual, cultural and physical life of the affected white nation are inconceivable. The next issue intends to await the complete officially announced details of the period from the beginning of March to the end of May 1921. – Rise up for the moral battle against the greatest shame for culture [*Kulturschmach*] of our century and perhaps of all time, brought about by the insane policy of hatred and the phrenetic sadism of the French nation!

Sept. 12-13, 1921 *Roman Observer*, page one:

"Zionism and Palestine" – dateline Paris, Sept. 9

... During the War Britain enlisted the Arabs in the struggle against the Turks, who were also their co-religionists, and promised King Hussein the establishment of a well-founded Arab kingdom. Afterwards they also made the famous Balfour promise to the Jews. Of these two promises, the first was just, but the second was not at all just, and thus was not realizable.

Palestine is our land; we have received it from our forefathers and we must hand it on to our posterity, and it is not the business of any power to interfere in the affairs of this our hereditary possession through the centuries. And if the Jews had some right over Palestine, they should have asserted it several hundred years ago. Kazem Jascia then said: We have suffered a bitter illusion. We rebelled against Turkey but fell into the hands of Jewish immigrants from Russia, from Poland, and from other countries imbued with the spirit of Bolshevism...

1922

Jan. 22, 1922 Pope Benedict XV dies.

Feb. 6, 1922 Achille Ratti is elected on the 14th ballot as Pope Pius XI (1922-1939).

Aug. 27, 1922   Cardinal Faulhaber's sermon to 100,000 German Catholics at a Pontifical Mass in Munich celebrated by Nuncio Pacelli:

...Compromises are unavoidable in the interplay of oppositions and interests. Superior to all compromises, however, are principles, like the eternal stars, and there comes a limit where we say: Up to here and no further! The Revolution was perjury and high treason, and it remains in history congenitally tainted and branded with the mark of Cain. Even if the upheaval brought some successes, even if it opened the way for adherents of the Catholic faith to higher offices far more than before, its moral character is not assessed by its results, for a misdeed may not be sanctified on the basis of its results.

Source: M. Faulhaber, *Stimmen*, pp. 25-34, reprinted in L. Volk, *Faulhaber Papers*, vol.1, pp. 278-279, note 3.

Sept. 2, 1922 Nazi newspaper on Cardinal Faulhaber's August 27th remarks:

"The Catholic Congress and National Socialism"

… At the Catholic Congress no other words received such frenetic applause as those of Cardinal Faulhaber when he summed up a true description of the "Berlin Jewish press" (by the way, he could rightly have given the same general description to the "Bavarian Courier"). With this remark, Cardinal Faulhaber took the concept of Jewish nationality and made it his own. For the Jewish press of Berlin ("Berlin Daily News," "Forward," "Freedom," "Red Banner," "Midday News," "World on Monday," "Financial Courier," etc.) includes religious and non-religious Jews. Until now Churchmen have spoken of Jews only in a religious sense, not in a racial or tribal sense. In this instance, however, the former sense was replaced by the racial sense, on the part of a high authority. (Though in another instance, granted, it was not: concerning the "Black Shame" in the Rhineland, Cardinal Faulhaber spoke of "pagans and Mohammedans" instead of negroes).

In what concerns Bavaria and Berlin, the words "perjury and high treason" of the Revolution dealt a resounding blow to the entire policy of the self-styled Christian and Catholic Center Party, and thereby also to the shady dealings of Dr. Wirth. These words from one of the highest Catholic dignitaries are naturally not a spontaneous temperamental utterance, but rather were the fruit of thorough discussion among leaders… One will have assumed that the elements led by the successor to Matthias von Biberach, already too closely bound to the party of Oscar Cohn, were becoming uncomfortable and that a change in the nationalist camp should be induced. However that may be, the fact is that the ten thousand representatives of Catholicism who were in conflict both with Jew-Berlin (with its Center Party head) and with German Bavaria (unfortunately still with the other Gorgon head) have placed themselves on the side of the latter…

The third politically remarkable fact was Cardinal Faulhaber's talk about "The Peacemaking Power of the Church." That was above all a criticism of the League of Nations, which we welcome…

These words were greeted with great applause. They express what National Socialists have been proclaiming day after day in public meetings, what the "*Volkisch Observer*" is often proclaiming, as the only such newspaper in Munich…

In any case it is now established that the head of the Church hierarchy has placed himself behind the *Volkisch* critique. From that also follows, if it is really intended earnestly and not just as the exertion of a small bit of political pressure, a relentless struggle against this international plague of the world finance markets.

And this *Volkisch* shot against this international conspiracy is one of the most important program points of National Socialism…

Source: *Volkisch Observer*, Sept. 2, 1922, page one. See Complete Timeline for full translation.

Oct. 21, 1922 *Catholic Civilization*, vol. 4, pages 111-121:

"World Revolution and the Jews"

... Who is directing? ... Who drives this mess of parties, laws, lodges, who guides this movement of world revolution that upends human society from one end of the world to the other?

Sinister voices arise on many sides to accuse the synagogue. A wolf remains always a wolf ... A profane hand has also brought to light secrets that bear the mark of the ghetto. Evidence or falsifications? It will be difficult, as always, to dispel the darkness in which Israel is jealously enveloped...

Today Russia is the field of battle where the world empire of tomorrow is being decided... those ringleaders who in order to implement their crazy utopia betray the country and assassinate the nation. Who are they?

The reader does not expect an answer from us. For too long they have been sadly famous even here across the Alps, the kabbalistic names of the rabble-rousers who hold themselves out as founders of the Communist International in Moscow, which they vaunt as the paradise of future human society. But if passing beyond the names, we look at them directly in the face to recognize who they are, it turns out to be a very strange fact that the greatest number, according to what is said, of the members of the governing body of the Communist Republic in Russia are not indigenous Russians, but Jewish intruders, who almost always take measures, however, to conceal their original name under the guise of a Slavic type name. In a booklet published in 1920 by the Society "Unity of Russia," we find a long list naming all the members of the Council, of the Commissions and delegations, of the Committees, Commissars, Central Offices, of which the organism of the State is constituted in the establishment of the Communist government. This list has been disseminated in every language, in every country, without contradiction: its information presents matters of value such that, in addition to its first origin, its peaceful notoriety accredits at least its substantial veracity.

Now in that list of more than 545 names of the holders of the governing offices of the State, citizens of Russian ethnicity are not more than 30: those of the Jewish race are a striking 447; the rest are scattered among Latvians, Finns, Germans, Armenians, Poles and other peoples that made up the Russian Empire... Yet today this tiny minority has invaded every avenue of power and imposes its dictatorship on the nation. And what a dictatorship!

... Thus from all this information one fact is clear and manifest: this breed which until yesterday lay in blind alleys, at the lowest levels of Russian life, all of a sudden is transformed and in possession of the throne ... How to explain this strange reversal of things, this calculated eruption, sages who take over unfailingly all the organs and machinery of society, so that one can say that in Russia – a unique example – the yoke of another nation, the Jews, has been imposed on the Slavs?

A full translation is in the Complete Timeline at Oct. 21, 1922.

Oct. 22-29, 1922   Italian Fascists march on Rome, resulting in the King of Italy appointing Mussolini as Prime Minister.

Nov. 25, 1922   Vice Consul Murphy's political situation report to the U.S. State Department included this section on Hitler and the Nazi Party:

The third inquiry made by the Socialists, probably of the greatest current interest, deals with the attitude of the Government toward the activities and breaches of the public peace caused by the national [sic] Socialists Workmen's party.   This interpolation was based on the claim of the United Socialists that armed bands of the national Socialists organization were terrorizing the Government; that the police sympathized with the activities of the organization and offered no resistance to it; that Hitler's strength had been greatly fortified by Mussolini's success which Hitler is attempting to imitate in Bavaria with the sympathy of the Government or at least without its active opposition.   The Socialists claimed that action should be taken against Hitler's organization under the special laws for the protection of the Republic.

The Government through its Minister of Justice in its reply characterized the National Socialist movement as a natural effect of the burdens imposed upon Germany during the past four years, and a natural reaction against the view of the United Socialists that the German people were justly bound to perform the conditions of the Treaty of Versailles.   He stated that the Government was, however, holding the movement under control and within reasonable bounds; the movement had a constitutional right to exist; the rumors of counter revolution founded upon the activities of Hitler's organization were not supported by acts of violence on the part of the organization; the responsibility for such disorders as had occurred could be attributed just as well to misdemeanors on the part of United Socialist workingmen as to members of the Hitler group.

My observation leads me to the conclusion that the so-called Bavarian Mussolini – Hitler, concerning whose activities the Department was advised in my report No. 221 of November 10, is countenanced by the government because he through his organization provides vent for the inevitable outcroppings of public discontent which lie so near the surface of things in Bavaria during this period of economic disorder. He is an opportunist quick to appeal to popular prejudice, as is demonstrated in his campaign against the Jews, but it does not seem that he has developed sufficiently to play the larger role of dictator which is his avowed ultimate aim.   He is content to progress slowly and submit to the control of the present government, and the government seems likewise content to have a useful tool which provides an exhaust for the element which craves attendance at the usual beer-hall assemblies to listen to denunciation of the Jews, the Entente in general and France in particular, to the condemnation of the Treaty of Versailles, and such 'Schlagwörter' [catchwords] as the "Berliner Judische Räterrepublik" [Berlin Jewish Soviets-Councils Republic] and a vivid portrayal of its economic woes…

Source: US NARA M336, R18, pp. 256-258.

1923

Jan. 3, 1923 Nazi Party's newspaper announces their goal for 1923 is to overthrow the "November Criminals," namely the Weimar Republic.

Mar. 3, 1923 Vice Consul Murphy's political situation report to Washington:

National Socialist German Workmen's Party (Hitler).

Campaign against Socialism, Profiteers (meaning thereby all Jews), Hunger, Poverty and the Parliamentary system of Government.

If the same amount of agitation, as is today the case in Bavaria, was indulged in and directed against the same objects among a people of more volatile temperament, serious explosions would have long since occurred. At the regular weekly meetings held by Hitler's organization throughout the state enough sparks are struck to build a nation-wide conflagration but they fall among green timber.

The speakers at the meetings invariably adopt the well-worn tactics of opposing everything that readily arouses popular antagonism, viz., the errors committed by the socialists, the weakness of the government, the 'Einheitsfront' fake, the vicious party system, the illusion of Bolshevism, the evils of 'unearned increment' and above all the Jews. Upon the hands of the latter are heaped not only the sins of Germany but of the entire world, and to them are attributed the economic woes of the entire people.

The only published platform of the party, a copy of which is transmitted with this report, contains twenty-five planks, but fundamental throughout is opposition to the Jews...

For the Department's information there is also attached a copy of a recently taken photograph of members of the Hitler storm troops (Sturmtruppen) which are estimated at four thousand, showing the Swastika (Hakenkreuz) – the organization's symbol – as well as the slogan "Germany Awake" (Deutschland Erwache). These are all young men who maintain military discipline and drill regularly in the country. They are divided into groups of hundreds, the leader of each of which receives the insignia of a metal star worn on the cap. The colors are red, white and black with the eagle. Members may also wear distinctive arm bands in these colors with Swastika...

Source: US NARA M336 Roll 18, pp. 682ff. (underlining in original). Fuller version in Complete Timeline.

Nov. 8-9, 1923 "Beer Hall Putsch" in Munich by Hitler, Ludendorff and followers is put down by force; approximately two dozen are killed in total from both sides.

Nov. 9, 1923 Bavaria Ambassador Ritter zu Groenesteyn's cable from Rome:

Groenesteyn to the Bavarian State Foreign Ministry, Munich, November 9, 1923

Re: The Ludendorff-Hitler Putsch in Munich

The first news of the Ludendorff-Hitler Putsch in Munich had already been published in this country's morning press when I paid my visit to the Cardinal Secretary of State this morning at the usual diplomatic reception.

The Cardinal appeared to be much alarmed by the news and especially expressed the fear that the name Ludendorff in connection with these events would provoke the French and offer them a welcome opportunity to proceed with new arbitrary and forceful collective punishment against Germany and against Bavaria in particular. Also, moreover, the Cardinal deplored a violent revolution of this sort because, even if by all appearances it was not motivated by the cause of separatism, it could still produce great dangers for Bavaria and the Reich, as it could cause unforeseeable results even beyond the borders of Germany. Therefore it is to be hoped and desired that a solution to this untoward incident be found as soon as possible, to re-establish lawful conditions for the good of Bavaria and the Reich.

The Cardinal had not yet received any reports from the Nuncio in Munich, and so it was entirely understandable that His Eminence would refrain from any further judgment about the foregoing press accounts. He raised only one other issue: what might become now of the Bavarian Concordat, if it should really come to a dictatorship in Bavaria.

In the Vatican they seem to be in considerable doubt whether it would be possible to conclude a Concordat with a dictator, because it is to be suspected that its validity under law could be subsequently disputed by the representatives of the people. Lacking instructions, and since the issue is not really pressing, I demurred to express myself on this…

Source: *Bayerisches Hauptstaatsarchiv*, "Akten der Gesandtschaft beim Päpstlichen Stuhl," [Bavarian Main State Archive, Files of the Embassy to the Papal See], no. 996, pp. 71-72. See also Besier and Piombo (2007), pp. 32, 217 & note 265.

1924

Mar. 29, 1924 Bavaria-Vatican Concordat is signed by Nuncio Pacelli and governing authorities of the State of Bavaria.

1925

1925 Cardinal Faulhaber's book *Deutsches Ehrgefühl und Katholisches Gewissen*, or "The German Sense of Honor and the Catholic Conscience," is published; it includes the words he spoke to a gathering of Catholic academics in the Lowenbrau Beer Hall in Munich on Feb. 15, 1924:

… Thesis 2. A Fascistic wave is flowing through the nations, summoned forth by the bankruptcy of the Socialist worldview. At its purest and for that reason most successful, the Fascist wave has opened a way in Italy … Even though underlings have here and there, on their own responsibility, committed or tolerated severe, even bloody excesses against Catholic association houses and gathering places of the Catholic movement, still the supreme head of Italian Fascism has up to now restrained with a firm hand the spirits of culture war against the Church, and has built his work in peace with the Church…

In America the Fascist stream is divided into two currents: While the Legionnaries take up the Pan-American concept with all means and not always with pure spiritual weapons, but still without taking a frontal position against the Roman Church, beside them the secret society of the Ku Klux Klan has been formed, which steps forth with fire and sword against all positive religions and which turns with special severity against the Roman Catholic religion...

Adolf Hitler knew better than the *Diodochs* of his movement that German history did not first begin in 1870 or in 1517, that for the re-establishment of the German *Volk* the sources of strength of Christian culture are indispensable, and that this work of re-establishment cannot be accomplished with the cult of Wotan and hatred of Rome. As a man of the *Volk* he also knew the soul of the South German *Volk* better than others, and knew that with a movement whose flip-side is struggle against Rome, the soul of the *Volk* will not be won over. There is a deeply moving tragedy in the fact that the originally pure spring became poisoned by later influences and by culture war against the Church...

Note: The "Diodochs" were the lieutenants of Alexander the Great. In context, the reference is to non-Catholic and anti-Catholic leaders of the Nazi-*Volkisch* coalition: Ludendorff, Rosenberg, and SA leader Ernst Röhm. The implicit equating of Hitler with Alexander the Great was probably not lost on an academic audience.

1928

May 19, 1928 *Catholic Civilization*, "The Jewish Peril and the 'Friends of Israel,'" May 19, 1928, vol. 2, pp. 335-344:

Our readers are aware of the news in our preceding issue about the decree of March 25th promulgated by the Sacred Congregation of the Holy Office, condemning the association named the "Friends of Israel." (1928, vol 2, p.171) ...

But turning to the point of the document as to the Jewish peril, it threatens the entire world by its pernicious infiltration or harmful interference, particularly among Christian peoples, and even more especially among Catholics and Latins, where the blindness of the old liberalism has mostly favored the Jews, while persecuting Catholics and religious most of all. The danger is more urgent every day ...

Thus, for example, while excluding the overly facile readiness of some who want to attribute to the Jews all the guilt for the worst events that have affected modern society, and Europe in particular, as seen for example in the question of Bolshevism; we have tried to make clear in these pages how much guilt and how much influence Jews had in the Russian Revolution, as in the French, and recently in Hungary, with all its bloodshed, cruelty and savage horrors; hence the resulting collapse of the great Moscow empire and the dictatorial tyranny of Bolshevik criminality, which menaces Europe...

See Complete Timeline for full translation.

1929

Feb. 11, 1929 Lateran Accords between the Vatican and Mussolini.

Feb. 22, 1929 Hitler's speech about the Lateran Accords, as published on the front page of the Nazi Party's newspaper:

For if the Church today has come to an understanding with Fascist Italy, which was unthinkable with liberal democratic Italy, then it is conclusively demonstrated that the Fascist realm of ideas is more closely related to Christendom than is the Jewish-liberal one, much less the atheistic-Marxist one, with which the self-styled Catholic Center Party feels so closely bound today, to the detriment of that same Christendom and of our German *Volk*. If the Pope today comes to such an understanding with Fascism, then he is at least of the view that Fascism and thereby Nationalism are acceptable for the faithful and are compatible with the Catholic faith…

Source: *Volkisch Observer*, Feb. 22, 1929, page one. See Complete Timeline.

1931

Aug. 1931 Cardinal Pacelli's words to German Chancellor Heinrich Brüning in a private meeting in Rome:

Pacelli broached the matter of the Reich Concordat… Pacelli thought I should just form a government with the Right with a view toward a Reich Concordat and make it clear in the process that a Concordat was to be concluded immediately. I retorted that he was misperceiving the political situation in Germany and above all the real nature of the Nazis…

He thought he had to repeat his request that I enter into a coalition with the Nazis. I explained to him that all the attempts to enter a coalition with the Right in a responsible manner for the nation and the people had failed. He misperceived the nature of Nazism. The Social Democrats in Germany were not religious, but they were tolerant, while I was so far convinced that the Nazis were neither religious nor tolerant.

Source: Heinrich Brüning, *Memoiren 1918-1934* [Memoirs] (1970), pp. 358-359.

1933

Jan. 30, 1933 Hitler comes to power as Chancellor of Germany, appointed by President Paul von Hindenburg.

Apr. 1, 1933 First nationwide Nazi-organized boycott of Jewish businesses in Germany.

July 20, 1933 Vatican-Germany Concordat is signed in Rome.

Aug. 19, 1933 A British diplomat in Rome reports to London that Cardinal Pacelli has told him privately that he abhors Nazi antisemitism, totalitarianism and terror, and that he only signed the Concordat because the Catholic Church had a gun to its head. See Complete Timeline.

Sept. 10, 1933 Vatican-Germany Concordat is ratified and goes into effect.

Nov. 18, 1933 *Catholic Civilization* describes the Vatican-Germany Concordat as a "great moment" for Germany and all of Christian Europe. Excerpts:

... However, we now conclude, to be brief, with our confrère from France, after recalling the noted objections, how "we believe that the Holy See has considered the matter more and better than anyone else, but may have equally good reasons that are firm and wise and weighty to pass over a concern, for the purpose of a great good."

For the purpose of this good it is therefore the obligation, for every honest citizen, and more so for every Catholic, to cooperate with all their energy, promoting better understanding along with the application of the terms and laws of the Concordat, without which the simple promulgation of a new legal statute would certainly not be a great thing. And we have said "new" not because all the ecclesiastical rights and liberties that it recognizes were given to the Church for the first time in Germany: those, as we well know, were for the most part recognized in other Concordats made with the various provinces or individual states (*Länderkonkordate*), as was mentioned above; but because a new and more solemn recognition was added to the former juridical status – on the schools question, for example, the rights of Church organizations, etc. – thus new force and range throughout the German Reich, and with this, hope is established for the future, if the rulers are not lacking in a sense of good faith and integrity, which must be assumed in all honest contracting parties, and much more in the men of the German Government, who are well aware of the terrible "present hour." Nor should one vainly skip by the "great hour" that is passing, for we can truly call it "a historical and providential hour" for Germany. But why not also add: for Christian Europe and for all the civilized world?

See Complete Timeline for full translation.

1934

May 14, 1934 Cardinal Pacelli's note responding to a German "Promemoria" that protested about the German Bishops' resistance to the swastika:

... The Promemoria maintains that the scruples of the Bishops against the hoisting of the swastika flag on the churches should be seen as "a deplorable lack of sympathy" with the new reality of the nation. Anyone familiar with the many un-Christian or even anti-Christian meanings that often have been and are being given to this symbol by National Socialists, will be able to understand that the Bishops' scruples were and are justified. To see in this any kind of hostile attitude toward the state is false. Beginning on the day when the swastika is no longer connected by its partisan champions with meanings and missions whose anti-Christian tendency offends the faithful, the resistance based on religious considerations will diminish of its own accord. It should also be considered that in other countries where relations between Church and State are amicable – countries with no less claim to be "authoritarian" states – the display of national flags on the churches has never been demanded, as for example in Italy. Anyone who appreciates the character of the Catholic Church as house of God and abode of the eucharistic presence and the liturgical sacrifice will understand the reasons why the truly religiously sensitive person must wish that this realm, dedicated to the eternal, not be dragged into the din and conflict of the day. A Catholic way of expressing solidarity with the people on patriotic holidays will never be rejected if the bishops are allowed freedom to find the forms that they consider appropriate.

Source: Albrecht, ed. (1965-1980), vol. 1, pp. 138-139.

June 6, 1934 German Bishops prepare a joint pastoral letter, denouncing some aspects of Nazi rule, including the Nazi regime's insistence on unconditional obedience. See Complete Timeline.

June 17, 1934 Papen gives a speech critiquing some trends in the Nazi Party associated with Ernst Röhm, head of the SA; the speech is covered by the *Roman Observer* and *Catholic Civilization*. See Complete Timeline.

June 29, 1934 German Bishops reach agreement with Hitler and top Nazi officials for implementation of the Concordat and protection of Catholic associations that are part of Catholic Action. See Complete Timeline.

June 30, 1934 Night of the Long Knives: Hitler's henchmen kill the SA leadership and many others on Hitler's kill list, including the most prominent German leader of Catholic Action and other prominent Catholics. See Complete Timeline for coverage of these events in the *Roman Observer*.

July 13-16, 1934 Newspapers throughout Argentina cover Buenos Aires Province banning public display of the swastika flag. See Complete Timeline.

July 25, 1934 Nazi coup attempt in Vienna fails, but kills the Catholic ruler of Austria, Engelbert Dollfus.

July 28, 1934 To calm international outrage over the assassination of Dollfus, Hitler appoints Papen as new German Ambassador to Austria. See Complete Timeline for coverage in the *Roman Observer*.

Aug. 2, 1934 German President Hindenburg dies and Hitler usurps the office, thus gaining absolute dictatorial power. See Complete Timeline for coverage in the *Roman Observer*.

Aug. 4, 1934 *Roman Observer*, page one:

"The New Responsibility of Hitler as Assessed by the French"

Dateline Paris, Aug. 3

Hitler, head of the National Socialist Party and Chancellor of the Reich, has now become President of the Reich and has an absolute power that no Emperor or King has possessed in Germany. He is Head of the people and of the State, and his will becomes the raison d'état. He is truly the sole master of the destiny of Germany. The Nazi regime thus wields the totality of power. Death has taken away the only man whose moral authority still prevailed, in the eyes of the German people, over the person of the Fuhrer, and who, by the major powers within his ambit, could give orders to Hitler. These are now his alone, and his responsibility increases.

Great importance should be attributed to the words spoken by Hess in the afternoon. It is striking indeed that in his eulogy for the Marshal [Hindenburg] he emphasized only his military glory and his decision to call Hitler to power. A decisive struggle is beginning for a total renewal.

No one could now prevent Hitler from completely carrying out the famous program of February 23, 1920.

The original idea of National Socialism, proclaimed at the outset of the movement, will enter into a decisive phase of realization.

Aug. 30, 1934 *Criterio*, Catholic journal in Buenos Aires, runs lead story on Nazi persecution of Catholic Church. See Complete Timeline.

Sept. 28, 1934 *Roman Observer* article on page 3 about Bishop Hudal's message, including Germany's "mission," juxtaposed with a photograph of Cardinal Pacelli:

"Rome, Christianity and Germanism: At a Lecture by Bishop Hudal in Trier"

In the course of a recent conference of the Görres Society in Trier, a lecture was given by His Excellency Bishop Hudal, Rector of the College of St. Mary of the Anima in Rome. His chosen theme is of the greatest current relevance and – at the present moment in Germany – is extremely delicate: "Rome, Christianity and the German People." The select audience of this leading academic association of German Catholics, including most notably the Bishop of Trier, the President of the State of Rhineland, and Duke John George of Saxony, followed Bishop Hudal's talk with rapt attention and warmly applauded him in agreement and gratitude…

Rome and the German people, working in concord in past times, built a new ideal of civilization upon the civilization of old, and more recently they have been seeking since the 16th century to draw closer. This aspiration to draw near again, to collaborate in a new concord for new tasks, represents the tragic impulse – because it still remains unfulfilled – in the history of the German people…

The German people have a mission all their own, which is to mediate between East and West and to act as a trusted bulwark against Bolshevism. For its part, the mission of Rome will always remain the same, which is to act as a *faro delle genti* [Latin: light to the nations]…

Full translation, original document, and accompanying photograph of Cardinal Pacelli are in the Complete Timeline at Sept. 28, 1934.

Oct. 1, 1934 Buenos Aires daily newspaper *La Prensa* article on page 12 describes swastika blessing ceremony by Archbishop Copello on Sept. 30, 1934. See Complete Timeline.

Oct. 15, 1934 *La Prensa*, page 9, on the Pontifical Mass of Oct. 14th with swastika flag in honor guard near the altar:

"Flags and Pendants of the Foreign Delegations Surrounded the Christian Altar"

From early on, the foreign pilgrim groups that had come to Buenos Aires were arriving at the central point of the ceremonies to attend the culmination of religious commitment. While groups of the faithful, some numerous, others smaller, but all enthusiastic, were finding their places in the areas reserved for each group, the flag-bearers, with emblems and pendants, ascended the steps of the platform, to form in the foreground an honor guard for the symbol of Christianity.

The monument then took on the appearance, as the ceremony began, of a large international trophy decorated with the most widely recognized national colors in the western world.

The Vatican flag, in the midst of all the others; multiple Argentine flags; the French with its bow of crepe; the British next to the American; the German with the cross of the National Socialist regime; each, in sum, adding its own particular significance to a most eloquent meaning for the enormous crowd of people straining to take in all that was happening.

1935

Jan. 15, 1935 Pope Pius XI's letter to Hitler, translated from the original German:

To the most honorable and illustrious

Herr Adolf Hitler,

Supreme Fuhrer and Chancellor of the German Reich,

The most honorable and illustrious Pope Pius XI offers his greetings and well wishes.

For the informal transmittal of the official letter in which You [*Du*] recently put Us on notice that following the passing away of the outstanding and unforgettable Herr Paul von Beneckendorff und Hindenburg, by the law of August 1st of last year, the office of Reich President was consolidated into one with that of Reich Chancellor and You thereby became the Supreme Fuhrer of the German Reich, We express to You Our grateful thanks. With joy We took note of the sentence in Your letter: "It lies very close to Your heart, that the ties that bind Germany with the Apostolic See might not only continue but be continually made closer." Since now in fact a true peace between ecclesiastical and worldly authority contributes optimally to the well-being of the people, We will most eagerly strive that, after overcoming the still existing difficulties, so far as it is within Our power, Your desire for the common good will be crowned with auspicious success.

For that We implore Almighty God, that He may impart to You, most honorable and illustrious man, and to the whole German people, His efficacious help.

Given in Rome, at St. Peter's, January 15th of the year MCMXXXV, in the thirteenth year of Our pontificate.

Pope Pius XI

Source: Albrecht (1965-1980), vol. 3, p.73.

July 15-21, 1935   *Der Stürmer* publishes photograph of swastika blessing by Archbishop Copello and related articles.

Article above and below the photograph: "Hatred Extending Beyond the Grave"

Many have already forgotten: when Gauleiter Peter Gemeinder died, the clergy of the Roman Catholic Church refused to give the Catholic Peter Gemeinder a church funeral.   They refused to do it because the deceased was a National Socialist. Because he was a man who hated the crime of the post-War era that was brought about by the Jews and Jews' lackeys, and fought so that things would become better. Because he was a person who honored Priests and hated Pfaffen.   That is why a church funeral was denied to National Socialist Peter Gemeinder.

Hatred extending beyond the grave...

In the free state of Danzig a Hitler Youth leader died. Because he was Catholic, his mother wanted to have him buried according to Catholic custom. The pastor refused to give the deceased Hitler Youth a church funeral, if his comrades were to be present. No Hitler Youth, whether Catholic or Protestant, may step into the cemetery or the church. No Hitler Youth flag may bedeck the bier of the dead comrade. If these demands were not satisfied, so wrote the pastor to the hard-pressed mother one day after the death of her son, then the burial could not take place.

Hatred extending beyond the grave...

Article to the right of the swastika blessing photograph:

"Who Governs Russia"

Excerpted from the anti-Jewish Belgian newspaper "L'Assaut" no. 18 of May 3, 1935

This question receives a categorical answer through the following enumeration of the approximately 550 upper and highest level officials of the Soviet paradise. There are 447 Jews without a fatherland, 30 Russians, 34 Latvians, 22 Armenians, 12 Germans, 3 Finns, 2 Poles, 1 Georgian, 1 Czech, 1 Hungarian.

These figures are excerpted from the official Russian daily press, such as Isvestia, Golos Truda and Rote Zeitung.

Aug. 3, 1935 *Catholic Civilization* on *El Kahal* by "Hugo Wast":

"Gold, Money and the Jews (H. Wast)"

… The thesis of the novel, in two parts, is the following: … The basis of money and thus of commerce and politics of the nations, in the whole world, is gold. Gold, for the most part, that is three-quarters, is hoarded and "controlled" by the Jews, who crave and seek to acquire the remaining fourth and so possess all the world's gold. So the Jews, the bosses who control the gold and thus the value of money, effectively control commerce and channel economic crises, actually guiding politics and deciding about war: everything in order to completely enslave Christians, destroy Christianity and establish Jewish world domination, which personifies their long-awaited "Messiah." The present economic crisis is, in fact, according to Wast, the result of the Jewish hoarding of gold. To shake off this domination it is necessary to dethrone gold, "the only god of the Jews," by devaluing it as the basis of money and reducing it to its industrial value, like all other metals. Down with gold, god of the Jews, bogus idol of the world! But how?

Here the fertile imagination of the novelist comes into play with a supposition, not far-fetched, which he presents powerfully with all the appearance of a real current event. The scene is set in the great metropolis of Buenos Aires, where the Jews, who numbered only 366 of 443,000 inhabitants in 1887, have grown so numerous (not specified precisely, because the last census did not take note of religion), increasing constantly, to the point that Wast claims Buenos Aires is the third city of the Jewish world after New York and Warsaw. They dominate because of the great Jewish bankers and the Synagogue with its Kahal, or supreme council, which maintains the unity of the Jews; so that even the richest among Christians are inevitably undermined by the usury of the Jews, the hoarding of gold and the holding of money…

This is not an antisemitic novel. Wast does not proclaim any crusade or any persecution against the Jews. It is much more a warning to Christians, especially those of Latin America: "That the Jew among you not mock you" (Par. 5, 81). It is a clear affirmation of living faith culminating in the memorable Eucharistic Congress, the richest thus far of the wonders of Grace of the true and only King of the world, Jesus Christ. In sum, if not a solution of economic questions, this is at least a balanced satire, not unworthy to stand in comparison with the *Utopia* of St. Thomas More.

See Complete Timeline for full translation.

Last page of author Hugo Wast's Introduction to *El Kahal*:

… the great financial battle will first lead to crisis, then to war and, finally, to revolution.

The Jew foments it, directs it, subsidizes it, and after making a *tabula rasa* of the Christian state, suffocates it and installs himself in the empty capital, to govern under the inspiration of the Kahal, the precursor of the Antichrist.

The Russian Revolution is a current and complete example…

And this is the reason that among all the peoples, the cry "death to the Jew!" has almost always been synonymous with "long live the fatherland!"

Because two nationalities cannot coexist in the same nation.

Cover and Contents of *El Kahal* and its companion novel, *Oro*, can be seen in the Complete Timeline at Aug. 3, 1935.

Sept. 15, 1935 *Roman Observer*, page one:

"Goebbels Against Communism"

Minister Goebbels also spoke at the Congress yesterday, refuting an article that appeared in a London newspaper under the title "Two Dictators," in which a parallel was drawn between the Nazi and Soviet regimes. The minister emphasized the fundamental difference between Communism and Nazism, irreconcilable doctrines, the one destructive of culture and the other constructive and uplifting for higher national and social values. Then Goebbels gave a detailed presentation of the Communists' methods and their results in the economic and social life of Russia, as well as the bloody battle that Nazism was obliged to sustain in order to prevent Communism from becoming established in Germany and transforming it into a danger and threat to Europe and the whole world. The minister denounced Judaism as the original cause of Bolshevism, demonstrating with citations and names that in all the countries where there are revolutionary disorders, the Communist tendency of the Jewish elements has played an important part in their preparation and their execution.

Sustaining its battle against Communism without ceasing and without compromise, Germany and its head are carrying out a mission for which all the nations should be grateful. The period of Communist revolution continues menacingly for all peoples. Without presuming to intrude in the internal politics of any country or to give counsel to any government, Germany is raising its voice of warning to all the nations against the gravity of the danger that Communism, of Jewish inspiration, represents for their culture and their existence.

Note: A translation of the *Roman Observer's* page one report on three Hitler speeches, which immediately precedes this article, is in the Complete Timeline at Sept. 15, 1935. Vatican newspaper coverage of the Nuremberg Laws enacted that day, and their subsequent implementation, can be found in the Complete Timeline entries following Sept. 15, 1935.

1936

June 19, 1936 Franz von Papen presents a pre-publication copy of Bishop Hudal's book *The Foundations of National Socialism* to Hitler and Goebbels in a private meeting in Germany. Excerpt of book:

... As Christians and Catholics, we have not the slightest reason to defend that Jewry which, after the World War, seized hold of the leadership of the worker masses under the banner of Marxism, and misused that leadership richly enough for their own selfish ends; yet, only because we condemn every injustice, we avoid any generalization, as if in history it is only Judaism that has been responsible for social and political abuses. (pp. 92-93)

July 17, 1936 Start of Spanish Civil War.

Nov. 4, 1936 Cardinal Faulhaber has a three-hour meeting with Hitler at Hitler's retreat on the Obersalzberg mountain near Berchtesgaden. See Complete Timeline.

Dec. 24, 1936 Christmas Eve pastoral letter of the German Bishops exhorts Catholics to support Hitler and the "religious and Church task" of defending against the "monstrous danger" of Bolshevism. See Complete Timeline.

1937

March 1937 Pope Pius XI's encyclical *Mit Brennender Sorge* is read from pulpits in Germany, denouncing Germany's violations of the Concordat and promotions of neo-pagan propaganda, while endorsing the effort to build a *Volksgemeinschaft* [national community of the *Volk*] and exhorting the German people to fulfill their providential calling. See Complete Timeline.

1938

Nov. 8-9, 1938 *Kristallnacht*, the Night of Shattered Glass.

Nov. 20, 1938 Father Charles Coughlin begins nationwide broadcasts of the Jewish-Communist conspiracy theory in America.

1939

Jan. 30, 1939 Hitler invokes the Jewish-Communist conspiracy theory, declaring to the German Reichstag that war in Europe will mean extermination of European Jews.

Feb. 10, 1939 Pope Pius XI dies.

Mar. 1, 1939 Eugenio Pacelli is elected as Pope Pius XII (1939-1958).

Mar. 12, 1939 Cardinal Copello stands at the right hand of the Papal throne during the coronation of Pope Pius XII.

Mar. 13, 1939 Monsignor Jozef Tiso, the leading political figure of Slovakia, flies to Germany and meets with Hitler.

Mar. 14, 1939 With Tiso back in Slovakia, the province of Slovakia secedes from Czechoslovakia.

Mar. 15, 1939 Germany invades the remainder of Czechoslovakia and takes over the country within a day.

Apr. 7, 1939 Italy invades Albania and takes over the country within a week.

Aug. 23, 1939 Germany and Soviet Union sign the Hitler-Stalin Pact, a mutual non-aggression treaty.

Sept. 1, 1939 Germany and Slovakia invade Poland.

Sept. 3, 1939 Great Britain and France declare war on Germany.

Sept. 17, 1939 Soviet Union invades Poland and occupies the eastern portion of the country.

1940

June 10, 1940 Italy declares war on France and Great Britain.

June 22, 1940 France surrenders to Germany.

1941

June 22, 1941 Hitler invokes the Jewish-Communist conspiracy theory in his proclamation to the German people upon Germany's invasion of the Soviet Union.

June 25, 1941 Nazi Propaganda Ministry issues orders to the German press to emphasize the Jewish-Communist conspiracy theory.

Oct. 2, 1941 Hitler invokes the Jewish-Communist conspiracy theory in his proclamation to German troops on the Eastern Front.

Nov. 20, 1941 German General von Manstein invokes the Jewish-Communist conspiracy theory in his Order of the Day.

Dec. 7, 1941 Japanese attack on Pearl Harbor brings the United States into World War II.

Notes

References to the Complete Timeline can be found online at the Galebach Law Office website: http://investigation2.galebachlaw.com/itimeline.html.

References to the Abridged Timeline can be found in the preceding section of this book.

Chapter 1. A Bizarre Discovery

Page **2** Parents and children are on equal footing when it comes to repentance and forgiveness: see, e.g., Malachi 3:24 ("And he shall turn the heart of the fathers to the children, and the heart of the children to their fathers ...").

2 Holy Year 1934: Pope Pius XI declared 1933 a Holy Year and later extended it for a year.

2 About "umlauts": We include them the first time a German word like *Stürmer* appears, and then omit them, as in *Sturmer*. An umlaut affects the vowel's pronunciation, making "Händel," for instance, sound in German like "Hendel."

Chapter 2. The Photograph in *Der Sturmer*

Page **3** *Der Sturmer* issue no. 29 of 1935, with swastika blessing photograph, articles, and translations, can be found in the Complete Timeline at July 15-21, 1935.

4 The Nuremberg judgment against Streicher is online at the Jewish Virtual Library: www.jewishvirtuallibrary.org/jsource/Holocaust/JudgeStreicher.html.

Chapter 3. What Does It Mean?

Page **5** the swastika was flown alongside the black-white-red German tricolor: pursuant to a decree signed by Hitler and Hindenburg, Complete Timeline at March 12, 1933.

5 Legate's reception in Argentina, as reported in the Vatican newspaper: Complete Timeline at Oct. 9-16, 1934.

5 Copello was elevated to Cardinal: Complete Timeline at Dec. 7 and 16, 1935.

5-6 evidence that the Vatican's top representative in Germany monitored the *Sturmer* display case: Complete Timeline at July 31, 1935.

Chapter 4. Looking for Answers at the Holocaust Museum

Page **8** The other photographs of clergy and churches in close association with Nazi symbols can be found in Part 1, Ch. 1 of the Investigation published online at the Galebach Law Office website in 2013: http://investigation2.galebachlaw.com/index.html.

8 Books by Brown-Fleming (2006) and Barnett (1992) are identified in the Bibliography.

Chapter 6. Publishing a Historical Article ...

Page **11** Sources about Argentina and the Catholic Church include Ben-Dror (2008) and Ivereigh (1995).

11 German Bishops' policies: Complete Timeline at Sept. 10, 1924; Sept. 1930; Feb. 1931; Feb. 10, 1931; Mar. 29, 1933; and Aug. 29, 1933. A discussion of the German Bishops' policies can be found in Lewy (1964), pp. 8-15.

11 "symbol of the struggle against the Cross of Christ": Complete Timeline at Mar. 17, 1931.

12 Cabinet meeting with Hitler, Hindenburg and Papen: see Papen, *Memoirs* (1952), p.287, and German flag decree, Complete Timeline at Mar. 12, 1933.

Chapter 7. ...or Not

Page **13** Father Spicer on the dark side: *Hitler's Priests* (2008); and on the brighter side: *Resisting the Third Reich* (2004).

Chapter 8. Self-Publish Online!

Page **14** October 7, 2010 online publication of the photograph and questions: http://investigation.galebachlaw.com.

Chapter 9. The Photo Is Authenticated

Page **16** Argentine coverage of Night of the Long Knives: *Caras y Caretas*, July 7, Aug. 4, 1934.

16-17 Argentine Catholic coverage of Nazi persecution of Catholic Church: *Criterio*, Aug. 30, 1934; translation and original in Complete Timeline at Aug. 30, 1934.

18 The original *La Prensa* article is in the Complete Timeline at Sept. 30, 1934.

Chapter 10. Vatican Policy Toward Nazi Germany in 1934

Page **20** Cardinal Pacelli's diplomatic notes on behalf of the Vatican to the German Government are reprinted in Albrecht (1965-1980). The portion of Pacelli's note of May 14, 1934 about the swastika is in the Complete Timeline at May 14, 1934.

20 For the Night of the Long Knives and the Nazi assassination of the ruler of Austria, followed by Papen's appointment, together with coverage in the *Roman Observer* and *Catholic Civilization*, see Complete Timeline entries for June and July 1934.

21 For the Vatican newspaper's treatment of Hitler's usurpation of power, see the Complete Timeline at Aug. 4, 1934. *Catholic Civilization's* mention of the "radical modification" of the Weimar Constitution is found in the Complete Timeline at Aug. 18, 1934. The German Bishops' oath of loyalty and obedience to the "constitutionally formed government" of Germany is set forth in Article 16 of the Vatican-Germany Concordat; the German and Italian originals of the Concordat are linked from the Complete Timeline at July 20, 1933.

21 For the Vatican newspaper's coverage of Hitler and events at the Nazi Party Congress in Nuremberg, and immediately following, see the Complete Timeline at Sept. 5-10, 1934; Sept. 12; and Sept 13, 1934.

21 exchanged publicized visits with Hitler: Complete Timeline at Sept. 5-10, 1934, entry for Sept. 13, and Complete Timeline at Sept. 14, 1934 (*Volkisch Observer*, page one).

21 Abbot Schachleiter's attendance at the Nazi Party Congress was captured in a photograph, a stylized version of which can be seen on the cover of Conway (1968). Schachleiter also appears briefly in the Nazi propaganda film *Triumph of the Will*, which was filmed at the Nazi Party Congress of 1934.

21 The Vatican newspaper's articles about Bishop Hudal are in the Complete Timeline, Sept. 8 and 28, 1934. Excerpts of the article about Hudal's speech and Germany's "mission" are in the Abridged Timeline at Sept. 28, 1934.

21 Hudal is known for helping Nazi war criminals after World War II: Goni (2002); Sereny (1983); Steinacher (2011).

21 Hudal boasting about helping Nazi war criminals: Hudal (1976), p.21 ("All these experiences finally gave me the occasion to devote my entire charitable work after 1945 first and foremost to the former adherents of Nazism and Fascism, especially the so-called 'war criminals,' who were persecuted by Communists and 'Christian' Democrats, often by ways and means hardly different from those of their former adversaries; even though these accused persons were often personally completely innocent, being the implementers of orders from those in higher positions, and thus the scapegoats for the system going amiss. Here to help, many to save, without opportunistic and calculated considerations, selfless and brave, these at the time were the obvious demands of a true Christianity that knows no Talmud-hatred, but rather love, kindness and forgiveness, and that leaves final judgments about the conduct of individual persons not to political parties but to an eternal judge who alone can probe hearts, motivations and ultimate intentions.")

21 Hudal met personally with Pope Pius XI: Complete Timeline at Oct. 1934.

21-22 *Catholic Civilization* article about Hudal as a German patriot: Complete Timeline at Nov. 17, 1934.

22 *Catholic Civilization* series on Nazi antisemitism: Complete Timeline at Oct. 20, Nov. 3, 1934.

22 *Roman Observer* praised a new book by Bishop Hudal: Complete Timeline at Dec. 30, 1934, including excerpts from the book.

22 German Bishops helped produce Saar vote victory for Nazi Germany: see Bishops' statement in Complete Timeline at Dec. 26, 1934 and Goebbels' appreciation for the Bishops' statements in Complete Timeline at Jan. 8, 1935.

22 Pope Pius XI's letter to Hitler is in the Abridged Timeline and the Complete Timeline at Jan. 15, 1935.

Chapter 11. Cardinal Pacelli's Outreach in Buenos Aires

Page **23** passing reference to Pacelli and Thermann: Newton (1992), p.111.

23 Further details about Thermann, and the extensive efforts he and his wife made to Nazify German schools and associations in Argentina, can be found in a German work on the Nazi Overseas Organization by Jürgen Müller (1997).

23 Thermann's interrogation reports: Complete Timeline at Oct. 16, 1934.

24 *El Pueblo* received German propaganda subsidies: Complete Timeline at Oct. 16, 1934.

24 Identification of *El Pueblo* as a semi-official publication of the Church in Buenos Aires: Ivereigh (1995), p.80.

24 photographs of Cardinal Pacelli disembarking from a German Junkers JU-52 plane: Complete Timeline at Oct. 16, 1934; Official Proceedings, *XXXII Congreso Eucaristico Internacional* (Buenos Aires: Comité Ejecutivo, 1935), vol. 1, p.444.

24 Thermann was not a Catholic: his personnel file in the Political Archive of the German Foreign Office identifies him as *Evangelisch*, meaning Protestant (Lutheran).

Chapter 12. What Have Historians Said About This?

Page **25** See Bibliography for titles of Hitler biographies by Bullock (1971), Fest (1974), Kershaw (1998), Toland (1976), and Wilson (2012).

25 The only history mentioning Pacelli's interaction with Thermann: Newton (1992).

26 Sandmann, in addition to the German original (1965), can be found in Italian translation (1976).

Chapter 13. Vatican Policy Toward Nazi Germany in 1935

Page **27** *Catholic Civilization* article reviewing *El Kahal*: Complete Timeline at Aug. 3, 1935, along with images of the covers of *El Kahal* and *Oro*. Excerpts of the article and book are in the Abridged Timeline at Aug. 3, 1935.

28 *Roman Observer* front page article on "Goebbels Against Communism": Abridged Timeline and Complete Timeline at Sept. 15, 1935. The Complete Timeline includes other significant *Roman Observer* articles from before and after that date.

29 German original of the excerpt from Hudal's fall 1935 book: Complete Timeline at Sept. 24, 1935.

Chapter 14. What Historians Have Said ... or Not

Page 30 A leading history of the *Protocols*: Norman Cohn, *Warrant for Genocide* (1996).

30 U.S.Holocaust Memorial Museum exhibit: excerpts and description online at http://www.ushmm.org/information/exhibitions/museum-exhibitions/a-dangerous-lie-the-protocols-of-the-elders-of-zion.

30 A history of Catholic antisemitism in Argentina: Ben-Dror (2003, 2008).

30 Guenter Lewy (1964), p.281, citing *Klerusblatt* [Clergy Bulletin], Jan. 1936, and Hudal's *The Foundations of National Socialism*.

30 Sandmann (1965), p.211.

31 Lacroix-Riz (1996), pp. 148, 205, 259.

31 Three historians on Hudal: Godman (2008), pp. 43 (Hudal was an "outsider on the make"), p.78 (Hudal was a "self-appointed mediator" with Nazi Germany), p.79 ("Appeasement" and "alliance" with Nazi Germany were the strategy of Hudal not Pacelli), p.82 (Hudal was pursuing a "different approach to the Third Reich" than Cardinal Pacelli); Burkard (2007), p.81 and *passim* (article in German with title intelligible in English: "Bischof Alois Hudal: Ein 'Anti-Pacelli'?"); Wolf (2010), p.255 ("And Hudal fell from grace with the pope by 1936 at the latest. It may be that Pius XI had become so distrustful of him by 1934 ...").

Chapter 15. What to Do with the Evidence?

Page 32 Published online in October 2011 at the Galebach Law Office website: http://investigation2.galebachlaw.com/investigation20111004.pdf.

Chapter 16. A Nun Enters the Story

Page 33 biographer of Pacelli describes Stella Maris: Ventresca (2013), p.51.

Chapter 17. Consulting Experts in Archives

Page 35 *Der Sturmer* Special Edition for Nazi Party Congress, Sept. 1935: Complete Timeline at Sept. 1935.

36 *Flaggenfrage* and other Fauhaber files: Complete Timeline at Jan. 30, 1934.

37 evidence of Orsenigo's unavailing intervention: Complete Timeline at Feb. 19, 1934.

37 invitation to Hudal's consecration as Bishop: Complete Timeline at June 18, 1933.

37 Bishop Hudal's sermon on "The Fuhrer-ness of the Catholic Priesthood" is excerpted in the Complete Timeline at Nov. 1, 1934.

Chapter 18. Sister Pascalina Is a Player

Page 38 Cardinal Faulhaber's Pascalina file can be found in *Nachlass Faulhaber* [Faulhaber Papers], Munich Archdiocese Archive.

Chapter 19. Guillotines in Munich

Page 41 The film *Sophie Scholl: The Final Days* is readily available commercially, with English subtitles.

41 White Rose statements from "Flugblätter der Weissen Rose" [Leaflets of the White Rose], Geschwister Scholl Memorial Room, Justizpalast, Munich.

Chapter 20. New Experts: Engineers and Entrepreneurs

Page **43** Nazi regime's protest Promemoria: Complete Timeline at Mar. 14, 1934.

43 Cardinal Pacelli's reply: Abridged Timeline and Complete Timeline at May 14, 1934.

44 Articles from the *Roman Observer* and *Catholic Civilization* that were included in the presentation: Complete Timeline at Sept. 5, 1934; Sept. 9, 1934; Sept. 28, 1934; Aug. 3, 1935; and Sept. 15, 1935.

44 The utility of antisemitic propaganda for winning over secularized masses to support Catholic political movements was demonstrated in Austria by the Christian Social Party under the leadership of Karl Lueger, as reported, for instance, in *Catholic Civilization*: Complete Timeline at Aug. 15, 1896. The impact of antisemitic propaganda in France was evident during the Dreyfus Affair in the 1890s.

45 Pacelli had been Pius XI's lead negotiator with the Soviet Union: Besier and Piombo (2007), pp. 44, 48-50.

In addition to the entrepreneurs and engineers in this chapter, we are grateful to our son who is an engineer, with a broad knowledge of history, for his input.

Chapter 21. Our Family Gets on Board

Pages **47-48** Cardinal Faulhaber's Hudal files: File nos. 1395/1, 1395/2, and 1395/3 of *Nachlass Faulhaber* at the Munich Archdiocese Archive.

48 Cardinal Faulhaber's letter to Hudal mentioning avoidance of "civil war" is dated Sept. 24, 1924, and is found in file no. 1395/1 of *Nachlass Faulhaber*.

48 The unsuccessful effort of 1946 by the German-speaking Cardinals, i.e., those from Germany and Austria, to have Hudal removed from his position as Rector of the Anima in Rome, is reflected in a letter of June 17, 1951 from Cardinal Frings, Archbishop of Cologne, to Archbishop Montini, stating that "when all the German-speaking Cardinals were gathered in Rome in February 1946, we were unanimously of the opinion that a change in the leadership of the Anima College would be brought about, and that we were united upon the person of Prelate Dr. Weinbacher for the matter of a new appointment." A copy of this letter is in *Nachlass Faulhaber*, file no. 1395/3.

48 Contents of the *Nachlass Faulhaber*'s Pascalina file include correspondence and receipts from or involving Sister Pascalina, dated Apr. 19, 1948; May 1, 1948; May 2, 1948; May 10, 1948; and continuing through Sept. 25, 1948.

48 Sister Pascalina solves the paper problem in May 1948: Letter from Msgr. Roesch to Cardinal Faulhaber, May 1, 1948; Memorandum, May 3, 1948; Letter from Sr. Pascalina to Card. Faulhaber, May 10, 1948; all from Pascalina file, *Nachlass Faulhaber*.

48-49 The letter quoted at length from Sister Pascalina to Cardinal Faulhaber is dated Sept. 11, 1948, from the Pascalina file, *Nachlass Faulhaber*, Munich Archdiocese Archive.

Chapter 22. Berlin: Pinning Down the Flag Issue

Page **52** The article quoted at length is "The Flags of Hatred Can No Longer Fly Under the Skies of Our Liberty," *La Vanguardia*, July 15, 1934. English translations of other articles are in the Complete Timeline at July 13-15, 1934.

Chapter 23. Ember in the Ashes at the Bavarian Library

Page **53** Works by Eckart and Schrönghamer-Heimdal include Eckart's periodical *Auf Gut Deutsch*, or "In Plain German," and Schrönghamer-Heimdal's *Das Kommende Reich*, or "The Coming Kingdom," published in 1918.

54 When the Archbishop laid down rules: e.g., Complete Timeline at Feb. 15, 1920.

54 *Munich Catholic Church Newspaper* in 1919 on Jewish-Masonic conspiracy: Complete Timeline at March 2, 1919.

54 *Munich Catholic Church Newspaper* article on the destruction of Russian Czarism: Complete Timeline at Dec. 8, 1918.

54 The full "Jewish Imperialism" article is in the Abridged Timeline and the Complete Timeline at April 11, 1920.

Chapter 24. French Connection

Page **56** *Catholic Documentation* article: Excerpts in Abridged Timeline at Mar. 6, 1920. Entire article, original and translation, in Complete Timeline at Mar. 6, 1920.

56 Austrian Army "thoroughly infected by Jewry": Complete Timeline at Apr. 4, 1920.

Chapter 25. Hitler Piggybacks

Page **58** Poliakov (2003), vol. 4, p.279.

59 Front page of *Volkisch Observer* on the *Protocols*: Complete Timeline at Apr. 22, 1920.

59 small notice for the *Protocols*: Complete Timeline at Jan. 28, 1920.

59 historical work stating that a pre-publication copy of the *Protocols* was sent to the staff of the *Volkisch Observer* in late 1919: Kellogg (2008), p.68.

59 *Volkisch Observer* reprint of "Jewish Imperialism": Complete Timeline at Apr. 26, 1920.

59 Bavarian laws protecting copyright can be found in *Bayerns Gesetze und Gesetzbücher* [Bavaria's Laws and Statute Books], 1677-1889 *et seq.*, entries under the heading "Uhrheberrecht," meaning Copyright Law.

60 *Volkisch Observer* article calling for vengeance: Complete Timeline at Apr. 29, 1920.

60 The order by Munich Police Chief Ernst Pöhner imposing a ten-day publication ban on the *Volkisch Observer* for incitement to violence against Bavarian Jews was published in the *Volkisch Observer* itself when it resumed publication: Complete Timeline at Apr. 30, 1920.

60 collection of Hitler's writings and speeches: Jäckel and Kuhn, eds., *Hitler: Sämtliche Aufzeichnungen, 1905-1924* [Hitler: Collected Writings, 1905-1924, in German only]. For English translations of selected Hitler writings and speeches: Complete Timeline at Sept. 16, 1919 and Apr. 27, 1920.

60 Hitler's attacks on supposed Jewish control of finance and stock markets: Complete Timeline at Sept. 16, 1919, with English translations of Hitler's speeches and writings from October 1919 to mid-April 1920.

60 Hitler saying the Jewish press is preventing rapprochement between Germany and Russia, Apr. 17, 1920, Jackel and Kuhn, pp. 122-125.

60 Hitler's equating of Jews and Bolsheviks beginning on April 27, 1920 and continuing in June and August 1920: Complete Timeline at Apr. 27, 1920; June 2 and 6, 1920; Aug. 6, 1920; and Aug. 31, 1920; Jackel and Kuhn, pp. 126-128 et seq.

60 Kershaw (1998), p.245.

Chapter 26. Jewish-Communist Conspiracy Theory and the Holocaust

Pages **62-63** Hitler's two invocations of Jewish-Communist conspiracy theory found at Yad Vashem, Holocaust History Museum, are in the Complete Timeline at Jan. 30, 1939 and Oct. 2, 1941; General von Manstein's is in the Complete Timeline at Nov. 20, 1941.

63 The special SS killing units were called *Einsatzgruppen*, meaning "special action squads" or, more literally, "operation" or "commitment" groups. In addition to the obvious diversion of military and logistical resources represented by the *Einsatzgruppen*, Hitler's diversion of main force elements to the southern part of the Eastern Front in 1941 and again in 1942, rather than toward the Russian capital further north, may have been related to the "Jewish-Communism" rationale for his invasion. While the southern thrust took German forces toward the oil fields of the Caucasus, it also took them to large Jewish populations in the Ukraine, as well as a further possible route to Jewish populations in the Middle East via the Black Sea and Turkey.

Chapter 27. Meeting Experts at Yad Vashem

Page **64** Yad Vashem information and virtual tour: www.yadvashem.org.

Chapter 29. The Vatican Honors the Swastika

Page **68** The swastika flag photo on the cover of Dr. Ben-Dror's book can be found in the Complete Timeline at Oct. 14, 1934.

68-69 *La Prensa's* coverage of the swastika flag in the honor guard near the altar for the Pontifical Mass is in the Complete Timeline at Oct. 14, 1934. That Timeline entry also includes a photograph from the Eucharistic Congress showing the platform around the large cross where the Pontifical Mass was celebrated on October 14th.

69 Official Proceedings: *XXXII Congreso Eucaristico Internacional* (Buenos Aires: Comité Ejecutivo, 1935), vol. 1, pp. 328-345, "La Misa solemne de Pontifical."

Chapter 30. Taking Stock of the Evidence

Pages **70-71** The German academic group that hosted Bishop Hudal's speech was the Görres Society. The annual volume of its proceedings is entitled *Jahresbericht der Görres-Gesellschaft: 1934* [Annual Report of the Görres Society] (Cologne: J.P. Bachem Commission Publishers, 1935).

71 The full text of Goebbels' speech on Jewish Communism was published in the *Volkisch Observer* on Sept. 14, 1935, pages 1, 3, and 4. The banner headlines on page one were: "Meaningful Speech at the Congress against World Bolshevism: Bolshevism – The Declared Enemy of All Nations: The Reich Propaganda Minister on Moscow's Blood Guilt: A Sharp Reckoning." A heading within the article on page 4 proclaimed: "The Bolshevik International Is in Reality a Jewish International."

71 *Roman Observer* article on Hitler's new absolute power: Abridged Timeline and Complete Timeline at Aug. 4, 1934.

71 Nazi Party 25-point program: Complete Timeline at Feb. 24, 1920; excerpts in the Abridged Timeline at same date.

71 Hudal's new book in Dec. 1934: *Rom, Christentum und Deutsches Volk*, pp. 8-9; excerpts in Complete Timeline at Dec. 30, 1934.

72 Pope Pius XI's encyclical: *Quas Primas* (1925), para. 12.

72 Vatican newspaper lauded Hudal's book: Complete Timeline at Dec. 30, 1934.

72 *Mein Kampf*, pt. II, ch. 7, translation from the original German.

72 passage about the swastika in Cardinal Pacelli's diplomatic note: Complete Timeline at May 14, 1934.

72 German Bishops proclaimed Catholics were obligated to stand up for the greatness of Germany: Complete Timeline at Dec. 26, 1934.

72 Goebbels' appreciation for Bishops' statements: Complete Timeline at Jan. 8, 1935.

72 German Bishops five months earlier recognized ... undue pressure on the consciences of Catholics: Complete Timeline at Aug. 21, 1934 (Bishop Berning, quoted in the Nazi press on Aug. 19 telling Germans they had a duty to vote "yes" in the referendum confirming Hitler's usurpation of the German Presidency, felt compelled two days later to write a letter to his fellow Catholic Bishops regretting the undue pressure he exerted on Catholic consciences.)

73 Summary of Nuremberg Laws: Complete Timeline at Sept. 17, 1935.

73 Göring declared the swastika to be the anti-Jewish symbol of the world: *Time* magazine, Sept. 23, 1935, p.23.

73 Saavedra Lamas won the Nobel Peace Prize: www.nobelprize.org/nobel_prizes/peace/laureates/1936/lamas-facts.html.

73 Ambassador Thermann's chain of command: (1) to German Foreign Minister von Neurath, a professional diplomat who took office before Hitler came to power, with no documented sympathy for Streicher or his propaganda organ, and (2) to SS head Heinrich Himmler, who had his own propaganda newspaper, *Das Schwarze Korps*, "The Black Corps."

Chapter 31. Conspiracy Theory: How Central to the Holocaust?

Page **75** Quotation from Herf (2006), p.95.

75 Quotation from Cohn (1996), p.214.

75 Hitler's proclamation to the German *Volk* on the day of the invasion: Complete Timeline at June 22, 1941.

76 Hitler said if the Nuremberg Laws prove insufficient: Complete Timeline at Sept. 17, 1935.

76 The mutual non-aggression treaty between Nazi Germany and the Soviet Union, or the "Hitler-Stalin Pact," was signed on August 23, 1939, nine days before Germany invaded Poland, and a month before Russia did the same.

Chapter 32. National Archives: US, Britain and France

Page **77** relevant U.S. State Department documents: Complete Timeline at Apr. 27, 1917.

78 The 1919 State Department documents about the "Bolshevism and Judaism" article: Complete Timeline at Oct. 17, 1919; Oct. 21, 1919; Nov. 17, 1919; Nov. 25, 1919; and Nov. 28, 1919.

79 Boris Brasol's efforts in 1919-1920 are described in Baldwin (2001).

79 Lansing and Dulles: A further lead, which may be pure coincidence, concerns Allen Dulles, brother of John Foster and future head of the CIA (1953-1961). Allen Dulles was in Munich in early spring 1920 and reported from there. Complete Timeline at Apr. 10, 1920.

79 Two American publishers of the *Protocols* in 1920: Small, Maynard & Co. in Boston; Beckwith Co. in New York.

Chapter 33. Rosh Pina Means "Cornerstone"

Page **80** The Velodrome roundup of more than 25,000 Jewish Parisians by the French police, on behalf of the Nazis, took place on July 16 and 17, 1942.

81 The Galilee boat is exhibited at the Yigal Alon Museum alongside Kibbutz Ginosar on the Sea of Galilee, north of the city of Tiberias, Israel.

82 Neve Michael Children's Village can be visited online: www.nevemichael.com.

Chapter 34. Rome Annihilating Jews

Page **83** Flavius Josephus's history is *The Judean War*. A modern translation is Flavius Josephus, *Judean War*, trans. S. Mason (2008).

Chapter 35. Connecting the Dots: "Jewish-Communism" 1920-1938

Page **84** A series of Vatican newspaper articles on the threat of Russian Communism can be found in the Complete Timeline at Jan. 28, 1920. Additional series of articles appeared beginning in mid-April 1920, when Poland invaded the Ukraine; in May, when the Polish Army took Kiev; and from July 25 to mid-August, 1920, when a counterattack by the Red Army drove the Polish Army back to the gates of Warsaw. After a Polish victory in mid-August sent the Red Army retreating back to Russia, *Catholic Civilization* ran a lengthy article about the now-vanquished threat. That article is in the Complete Timeline at Oct. 2, 1920.

84 *Roman Observer's* "Jewish Peril" article: excerpts in Abridged Timeline at Oct. 15, 1920; fuller translation in the Complete Timeline at same date.

84 *Catholic Civilization's* three-part series on "Jewish Bolshevik" atrocities in the Ukraine: Complete Timeline at Nov. 20, 1920.

84 precursor to the Holocaust in the Ukraine in 1918-1920 is documented in Salo Baron, *The Russian Jew under Tsars and Soviets* (1975), pp. 181-186; Nora Levin, *The Jews in the Soviet Union Since 1917* (1988), esp. p.49; H.H. Ben-Sasson, ed., *A History of the Jewish People* (Cambridge: Harvard Univ. Press, 1976), esp. pp. 954-955.

84-85 favorable words about the murderous military forces, White Russians under General Denikin, Ukrainians under Petliura, and Polish Army: *Roman Observer* article of Jan. 30, 1920 praising Denikin, in Complete Timeline at Jan. 28, 1920; *Catholic Civilization* article in Complete Timeline at Oct. 2, 1920 (re alliance of Petliura and Polish Army).

85 Half a dozen *Roman Observer* articles during 1921: Abridged Timeline and Complete Timeline at Apr. 23, 1921; May 8, 1921; May 30-31,1921; June 18, 1921; July 4-5, 1921; and Sept. 12-13, 1921.

85 vehement *Catholic Civilization* article: Complete Timeline at July 15, 1922.

85 "World Revolution and the Jews": Complete Timeline at Oct. 21, 1922; excerpts in Abridged Timeline.

85 "Who Governs Russia?": Complete Timeline at July 15-21, 1935.

85 actual percentage of Jews among Russian Communists: Levin (1988) states that 5.2% of Communist Party members in the Soviet Union in 1922 were Jews, vol. 1, p.47. Levin states that 15-20% of delegates to Communist Party congresses from 1917 to 1922 were of Jewish ethnicity, vol. 1, p.49, citing Gitelman (1972), p.106; see also Bieberstein (2010), p.135. At one point in 1917, before the Revolution, five or six of 21 members of the Communist Central Committee in Russia were ethnic Jews. Levin, vol. 1, p.49; Bieberstein, pp. 135-136.

86 May 1928 *Catholic Civilization* article: Complete Timeline at May 19, 1928; excerpts in Abridged Timeline.

86 Father Hubert Wolf (2010), p.111.

86 *Catholic Civilization's* 1934 two-part series on "the Jewish Question" and Nazi antisemitism: Complete Timeline at Oct. 20, 1934 and Nov. 3, 1934.

86-87 Vatican newspaper's endorsement of Jewish-Communist conspiracy theory: Abridged Timeline and Complete Timeline at Sept. 15, 1935.

87 Vatican newspaper's notice about Hudal's new book: Complete Timeline at Nov. 13, 1936, together with news item on the same page about Jewish-Communism in Hungary.

87 Hudal's book presented by Papen to Hitler: Complete Timeline at June 19, 1936. See Ryback (2008), chapter about Hudal's book in Hitler's private library.

87 Encyclical *Mit Brennender Sorge*: Complete Timeline at Mar. 14, 1937.

88 Pope Pius XI's audience with Belgian pilgrims was covered in the *Roman Observer*, but without mention of his remarks concerning antisemitism.

88 Pope Pius XI's words about self-defense, together with words against antisemitism, reported in *Catholic Documentation*: Complete Timeline at Dec. 5, 1938.

88 adjacent article in *Catholic Documentation*: Complete Timeline at Dec. 5, 1938.

Chapter 36. The Impact of Newspapers

Page **89** Quotation from Archbishop Montini, later Pope Paul VI: G.B. Montini, "The Difficulties of 'L'Osservatore Romano,'" (1961) in G.B. Montini, *Discorsi e Scritti Milanesi 1954-1963* [Speeches and Writings in Milan, 1954-1963], (Brescia: Istituto Paolo VI), republished online at http://chiesa.espresso.repubblica.it/articolo/169841?eng=y. In May 2014, the Vatican announced that Paul VI would be beatified, one step short of canonization, in October 2014. What was Giovanni Battista Montini's role in the promotions of the Jewish-Communist conspiracy theory in the *Roman Observer* and *Catholic Civilization* in the 1930s, when he was involved in the Secretariat of State's oversight function? We have not addressed that question and do not know whether anyone else has.

89 Bergen quoted the *Roman Observer* to show the Vatican's position on issues: e.g., Complete Timeline at May 10, 1935.

89 Faulhaber cited the Vatican paper for the same purpose: e.g., Complete Timeline at Oct. 5. 1922 and March 2, 1932.

89 *Roman Observer* stood behind Faulhaber's controversial remarks: A front page article said Faulhaber had spoken "with the heart and mind of a priest." Complete Timeline at Oct. 1, 1922. Cardinal Faulhaber cited this article as evidence of the Vatican's support for him in a letter to the Bavarian Bishops four days later, Complete Timeline at Oct. 5, 1922. The Cardinal's controversial words about "perjury and high treason" are discussed in Chapter 37.

89 *Catholic Civilization* as described by a long-time member of its staff: Giuseppe DeRosa, *La Civiltà Cattolica: 150 Anni al Servizio della Chiesa 1850-1999* [*Catholic Civilization*: 150 Years in the Service of the Church] (Rome: La Civiltà Cattolica, 1999), chapter 4.

90 Dec. 7, 1919 Bavarian Bishops' pastoral letter on the bad press and articles following in *Munich Catholic Church Newspaper*: Complete Timeline at Dec. 7, 1919.

90 Scholarly study showing five percent of left-wing newspaper editors were Jewish: Donald Dietrich, *Catholic Citizens in the Third Reich* (1988), p.71. The *Munich Catholic Church Newspaper* article claimed a literary historian named Barel established that nearly three-fourths of German newspapers were in the hands of Jews. We have not been able to find any such person, or any such study.

90 *Catholic Documentation* was published by the House of the Good Press in France: see Complete Timeline at Feb. 15, 1919.

90-91 The "good press" was a Vatican initiative: see Complete Timeline at Easter 1907.

91 The "good press" was a designated priority for the Vatican Nuncio in Munich: Cardinal Gasparri to Pacelli's predecessor as Vatican Nuncio in Munich, Archbishop Aversa, Nov. 1916: "As His Eminence the Nuncio is well aware of the enormous influence that the press exerts on public opinion, and of its immense advantages, but also of the tremendous damage it does to the Holy See, to the Church, and to religion, He will therefore make every effort to support and propagate the good press." Wolf (2010), p.20, quoting "Instructions for Abp. Aversa," Nov. 1916, Archive of the Munich Nunciature, vol. 257, folder 10, pp. 1-108.

91 "Archbishop's Decrees": Complete Timeline at Feb. 15, 1920.

91 Vatican statement in 1916 rejecting discrimination against Jews: Complete Timeline at Feb. 9, 1916.

91 Social Democrat newspaper of Munich spoke out: Complete Timeline at May 23, 1920 and May 27-28-29, 1920.

Chapter 37: Connecting More Dots: Bavaria 1920-1923

Page **92** *Bavarian Courier*: *Bayerischer Kurier*, Apr. 13, 1920.

92 *Munich Catholic Church Newspaper* article "Not Jew-Hatred but Christian-Defense": Complete Timeline at May 2, 1920; excerpts in the Abridged Timeline.

92 Nazi-oriented paper's incitement to violence against Munich's Jewish community: *Volkisch Observer*, in Complete Timeline at Apr. 29, 1920.

93 propaganda campaign against Jews on front page of *Munich Catholic Church Newspaper*: Complete Timeline at May 9, 1920; excerpts in the Abridged Timeline.

93 The 25-point Nazi Party Program: Complete Timeline at Feb. 24, 1920; excerpts in the Abridged Timeline at same date.

93 Historian Emma Fattorini: *Germania e Santa Sede: Le Nunciature di Pacelli fra la Grande Guerra e la Repubblica di Weimar* [Germany and the Holy See: The Pacelli Nunciature between the Great War and the Weimar Republic] (1992).

93 Historian Fr. Hubert Wolf: *Pope and Devil* (2010) ("During his time in Germany Pacelli wrote to Rome daily, sometimes several times a day; thus far almost five thousand of his detailed reports have been identified in the Vatican Secret Archives.")

93 Nuncio Pacelli's negative comments about Nazism after the Beer Hall Putsch: Complete Timeline at Nov. 14, 1923 and Apr. 24, 1924; Rychlak (2010), pp. 45, 392-393. Prof. Rychlak also cites a report of Pacelli to Rome denouncing nationalism. (p.45) There is no indication this report mentions Hitler or Nazism. See Besier and Piombo (2007), pp. 34-35.

93 Rychlak writes that Pacelli spoke out publicly against Nazism and Hitler on at least 40 occasions as Nuncio (p.37): Nothing cited by Rychlak, and nothing found in other sources, shows Pacelli speaking publicly, or privately, against Nazism or Hitler before Nov. 1923. The one specific instance Rychlak cites from before Nov. 1923 (p.37) does not mention Nazism or Hitler; rather, it concerns non-Bavarian right-wing elements that have entered Bavaria. Rychlak says that Pacelli recognized and reported the threat of Nazism in 1923, before the National Socialists were even known as Nazis. (p.44) The report Prof. Rychlak cites is from Nov. 14, 1923, i.e., after the Putsch.

94 prominent Catholic priest's words against antisemitism picked up derisively in Munich's Nazi-oriented newspaper: *Volkisch Observer*, in Complete Timeline at June 9, 1920.

94 *Munich Post* article, "Opponents of the Spirit of Pentecost": Complete Timeline at May 23, 1920. The *Post* continued in a similar vein in articles that can be found in the Complete Timeline at May 27-28-29, 1920.

94 "greatest shame for culture": Abridged Timeline and Complete Timeline at Aug. 21, 1921.

94 Cardinal Faulhaber's "perjury and high treason" speech is excerpted in the Abridged Timeline and the Complete Timeline at Aug. 27, 1922.

94 Adenauer's remarks and the crowd's "consternation" were described in the *Münchner Neueste Nachrichten* [Munich Latest News]: Complete Timeline at Aug. 30, 1922.

94-95 blistering rebuke of Konrad Adenauer by Bavarian Baron Cramer-Klett: Complete Timeline at Apr. 26, 1923. Cramer-Klett was a friend of Pacelli: Ventresca (2013), pp. 70-71. See also Hildebrand (1994), p.120. Cramer-Klett appears in Cardinal Pacelli's notes of his audience with Pope Pius XI on Sept. 27, 1935, Vatican Archives, on microfilm at U.S.

Holocaust Memorial Museum, Record Group 76.002B, 430a, 343-355. Cramer-Klett also had the distinction of being personally featured in the *Munich Catholic Church Newspaper*: Complete Timeline at June 29, 1919.

95 Nazi newspaper's articles about Cardinal Faulhaber's Aug. 27, 1922 remarks: Complete Timeline at Aug. 30,, Sept. 2, and Sept. 23, 1922; excerpts in the Abridged Timeline at Sept. 2, 1922.

95 Nazi newspaper article calling Erzberger "Matthias von Biberach": Complete Timeline at Sept. 2, 1922.

95 Hitler's speeches invoking Jewish-Bolshevik conspiracy theory and denouncing the "November criminals" and the "Jewish press": Complete Timeline at Aug. 16, Aug. 17, Sept. 18, and Sept. 23, 1922.

95 *Catholic Civilization* published "World Revolution and the Jews": Complete Timeline at Oct. 21, 1922.

95 The March on Rome by Italian Fascist "blackshirts," i.e. stormtroops and thugs, which succeeded in gaining Mussolini the appointment by the King of Italy to become Prime Minister of Italy, occurred in the last week of October 1922.

96 Murphy's November 1922 reports about Hitler and the Nazi Party: Complete Timeline at Nov. 10 and 25, 1922. The first mention of the Nazis in any of Murphy's twice-monthly political situation reports from Munich to Washington is in the Complete Timeline at Oct. 23, 1922. Murphy's detailed, extensive reports about the Nazis' growth and paramilitary mobilization during 1923 are in the Complete Timeline at Jan. 14, Feb. 2, Mar. 3, May 13 and May 28, 1923. His reports are at U.S. National Archives Records Admin., M336, Roll 18.

96 Report of Father Lorenz Pieper joining Nazi Party: Complete Timeline at Apr. 28, 1923.

96 Examples of Father Pieper's pro-Nazi speeches in Bavaria in 1923: Complete Timeline at July 24, Aug. 24 and Aug. 28, 1923.

96 The Nazi SA event in Ingolstadt: announcement in Complete Timeline at Apr. 29, 1923; report in Nazi newspaper, Complete Timeline at May 1, 1923.

96 Nazi newspaper's weekly listing of Sunday Mass times in the Munich Archdiocese: the first occurrence appears in the Complete Timeline at Apr. 30, 1923. Another example, which added a special prayer for Hitler, is in the Complete Timeline at May 21, 1923. The weekly feature, as seen in the May 21 example, included the time of Sunday services of the Old Catholics and the Lutherans; the comparatively small number of those listings reflects the overwhelmingly Catholic character of Munich.

96 Examples of field masses and swastika blessing ceremonies: Complete Timeline at Apr. 29, May 1, June 12, July 11, Aug. 18 and Aug. 22, 1923. The Aug. 22 entry includes a reference to denial of permission for consecration of Nazi flags *inside* the church. The Diocese of Regensburg, Bavaria, forbade a diocesan priest to conduct a swastika blessing: Complete Timeline at Aug. 23, 1923.

96 The 1924 Bavarian Bishops' policy against blessing the flags of political organizations: Complete Timeline at Sept. 10, 1924.

97 Heinrich Held's letter to Faulhaber: Complete Timeline at Oct. 6, 1923.

97 Chancellor Stresemann's letter to Faulhaber: Complete Timeline at Oct. 13, 1923.

97 Faulhaber's reply to Stresemann: Complete Timeline at Nov. 6, 1923.

97 Hastings (2010) provides concise biographical information about many of the Catholic priests who supported the Nazi movement in 1923, noting the many who stopped supporting the Nazis after the Putsch, and some who later opposed the Nazis. Abbot Albanus Schachleiter,

Lorenz Pieper, and at least three other priests in Bavaria, Magnus Gött, Bernhard Stempfle and Josef Roth, did not stop supporting the Nazis. See Spicer, *Hitler's Priests* (2008), pp. 34-60.

97 Hastings describes the remaining Catholic Nazis as abandoning Catholicism after the Putsch, including details about Heinrich Himmler's practice of Catholicism before, and lack of same after, at pp. 144-162.

Chapter 38. "Pre-Existing Condition"?

Page **98** Hastings (2010), pp. 46-142.

98 German historians of the early Nazi movement: In addition to many histories in English, Steve examined the following German-language historical works dealing with the early Nazi Party or antisemitic trends in Germany at the time: Altmann (1971); Auerbach (1977); Blaschke (1997); Blau (1965); Cohen (1998); Deuerlein (1962, 1968, 1969); Fenske (1969); Franz-Willig (1974, 1975, 1993); Hesemann (2008); Hummel and Kissener (2009); Maser (1965); Pfahl-Traughber (1993); Tyrell (1975); Volk (1966).

98 Hitler's English-language biographies: Bullock (1971); Fest (1974); Hamann (1999); Kershaw (1998); Ryback (2008); Toland (1976); and Wilson (2012).

98 Kershaw mentions Faulhaber's August 27, 1922 speech in connection with events in 1925: Kershaw (1998), p.268.

98 recent biography of Eugenio Pacelli published by Belknap division of Harvard Univ. Press: Ventresca (2013), pp. 54-55.

99 Catholic Center Party flagship newspaper *Germania* in early 1919: Complete Timeline at Jan.-Feb. 1919.

99 *The German Spirit and Jew Hatred*: Complete Timeline at "Late 1919 to early 1920."

99 Statements by Erzberger and two Bavarian Bishops: Complete Timeline at "Late 1919 to early 1920."

100 Father Erhard Schlund's 1919 book on Bolshevism: Complete Timeline at "Late 1919."

100 Fritz Gerlich's 1920 book on Communism, *Der Kommunismus als Lehre vom Tausendjährigen Reich* [Communism as the Teaching of the Thousand Year Reign] (1920), p.227.

101 Faulhaber's Archdiocesan newspaper: Complete Timeline at Apr. 11, 1920; May 2 and 9, 1920; Nov. 21, 1920; and Dec. 12, 1920.

101 Archdiocesan paper on Jewish-Masonic conspiracy theory, and articles against Bolshevism, in 1919: Complete Timeline at Mar. 2, 1919; Mar. 16, 1919; May 18, 1919; May 25, 1919; June 1, 1919.

101 Munich's leading Catholic intellectual journal: *Historische-Politische Blätter für das Katholische Deutschland* [Historical-Political Papers for Catholic Germany]. The journal's article on the *Protocols* can be found in vol. 165, p.754.

101 Five authors of Jewish-Bolshevik conspiracy theory in Munich in the second half of 1919 and first three months of 1920: Dietrich Eckart and Alfred Rosenberg published in Eckart's periodical *Auf Gut Deutsch* [In Plain German]; Franz Schrönghamer-Heimdal published in the *Allgemeine Rundschau* [General Review]; Paul Bang published a book entitled *Judas Schuldbuch* [The Jews' Guilt-Book]; and the anonymous piece of Jewish-Bolshevik conspiracy theory appeared in the *Volkisch Observer*: see Complete Timeline at Feb. 25, 1920.

102 Churchill's February 1920 article: "Zionism versus Bolshevism: A Struggle for the Soul of the Jewish People," *Illustrated Sunday Herald*, Feb. 8, 1920, p.5. In 1935, however, Churchill dismissed the Nazis' accusation that the Jews were "the main prop of communism." Winston Churchill, "The Truth about Hitler," *The Strand*, Nov. 1935, pp. 10, 18.

102 Bavarian National Museum memorializing Jews as a respected element of the Bavarian people: see Staudinger (2007), pp. 28-31.

102 Wittelsbach monarchy elevating Jews and Protestants to the Bavarian nobility: For example, Jewish philanthropist Maurice de Hirsch, based in France, who financed the emigration of many thousands of Russian Jews to Argentina in the late 19th century, was from a Jewish family in Bavaria. His grandfather was ennobled by the Wittelsbach monarchy. His father was made a Baron by the Wittelsbachs. Adolf Hildebrand, a pre-eminent Bavarian artist and sculptor, had a Protestant father and Jewish mother. The Wittelsbachs ennobled him with a hereditary title, borne also by Catholic philosopher Dietrich von Hildebrand, Adolf's son.

102 Further evidence of the failure of antisemitic political movements to gain traction in Bavaria before the First World War can be found in Hastings (2010), pp. 24-25. A Christian Social Party was formed in Munich in 1900, modeled on the highly successful antisemitic party of the same name in neighboring Austria under Karl Lueger. Despite many other cultural similarities between Bavaria and Austria, the Christian Social Party failed politically in Bavaria. In the Munich municipal elections of 1908 and 1911, it polled only in the low single digits. For an academic study of antisemitic sentiments and propaganda in Bavaria, focused on the largely Protestant city of Nuremberg, from 1910 to 1933, see Kauders (1996).

102 Bavarians gave 0.3% of their votes to the antisemitic parties in 1912, while the rest of Germany gave more than eight times that percentage, 2.5%, to the antisemites: www.wahlen-in-deutschland.de/kuBayern.htm.

Chapter 39. Playing with Fire

Page **103** Historians on the Beer Hall Putsch: Deuerlein (1962, German); Flood (1989), pp. 483-565; Gordon (1972); Kershaw (1998), pp. 202-212; Large (1997), pp. 175-194; Schmidt (2000, German), pp. 73-83.

103 Vice Consul Murphy's telegram: Complete Timeline at Nov. 8-9, 1923.

103 Tripled membership: Kershaw (1998), p.190, states that Nazi Party membership increased by 35,000 from February to November 1923, to a total of around 55,000 before the Putsch.

103 "Our Mission for 1923" was the banner headline in the first 1923 edition of the Nazis' *Volkisch Observer*. "Down with the November Criminals!" was the banner headline ten days later. Complete Timeline at Jan. 3 and 13, 1923.

103 Nazi stormtroop strength growing from January to March 1923: Complete Timeline at Jan. 15, 1923 and Mar. 3, 1923.

103 *Volkisch Observer* headlines from Sept. to early Nov. 1923 included: "November Republic is Stealing from its Citizens..." – "the Republic Is Ripe for Collapse" – "The Revolution Is a Singular Theft" – "We Are Ready to Fight" – "The Collapse of the November Treason" – "Jewish Decomposition of Germany" – "The Announcement of the Patriotic Fighting League" – "The Imploding Reich Government" – Hitler's Appeal: "Combat Veterans!" against "the treason of the November Criminals" – "Adolf Hitler Entrusted with the Entire Political Leadership of the Fighting Formations" – "The Only Task: Rooting Out Marxist High Treason" – "A Victim of High Treason" – "The German Officer Since the Crime of November" – Berlin: "Fear of the National Socialist Movement" – Military appeal to "German Men!" and "Students!" See Complete Timeline at Sept. 12 through Nov. 6, 1923.

103-104 potential to spark a "nation-wide conflagration": Complete Timeline at Mar. 3, 1923.

104 Rychlak's examples prove the opposite: see Ch. 37, notes for p.93.

104 A history of the Beer Hall Putsch: Gordon (1972), p.448.

104 Cardinal Faulhaber's sermon: Complete Timeline at Nov. 4, 1923.

104 Faulhaber's reply to Stresemann: Complete Timeline at Nov. 6, 1923.

104-105 Matt's poster in translation: Complete Timeline at "Nov. 9, 1923 before dawn."

105 Matt was a reliable Catholic in the Bavarian cabinet: Schmidt (2000, in German), pp. 125-130 and passim.   Matt's role during the course of negotiations on the Vatican-Bavaria Concordat, and his role after the Putsch in quickly concluding the Concordat, can be seen in the Complete Timeline at Mar. 5, 1921; Mar. 21, 1921; May 28, 1921; Sept. 6, 1921; Nov. 14, 1921; Dec. 15, 1921; Apr. 15, 1922; June 3, 1922; July 10, 1922; July 23, 1922; Nov. 16, 1922; Dec. 28, 1922; Aug. 15, 1923; Sept. 4-5, 1923; Nov. 8, 1923; and Jan. 26, 1924; Mar. 20, 1924; and Mar. 29, 1924.   Pacelli's earlier efforts toward a Concordat, before Matt became *Kultusminister*, can be seen in the Complete Timeline at Feb. 4 and Mar. 9, 1920.

105 Some historians state that Matt was with Pacelli and Faulhaber on the evening of Nov. 8, 1923: e.g., Flood (1989), p.508.

105 Demonstrations against Cardinal Faulhaber went on for months: Complete Timeline at Nov. 14, 1923; Dec. 7 and 8, 1923; Dec. 28, 1923; Jan. 9, 1924; and Mar. 11, 1924.

105 Matt denied he was with Faulhaber and Pacelli: Schmidt (2000), pp. 74-75 and note 279.

105   Catholic Women's League offices and Catholic political leaders involved: Schmidt (2000), pp. 74-75. Ludendorff (1938), pp. 76-77, claimed that two prominent members of Bavaria's Catholic political party, Munich City Councilors Rauch and Scharnagl, drafted Matt's poster, and that Rauch went to the Archbishop's palace at 1:15 a.m. on Nov. 9 to discuss matters with Cardinal Faulhaber.   Ludendorff's biases undermine his credibility, and no confirmation of his claim appears in the histories we reviewed.

105 Bavarian division of the German Army in Munich failed to oppose the Putsch: Besier and Piombo (2007), p.34.

106 Cardinal Faulhaber's praise of Hitler and the originally pure Nazi spring: Complete Timeline at Feb. 15, 1924. The same words, appearing in his 1925 book together with praise for Mussolini, are in the Abridged Timeline and Complete Timeline at the beginning of 1925.

106 Ambassador Ritter zu Groenesteyn's report: Complete Timeline at Nov. 9, 1923; excerpts in the Abridged Timeline at the same date.

106 note from Faulhaber to Pacelli about the Vatican-Bavaria Concordat: Complete Timeline at Nov. 8, 1923.

107 German Government authorities, including Chancellor Wirth, informed Nuncio Pacelli a Bavarian State Concordat was not possible: Complete Timeline at Apr. 4, 1922 and July 23, 1922.

107 Bavarian Government authorities and local Church interests blocked Pacelli's proposals for a Concordat: Complete Timeline at Apr. 15, 1922; June 3, 1922; July 10, 1922; Sept. 5, 1922; Nov. 16, 1922; Dec. 28, 1922; Aug. 15, 1923; and Sept. 4-5, 1923.

107 threat that prompted Held and Stresemann to write Cardinal Faulhaber in October 1923: Complete Timeline at Oct. 6 and Oct. 13, 1923.

107 Thyssen book: *I Paid Hitler* (1941).

Chapter 40. "Jewish-Communism" and Father Coughlin

Page **108** published evidence from investigation in June 2013:

http://investigation2.galebachlaw.com.

109 collections of Father Coughlin's radio broadcasts: Charles Coughlin, *Radio Addresses* (1936); Charles Coughlin, *"Am I an Anti-Semite?"* (1939).

110 The centerpiece of Father Coughlin's radio address on Nov. 20, 1938: Coughlin, *"Am I an Anti-Semite?"* (1939), pp. 34-55. Excerpts are in the Complete Timeline at Nov. 20, 1938.

Two weeks later, Coughlin's radio address was entitled "Not Anti-Semitism but Anti-Communism." *Ibid.*, pp. 70-88.

110 Coughlin's weekly newspaper *Social Justice* summarized the March 6, 1920 *Catholic Documentation* article: Complete Timeline at Aug. 8, 1938.

111 flood of telegrams and letters to Coughlin's office about the attribution to the "American Secret Service," together with the attempted explanation: *Social Justice*, Dec. 12, 1938, p.8.

111 The book by Father Fahey in Ireland reprinting the 1920 *Catholic Documentation* article was excerpted in Father Coughlin's radio address of Nov. 20, 1938; see *"Am I an Anti-Semite?"* (1939), pp. 47-52.

111 Press speculation about Pacelli and Coughlin: e.g., headlines in the *New York Times*, Oct. 9, 1936, p.1 ("Cardinal Pacelli, Papal Envoy, Here" – "He Is Silent on Coughlin"); Oct. 10, 1936, p.5 ("Coughlin's Ticket Quits in the State" – "Cardinal Pacelli, Papal Envoy, Is Silent"); Oct. 16, 1936, p.1 ("Coughlin's Superior Is Guest of Roosevelt"); Nov. 6, 1936 ("Pacelli Lunches with Roosevelt" – "Press Interview Barred" – "Bishop Spellman, an Adviser, Checks Reporters as They Seek Expression of Views" ... on "Coughlin and similar topics of public interest"); Nov. 8, 1936, p.1 ("Coughlin Quits Air" – "Asserts Church Had No Part in Decision").

Chapter 41. Tracing a Common Thread

Page **112** The novels of Gustavo Martinez Zuviria under the pseudonym Hugo Wast, other than the antisemitic novels *El Kahal* and *Oro*, can be found in one volume under the title *Todas Las Novellas de Hugo Wast* [All the Novels of Hugo Wast] (1942). "Hugo Wast" is an anagram made from an alternative spelling of the author's first name: "Ghustawo."

112-113 examined Hudal's books: *Die Religiösen und Sittlichen Ideen des Spruchbuches* [The Religious and Moral Ideas of the Book of Proverbs] (1914); *Die Serbisch-Orthodoxe Nationalkirche* [The Serbian Orthodox National Church] (1922); and the collection of Hudal's sermons from the 1920s and early 1930s, *Vom Deutschen Schaffen in Rom* [Of German Work in Rome] (1933).

113 Gustavo Martinez Zuviria served as the President of the Press and Publicity Committee for the International Eucharistic Congress of 1934: *XXXII Congreso Eucaristico Internacional* [Official Proceedings of the 32nd International Eucharistic Congress] (Buenos Aires: Comité Ejecutivo, 1935), vol. 1, pp. 61, 400.

113 Alois Hudal consecrated as Bishop by Cardinal Pacelli personally: see translation of invitation sent by Hudal to Faulhaber for this event, Complete Timeline at June 18, 1933.

113 The number, and names, of Bishops consecrated personally by Eugenio Pacelli as Cardinal and as Pope Pius XII, and by Karol Wojtyla, as Cardinal-Archbishop of Krakow and as Pope John Paul II, can be seen on the website www.catholic-hierarchy.org, a site that is commonly relied upon by Catholic journalists.

113 on Eugenio Pacelli's watch as Nuncio: A Nuncio, in addition to serving as the Vatican's Ambassador to a nation state, is responsible "to follow attentively the life of the Church and her situation in society." Pope St. John Paul II, Address to Bishops of France, Feb. 27, 2004, www.vatican.va. See also Ezekiel 33:6; Fattorini (1992); Wolf (2010).

114 Fattorini's book about Nuncio Pacelli's early reports to Rome: Fattorini (1992).

114 Cardinal Gasparri's remarks were made to the Belgian Ambassador to the Vatican, according to Minerbi (1990), p.122: Complete Timeline at Dec. 1918.

114 report commissioned by Achille Ratti and forwarded by him to Rome, saying all Bolshevik leaders except Lenin are Jews: Complete Timeline at Nov. 22-23, 1918; described in Kertzer (2001), pp. 251-252.

Chapter 42. Why Did They Do It?

Page **115** Vatican's newspaper showering attention on Germany and Munich Catholicism, and praise on the Catholic press of Bavaria: see *Roman Observer* front page articles in Complete Timeline at Apr. 11, 1920; Apr. 18, 1920; and Apr. 30, 1920.

115 Vatican newspaper's praise in early May 1920 for Archbishop Faulhaber and Nuncio Pacelli, as well as Munich Archdiocese and Bavarian Catholic Press Association: Complete Timeline at May 6 and May 7, 1920.

115 October 15th direct promotion of Jewish-Communist conspiracy theory by the *Roman Observer*: Complete Timeline at Oct. 15, 1920.

116 *Roman Observer* coverage of the San Remo Conference: Complete Timeline at Apr. 18-30, 1920.

116 *Munich Catholic Church Newspaper* said that granting the mandate to Britain interfered directly with the rights of the Pope: Complete Timeline at May 9, 1920.

116 Eight *Roman Observer* front-page articles denouncing Zionism: Complete Timeline at June 9 to July 14, 1920.

116 *Munich Catholic Church Newspaper* on union of Christians and Muslims in the Holy Land: Complete Timeline at July 25, 1920.

116 Latin Patriarch of Jerusalem claimed to speak the entire non-Jewish population of Palestine: Complete Timeline at July 20, 1920.

116-117 *Roman Observer* articles in October and November 1920: Complete Timeline at Oct. 9, Oct. 15, and Nov. 7, 1920.

117 Vatican paper on Churchill and Jewish "national center" in Palestine: Complete Timeline at Apr. 7, 1921.

117 Front page article in *Roman Observer* equating Judaism with Bolshevism: Apr. 23, 1921.

117 Vatican newspaper blamed violence in Palestine on "Zionist invasion" and "Communist Jews": Complete Timeline at May 8, 1921.

117 Pope Benedict XV's words against the Jews attaining "preponderance and privilege" in Palestine: Complete Timeline at June 13, 1921.

117 Five *Roman Observer* articles on Palestine: Complete Timeline at June 18, 1921.

117 September 1921 *Roman Observer* front page article on Arab leader against Jewish immigrants: Complete Timeline at Sept. 12-13, 1921.

117 Cardinal Bourne: Complete Timeline at Oct. 15, 1921.

117 Series of seven articles on "Zionism and "Palestine" in the *Roman Observer*: Complete Timeline at Apr. 21, 1922. The article about the Patriarch of Jerusalem is at May 13, 1922.

117 Article on "The Jews of Poland": Complete Timeline at July 19, 1922.

118 *Catholic Civilization's* two attacks: Complete Timeline at July 15, 1922 and Oct. 21, 1922. The Oct. 21 article is excerpted in the Abridged Timeline.

Chapter 43. Rome, Jerusalem, and "Replacement Theology"

Page **119** Herzl's diary entries are excerpted in the Complete Timeline at Jan. 25, 1904.

120 Replacement theology rejected by the Second Vatican Council: *Nostra Aetate* (1965).

120 Devotees of replacement theology: e.g., Carroll (1987), pp. 52-53. Julian the Apostate's effort to rebuild the Temple in Jerusalem was recalled in the May 2, 1920 *Munich Catholic Church Newspaper* article in the Abridged Timeline and Complete Timeline at May 2, 1920.

121 Cardinal Gasparri told a French diplomat Samuel was going to Palestine for the sole purpose of supporting Zionism: Complete Timeline at June 27, 1920.

122 Articles in *Catholic Civilization*: Complete Timeline at May 20, 1922 and July 15, 1922. Earlier articles in the *Roman Observer* in 1922 are cited in notes to Chapter 42, above.

122 *Catholic Civilization* articles about Bolshevism containing nothing about Judaism: see, e.g., Complete Timeline at Dec. 17, 1927.

122 *Catholic Civilization's* 1928 article on the "Friends of Israel": Complete Timeline at May 19, 1928.

Chapter 44. The Vatican and the Treaty of Versailles
Page **123** Faisal-Weizmann Agreement: Complete Timeline at Jan. 3, 1919.

124 Pope Pius XI denounced separation of Church and State as "oppression" against the Church: e.g., Encylical *Dilectissima Nobis*, "On the Oppression of the Church in Spain," June 3, 1933, para. 6.

125 Italian historian describes report from Eugenio Pacelli referring to the Versailles Treaty as "an international absurdity": Fattorini (1992), pp. 163.

125 Edgardo Mortara case: Kertzer (2001), pp. 118ff.

125 *Munich Catholic Church Newspaper* on Ernesto Nathan: Abridged Timeline and Complete Timeline at May 9, 1920.

126 March 1919 article in *Munich Catholic Church Newspaper* saying "extremely painful" for Holy See: Complete Timeline at Mar. 23, 1919.

126 Articles encouraging worldwide mobilization of Catholics to oppose Zionism: Complete Timeline at July 25, Aug. 15, Aug. 22, Oct. 10, and Nov. 21, 1920.

126 Articles against separation of Church and State: Complete Timeline at Mar. 2, 1919; Aug. 3 and 24, 1919; and Nov. 2, 1919.

126 Against the Versailles Treaty and the exclusion of the Pope from the Peace Conference: Complete Timeline at July 27, 1919; Sept. 14, 1919; and Nov. 9, 1919.

126 First World War called the "Freemasons' War": Complete Timeline at Sept. 7, 1919.

126 the Pope "implicitly condemned" the Versailles Treaty: Complete Timeline Mar. 7, 1920.

126 dozen articles on Czechoslovakia: Complete Timeline at Apr. 20, June 1 and 8, Aug. 24, Sept. 14 and Nov. 9, 1919; and Feb. 15, July 4, Aug. 1, Oct. 3, Nov. 21 and Dec. 12, 1920.

126 calling Masaryk's wife and daughter Jewish: Complete Timeline at Nov. 9, 1919.

126 first issue of *Catholic Documentation*: Complete Timeline at Feb. 15, 1919.

127 rough early form of Jewish-Bolshevik propaganda: Complete Timeline at Aug. 2, 1919.

127 strategy for countering the "Jewish invasion" of Palestine: Complete Timeline at Jan. 31, 1920.

127 *Catholic Documentation* tarred Masaryk with Marxism and Bolshevism in lengthy article predicting early demise of Czechoslovakia: Complete Timeline at Nov. 20, 1920.

Chapter 45. Taking Off the Gloves
Page **128** Vatican providing crucial support to Mussolini from 1922 through the 1930s: Kertzer (2014), pp. 29-30, 47-59, 74-77, 86-87, 98-113, 132-133, 237-239.

128 *Catholic Civilization's* role in signaling Vatican support for Mussolini: see Kertzer (2014), pp. 47-48, 75-77, and Complete Timeline at Oct. 21, 1922; Summer 1924; Aug. 2, 1924; and Aug. 16, 1924.

128-129 *Roman Observer* instructing Italian Catholics that conscience requires them to obey instructions not to support the Socialist opposition to Mussolini: Complete Timeline at Sept. 12 and 14, 1924.

129 Priests in Italy celebrated mass and conducted ceremonial services for the Fascists and their uniformed paramilitary formations: Kertzer (2014), pp. 178-179 ("the Catholic clergy played a crucial role in lending the Duce cult a religious flavor, promoting a heady mix of Fascist and Catholic ritual. Priests were an integral part of the Fascist youth organizations...")

129 Vatican tolerated Fascist violence while its newspaper pretended Mussolini was opposed to it: Kertzer (2014), pp. 48, 56.

129 *Roman Observer* objected to Italy's racial laws only as to infringement of Church control of marriage: Complete Timeline at Nov. 15, 1938.

129 Pope Pius XI plied Mussolini with elements of Jewish-Communist conspiracy theory: Kertzer (2014), p.186.

130 Hitler's speech on the implications of the Lateran Accords between the Vatican and Mussolini: Complete Timeline at Feb. 22, 1929.

130 Cardinal Pacelli instructed a Catholic Chancellor of Germany to form a coalition with the Right: Complete Timeline at Aug. 1931.

130 Father Ludwig Kaas's article praising Italian Fascism as a model for other countries: Complete Timeline at Nov. 1932.

130 Kertzer concludes that Cardinal Pacelli was more pro-Fascist than Pope Pius XI: Kertzer (2014), p.352.

130-131 *Catholic Civilization* on the Vatican-Germany Concordat: Complete Timeline at Nov. 18, 1933.

131 "I rejoice in the greatness of Germany": Friedländer (1966), p.16.

131 German official wrote that the Vatican's Nuncio expressed his hope the Germans would march into Paris by way of Versailles: Friedländer (1966), p.54.

Chapter 46. Ruling from Rome

Page **132** *Nostra Aetate* (1965), para. 4, re rejection of replacement theology: "True, the Jewish authorities and those who followed their lead pressed for the death of Christ; still, what happened in His passion cannot be charged against all the Jews, without distinction, then alive, nor against the Jews of today. Although the Church is the new people of God, the Jews should not be presented as rejected or accursed by God, as if this followed from the Holy Scriptures. All should see to it, then, that in catechetical work or in the preaching of the word of God they do not teach anything that does not conform to the truth of the Gospel and the spirit of Christ."
– and para. 4, re rejection of antisemitism: "Furthermore, in her rejection of every persecution against any man, the Church, mindful of the patrimony she shares with the Jews and moved not by political reasons but by the Gospel's spiritual love, decries hatred, persecutions, displays of anti-Semitism, directed against Jews at any time and by anyone."

132 *Gaudium et Spes* (1965), para. 73, re affirmation of human rights: "The present keener sense of human dignity has given rise in many parts of the world to attempts to bring about a politico-juridical order which will give better protection to the rights of the person in public life. These include the right freely to meet and form associations, the right to express one's own opinion and to profess one's religion both publicly and privately. The protection of the rights of a person is indeed a necessary condition so that citizens, individually or collectively, can take an active part in the life and government of the state… However, those political systems, prevailing in some parts of the world are to be reproved which hamper civic or religious freedom, victimize large numbers through avarice and political crimes, and divert the exercise of authority from the service of the common good to the interests of one or another faction or of the rulers themselves."

132 *Dignitatis Humanae* (1965), para. 3, re championing of freedom of conscience: "On his part, man perceives and acknowledges the imperatives of the divine law through the mediation of conscience. In all his activity a man is bound to follow his conscience in order that he may come to God, the end and purpose of life. It follows that he is not to be forced to act in a manner contrary to his conscience. Nor, on the other hand, is he to be restrained from acting in accordance with his conscience, especially in matters religious. The reason is that the exercise of religion, of its very nature, consists before all else in those internal, voluntary and free acts whereby man sets the course of his life directly toward God. No merely human power can either command or prohibit acts of this kind."

132 *Roman Observer* on the "Grandiose Homage of the Metropolis": Complete Timeline at Oct. 9-16, 1934.

132 homage of Manchukuo to Pope Pius XI: Complete Timeline at Sept. 11, 1938. Manchukuo bordered on the Jewish Autonomous Oblast, the territory opened by Stalin in the mid-1930s for Jews in the Soviet Union to settle.

132 passage written by one of Cardinal Pacelli's subordinates: Domenico Tardini, "San Tommaso d'Aquino e la romanità" [St. Thomas Aquinas and Roman-ness], *Rivista di filosofia neoscolastica* [Review of Neo-Scholastic Philosophy] (1937), vol. 39, p.14, quoted in Godman (2004), p.23. Tardini held positions in the Vatican Secretariat of State from the 1920s through the 1950s. He became Vatican Secretary of State in 1958 under Pope John XXIII.

133 Pope Pius XI's words to the crowd: Official Proceedings, *XXXII Congreso Eucaristico Internacional* (1935), vol. 1, pp. 332-335.

133 Kertzer shows Cardinal Pacelli, Pizzardo and Tardini supporting Italy's invasion of Ethiopia: Kertzer (2014), pp. 215-216, 223.

133 document appointing Pacelli as Legate: Official Proceedings, vol. 1, pp. 158-162. Kaas did not return to Germany after his departure for Rome in 1933.

133 *Catholic Civilization's* article about the Vatican-Germany Concordat: Abridged Timeline and Complete Timeline at Nov. 18, 1933.

134 September 1934 *Roman Observer* article stating Germany's "mission": Abridged Timeline and Complete Timeline at Sept. 28, 1934.

134 Pope Pius XI repeatedly giving instructions to Mussolini: Kertzer (2014), pp. 53, 88, 141, 167-172, 191-192, 204, 239, 294.

134 Roman Catholic Church was a "perfect society": Pope Leo XIII's Encyclical *Immortale Dei* (1885).

134 the Kingdom of Christ on earth: Encyclical *Quas Primas*, excerpts in the Complete Timeline at Dec. 11, 1925.

134 Hudal's devotion to Rome: Alois Hudal, *Vom Deutschen Schaffen in Rom* [Of German Work in Rome] (1933), p.13.

135 Pacelli likewise evinced a strong Roman patriotism: Cardinal Eugenio Pacelli, "The Sacred Destiny of Rome," in E. Pacelli, *Discorsi e Panegirici (1931-1938)* [Speeches and Panegyrics] (Vatican City: 1956), p.514.

135 "Eugenio Pacelli, Roman": Ventresca (2013), p.7.

136 "My kingdom is not of this world": Gospel of John 18:36.

Chapter 47. Accountable to No Man

Pages **136-137** Kertzer: p.352.

137 Ventresca: p.138.

137 *We Remember: A Reflection on the Shoah* can be found at the Vatican website: www.vatican.va/roman_curia/pontifical_councils/chrstuni/documents/rc_pc_chrstuni_doc_160 3198_shoah_en.html.

137 Pope Symmachus, "accountable to no man": Carroll (1987), pp. 143-144.

138 Lord Acton quote: John Dalberg-Acton, *Historical Essays & Studies* (London, Macmillan, 1907), p.504 (Letter to Bishop Creighton: "… You say that people in authority are not to be snubbed or sneezed at from our pinnacle of conscious rectitude… I cannot accept your canon that we are to judge Pope and King unlike other men, with a favourable presumption that they did no wrong…")

138 the Council should be interpreted in a spirit of "continuity" rather than "discontinuity" with the past: Pope Benedict XVI, Address to the Roman Curia, Dec. 22, 2005.

Chapter 48. Did Hitler and Pacelli Ever Meet?

Page **139** Prinz Konstantin von Bayern, *Der Papst* (1952), p.93.

139 German defender of Pope Pius XII: Michael Hesemann, *Der Papst der Hitler Trotzte* (2008), p.69.

139 Sister Pascalini told a Boston author: Paul Murphy, *La Popessa* (1983), pp. 51-52.

139 passage has been seldom cited: The only citation we found to this passage is in a work by an English Catholic author, Gerald Noel, *Pius XII: The Hound of Hitler* (2008). The only other citation to Murphy's book that we found is in Rychlak's *Righteous Gentiles.*

139 Hitler's documented rantings in late 1919 and early 1920: these can be found, in English translation, in the Complete Timeline at Sept. 16, 1919.

139-140 contains ideas found in *Catholic Civilization*: compare Hitler's first documented antisemitic statement, in the Complete Timeline at Sept. 16, 1919, with the article in the Complete Timeline at Jan. 1, 1881.

140 Pacelli wrote a carefully crafted letter: A translation of this letter, together with an image of the draft letter extensively edited in Pacelli's handwriting, can be found in Wolf (2010), pp. 135-136, including this final line: "I need not add that during my stay in Bavaria I myself have never had any sort of personal contact with him."

140 private conversation of Pacelli with British diplomat: reported by that diplomat, Ivone Kirkpatrick, to the British Foreign Office, as seen in the Complete Timeline at Aug. 19, 1933.

140 explanation of the Concordat in *Catholic Civilization*: Complete Timeline at Nov. 18, 1933; excerpt in Abridged Timeline at same date.

141 one of the most pre-eminent Catholic philosophers of the 20th century: J. Ratzinger, Foreword, in Alice von Hildebrand, *Soul of a Lion* (2000), p.9.

141 Pacelli's words to Dietrich von Hildebrand, in Hildebrand's memoirs: Complete Timeline at Jan. 1935; Hildebrand, *Memoiren und Aufsätze gegen den Nationalsozialismus* [Memoirs and Essays against National Socialism] (1994), pp. 120-121.

141 Hildebrand's words in May 1934: *ibid.*, pp. 220-223, reprinting Hildebrand, "The Distinguishing of Spirits," *Christliche Ständestaat*, May 27, 1934.

Chapter 49. The Train Stops at Auschwitz

Page **142** Faulhaber highlighted the "Legionnaires": Complete Timeline at 1925.

143 Pascalina's postcard: Schad (2007), pp. 67-68.

143 Cardinal Faulhaber on the Menzingen order: Faulhaber to Pascalina, Sept. 24, 1948, Pascalina File, Faulhaber Papers, Munich Archdiocese Archive.

144 Decisions of the Allies not to bomb Auschwitz and rail line: A visit to the British War Museum in London, by one of our sons, found an informative display about this matter.

144 because we are human: Acts 10:34 ("'I now really understand,' Peter said, 'that God has no favourites, but that anybody of any nationality who fears him and does what is right is acceptable to him.'")

Chapter 50. Prologue as Epilogue

Page **145** *Catholic Civilization* heralded the writings of Dr. Bataille, Miss Diana Vaughan and Taxil: Complete Timeline at Sept. 19, 1896.

146 St. Thérèse of Lisieux wrote a letter to "Diana Vaughan," enclosing a photograph of herself dressed as Joan of Arc for a convent play: Ahern (1998), pp. 98-100.

146 "Dr. Bataille" on Jewish control of Masonic movement: excerpts of *Le Diable au XIXe Siècle* are translated in the Complete Timeline at 1894.

147 *Catholic Civilization's* coverage of the Leo Taxil hoax: Complete Timeline at May 1, 1897 and May 15, 1897.

We are grateful to our daughter and son-in-law who focused on the history of the *Protocols* with us, and to our grandchildren, who brought us joy and laughter during the process.

Bibliography of Works Cited

A complete Bibliography of works consulted is online at the Galebach Law Office website: http://investigation2.galebachlaw.com/ibibliography.

Ahern, Patrick, *Maurice and Therese: The Story of a Love* (New York: Doubleday, 1998)

Albrecht, Dieter, ed., *Der Notenwechsel Zwischen dem Heiligen Stuhl und der Deutschen Reichsregierung*, [The Note Exchange Between the Holy See and the German Reich Government] (Mainz: Matthias-Grünewald, 1965-1980)

Altmann, Wolfgang, *Die Judenfrage in Ev. und Kath. Zeitschriften Zwischen 1918 und 1933* [The Jewish Question in Protestant and Catholic Journals between 1918 and 1933] (Munich: Univ. of Munich dissertation, 1971)

Auerbach, Helmuth, "Hitlers Politische Lehrjahre und die Münchener Gesellschaft 1919-1923," [Hitler's Political Apprentice Years and Munich Society] *Vierteljahrshefte für Zeitgeschichte* [Contemporary History Quarterly] (1977), vol. 25, pp. 1-45

Bajohr, Frank and Michael Wildt, eds., *Volksgemeinschaft: Neue Forschungen zur Gesellschaft des Nationalsozialismus* [*Volk* Community: New Research on the Society of National Socialism] (Frankfurt am Main: Fischer, 2009)

Baldwin, Neil, *Henry Ford and the Jews: The Mass Production of Hate* (New York: Public Affairs, 2001)

Bang, Paul, *Judas Schuldbuch* [The Jews' Guilt-Book] (Munich: Deutscher Volks-Verlag, 1919)

Barnett, Victoria, *For the Soul of the People: Protestant Protest Against Hitler* (New York: Oxford Univ. Press, 1992)

Baron, Salo, *The Russian Jew under Tsars and Soviets* (New York: Macmillan, 1976)

Bataille, Docteur (pseud. of Jogand-Pagès), *Le Diable au XIXe Siècle* [The Devil in the 19th Century], vol. 2 (Paris: Delhomme et Briguet, 1894)

Bayern, Konstantin Prinz von, *Der Papst: ein Lebensbild* [The Pope: a Sketch of his Life] (Munich: Kindler, 1952)

Ben-Dror, Graciela, *Católicos, Nazis y Judios* [Catholics, Nazis and Jews] (Buenos Aires: Ediciones Lumiere, 2003)

Ben-Dror, Graciela, *The Catholic Church and the Jews: Argentina, 1933-1945* (Lincoln: Univ. of Nebraska Press, 2008)

Besier, Gerhard and Francesca Piombo, *The Holy See and Hitler's Germany*, trans. W.R. Ward (Basingstoke: Palgrave Macmillan, 2007)

Bieberstein, Johannes Rogalla von, *"Jüdischer Bolschevismus": Mythos & Realität* ["Jewish Bolshevism": Myth and Reality] (Graz: Ares, 2010)

Blaschke, Olaf, *Katholizismus und Antisemitismus im Deutschen Kaiserreich* [Catholicism and Antisemitism in the German Kaiser Reich] (Göttingen: Vandenhoeck and Ruprecht, 1997)

Blet, Pierre, S.J., et al., eds., *Actes et Documents du Saint Siège Relatifs à la Second Guerre Mondiale* [Acts and Documents of the Holy See Concerning the Second World War] (Vatican City: Libreria Editrice Vaticana, 1965-1981)

Brown-Fleming, Suzanne, *The Holocaust and Catholic Conscience* (Notre Dame: Univ. of Notre Dame Press, 2006)

Brüning, Heinrich, *Memoiren 1918-1934* [Memoirs 1918-1934] (Stuttgart: Deutsche Verlags-Anstalt, 1970)

Bullock, Alan, *Hitler: A Study in Tyranny* (New York: Harper, 1971)

Burkard, Dominik, "Bischof Alois Hudal: Ein 'Anti-Pacelli'?," *Zeitschrift für Religions- und Geistesgeschichte* [Journal for Religious- and Intellectual-History] (Jan. 2007)

Burkard, Dominik, *Häresie und Mythus des 20. Jahrhunderts* [Heresy and the Myth of the 20th Century] (Paderborn: Schöningh, 2005)

Burleigh, Michael, *The Third Reich: A New History* (New York: Hill and Wang, 2000)

Bytwerk, Randall, *Julius Streicher* (New York: Stein and Day, 1983)

Carroll, James, *Constantine's Sword* (Boston: Houghton Mifflin, 2001)

Carroll, Warren, *The Building of Christendom* (Front Royal: Christendom College Press, 1987)

Chenaux, Philippe, *Pie XII: Diplomate et Pasteur* [Pius XII: Diplomat and Pastor] (Paris: Cerf, 2003)

Chenaux, Philippe, "Pacelli, Hudal et la Question du Nazisme (1933-1938)," *Revista di Storia della Chiesa in Italia* [Review of Church History in Italy], vol. 57 (2003), pp. 133-154

Cohen, Susan, ed., *Antisemitism: An Annotated Bibliography* (Munich: Saur, 1998)

Cohn, Norman, *Warrant for Genocide: The Myth of the Jewish World Conspiracy and the Protocols of the Elders of Zion* (London: Serif, 1996)

Connelly, John, *From Enemy to Brother: The Revolution in Catholic Teaching on the Jews, 1933-1965* (Cambridge: Harvard Univ. Press, 2012)

Conway, John, *The Nazi Persecution of the Churches, 1933-1945* (New York: Basic Books, 1968)

Conway, John, "The Vatican, Germany, and the Holocaust," in Peter Kent and J.F. Pollard, eds., *Papal Diplomacy in the Modern Age* (Westport: Praeger, 1994).

Coppa, Frank, *The Papacy, the Jews, and the Holocaust* (Washington: Catholic Univ. Press, 2006)

Cornwell, John, *Hitler's Pope* (New York: Viking, 1999)

Coppa, Frank, *Controversial Concordats* (Washington: Catholic Univ. Press, 1999)

Coughlin, Charles, *"Am I an Anti-Semite?"* (Detroit: Condon Printing Co., 1939)

Coughlin, Charles, *Radio Addresses* (Detroit: Radio League of the Little Flower, 1936)

Dalberg, John (Lord Acton), *Historical Essays and Studies* (London: Macmillan, 1907)

Dalin, David, *The Myth of Hitler's Pope: How Pope Pius XII Rescued Jews from the Nazis* (Washington: Regnery, 2005)

DeRosa, Giuseppe, *La Civiltà Cattolica: 150 Anni al Servizio della Chiesa 1850-1999* [*Catholic Civilization*: 150 Years in the Service of the Church] (Rome: La Civiltà Cattolica, 1999)

Deuerlein, Ernst, *Der Aufstieg der NSDAP in Augenzeugenberichten* [The Rise of the Nazi Party in Reports of Eyewitnesses] (Düsseldorf: Karl Rauch Verlag, 1968)

Deuerlein, Ernst, *Der Hitlerputsch* (Stuttgart: Deutsche Verlags-Anstalt, 1962)

Deuerlein, Ernst, *Hitler: Eine Politische Biographie* (Munich: List, 1969)

Dietrich, Donald, *Catholic Citizens in the Third Reich* (New Brunswick, NJ: Transaction Books, 1988)

Domarus, Max, ed., *Hitler: Speeches and Proclamations 1932-1945*, trans. Wilcox and Gilbert (Wauconda, IL: Bolchazy-Carducci, 1992)

Epstein, Klaus, *Matthias Erzberger and the Dilemma of German Democracy* (Princeton: Princeton Univ. Press, 1959)

Fattorini, Emma, *Germania e Santa Sede* [Germany and the Holy See] (Bologna: Società Editrice il Mulino, 1992)

Fattorini, Emma, *Hitler, Mussolini and the Vatican* (Cambridge UK: Polity, 2011)

Faulhaber, Michael von, *Deutsches Ehrgefühl und Katholisches Gewissen* [The German Sense of Honor and the Catholic Conscience] (Munich: Pfeiffer, 1925)

Faulhaber, Michael von, *Judaism, Christianity and Germany* (New York: Macmillan, 1934)

Faulhaber, Michael von, *Judentum Christentum Germanentum* [Judaism Christianity German-ness] (Munich: Huber, 1934)

Feldkamp, Michael, *Pius XII und Deutschland* [Pius XII and Germany] (Goettingen: Vandenhoeck und Ruprecht, 2000)

Fenske, Hans: *Konservativismus und Rechtsradikalismus in Bayern nach 1918* [Conservatism and Rightwing Radicalism in Bavaria After 1918] (Berlin: Verlag Gehlen, 1969)

Fest, Joachim, *Hitler*, trans. R. and C. Winston (New York: Harcourt Brace Jovanovich, 1974)

Flannery, Edward, *The Anguish of the Jews* (New York: Paulist Press, 1985)

Flood, Charles, *Hitler: The Path to Power* (Boston: Houghton Mifflin, 1989)

Ford, Henry, *The International Jew* (Dearborn, MI: Dearborn Publishing Co., 1920)

Franz-Willig, Georg, *Krisenjahr der Hitlerbewegung, 1923* [Crisis Year of the Hitler Movement] (Oldendorf, Schütz, 1975)

Franz-Willig, Georg, *Nationalsozialismus* [National Socialism] (Rosenheim: Deutsche Verlagsgesellschaft, 1993)

Franz-Willig, Georg, *Ursprung der Hitlerbewegung 1919-1922* [Origin of the Hitler Movement] (Oldendorf: Schütz, 1974)

Friedländer, Saul, *Nazi Germany and the Jews, Volume I: The Years of Persecution, 1933-1939* (New York: Harper Collins, 1997)

Friedländer, Saul, *Pius XII and the Third Reich*, trans. C. Fullman (New York: Knopf, 1966)

Gallagher, Charles, *Vatican Secret Diplomacy* (New Haven: Yale Univ. Press, 2008)

Gerlich, Fritz, *Der Kommunismus als Lehre vom Tausendjährigen Reich* [Communism as the Teaching of a Thousand Year Kingdom] (Munich: Verlag Hugo Bruckmann, 1920)

Gerlich, Fritz, *Der Kommunismus in der Praxis* [Communism in Practice] (Munich: Süddeutschen Monatshefte G.m.b.H., 1919)

Gitelman, Zvi, *Jewish Nationality and Soviet Politics* (Princeton: Princeton Univ. Press, 1972)

Godman, Peter, *Hitler and the Vatican* (New York: Free Press, 2004)

Goldhagen, Daniel Jonah, *Hitler's Willing Executioners* (New York: Knopf, 1996)

Goldhagen, Daniel Jonah, *A Moral Reckoning: The Role of the Catholic Church in the Holocaust and its Unfulfilled Duty of Repair* (New York: Knopf, 2002)

Goni, Uki, *The Real Odessa: How Peron Brought the Nazi War Criminals to Argentina* (London: Granta, 2002)

Gordon, Harold, Jr., *Hitler and the Beer Hall Putsch* (Princeton: Princeton Univ. Press, 1972)

Hamann, Brigitte, *Hitler's Vienna: A Dictator's Apprenticeship*, trans. T. Thornton (New York: Oxford Univ. Press, 1999)

Hastings, Derek, *Catholicism and the Roots of Nazism* (Oxford, Oxford Univ. Press, 2010)

Hay, Malcolm, *The Foot of Pride* (Boston: Beacon Press, 1950)

Helmreich, Ernst, *The German Churches Under Hitler* (Detroit: Wayne State Univ. Press, 1979)

Herf, Jeffrey, *The Jewish Enemy: Nazi Propaganda During World War II and the Holocaust* (Cambridge: Belknap. Harvard Univ. Press, 2006)

Hesemann, Michael, *Der Papst, der Hitler Trotzte: Die Wahrheit über Pius XII* [The Pope Who Defied Hitler: The Truth about Pius XII] (Augsburg: Sankt Ulrich Verlag, 2008)

Hildebrand, Alice von, *The Soul of a Lion: Dietrich von Hildebrand* (San Francisco: Ignatius Press, 2000)

Hildebrand, Dietrich von, *Memoiren und Aufsätze gegen den Nationalsozialismus* [Memoirs and Essays against National Socialism] (Mainz: Matthias-Grünewald-Verlag, 1994)

Hitler, Adolf, *Mein Kampf*, trans. R. Manheim (Boston: Houghton Mifflin, 1943; London: Pimlico, 1992)

Hochhuth, Rolf, *Der Stellvertreter* [The Deputy or The Vicar] (Reinbek: Rowohlt, 1963)

Hudal, Alois, *Deutsche Kulturarbeit in Italien* [German Cultural Activity in Italy] (Münster: Aschendorff, 1934)

Hudal, Alois, *Deutsches Volk und Christliches Abendland* [The German *Volk* and the Christian West] (Innsbruck: Tyrolia, 1935)

Hudal, Alois, *Die Grundlagen des Nationalsozialismus* [The Foundations of National Socialism] (Leipzig: Gunther, 1937, 5th ed.)

Hudal, Alois, *Katholizismus in Oesterreich* [Catholicism in Austria] (Innsbruck: Tyrolia, 1931)

Hudal, Alois, *Die Religiösen und Sittlichen Ideen des Spruchbuches* [The Religious and Moral Ideas of the Book of Proverbs] (Rome: Papal Biblical Institute Press, 1914)

Hudal, Alois, *Rom, Christentum und Deutsches Volk* [Rome, Christianity and the German *Volk*] (Innsbruck: Tyrolia, 1934)

Hudal, Alois, *Römische Tagebücher: Lebensbeichte eines Alten Bischofs* [Roman Diaries: The General Confession of an Old Bishop] (Graz: Stocker, 1976)

Hudal, Alois, *Die Serbisch-Orthodoxe Nationalkirche* [The Serbian Orthodox National Church] (Graz: Moser, 1922)

Hudal, Alois, *Der Vatikan und die Modernen Staaten* [The Vatican and Modern States] (Innsbruck: Tyrolia, 1935)

Hudal, Alois, *Vom Deutschen Schaffen in Rom* [Of German Work in Rome] (Innsbruck: Tyrolia, 1933)

Hummel, Karl-Joseph and Michael Kissener, eds., *Die Katholiken und das Dritte Reich* [Catholics and the Third Reich] (Paderborn: Ferdinand Schöningh, 2009)

Hürten, Heinz, *Deutsche Katholiken, 1918-1945* [German Catholics] (Paderborn: F. Schöningh, 1992)

Hurwitz, Ariel, *Jews Without Power: American Jewry During the Holocaust* (New Rochelle: MultiEducator, 2011)

Hurwitz, Cipora, *Forbidden Strawberries*, trans. G. Forman (New Rochelle: MultiEducator, 2010)

Ivereigh, Austen, *Catholicism and Politics in Argentina, 1810-1960* (Oxford: St. Martin's, 1995)

Jäckel, Eberhard, and Axel Kuhn, eds., *Hitler: Sämtliche Aufzeichnungen, 1905-1924* [Hitler: Collected Writings] (Stuttgart: Deutsche Verlags-Anstalt, 1980)

Jogand-Pagès, Gabriel (pseudonym Docteur Bataille), *Le Diable au XIXe Siècle* [The Devil in the 19th Century], vol. 2 (Paris: Delhomme et Briguet, 1894)

Jones, Nigel, *The Birth of the Nazis* (New York: Carroll & Graf, 2004)

Katz, Jacob, *From Prejudice to Destruction: Anti-Semitism, 1700-1933* (Cambridge: Harvard Univ. Press, 1997)

Katz, Jacob, *Jews and Freemasons in Europe*, trans. L. Oschry (Cambridge: Harvard Univ. Press, 1970)

Kellogg, Michael, *The Russian Roots of Nazism* (Cambridge: Cambridge Univ. Press, 2008)

Kent, Peter, and J.F. Pollard, eds., *Papal Diplomacy in the Modern Age* (Westport, CT: Praeger, 1994)

Kershaw, Ian, *Hitler, 1889-1936: Hubris* (London: Allen Lane, 1998)

Kertzer, David, *The Pope and Mussolini* (New York: Random House, 2014)

Kertzer, David, *The Popes against the Jews* (New York: Knopf, 2001)

Lacroix-Riz, Annie, *Le Vatican, l'Europe et le Reich de la Première Guerre Mondiale à la Guerre Froide* [The Vatican, Europe and the Reich from the First World War to the Cold War] (Paris: Armand Colin, 1996)

Lamm, Hans, ed., *Von Juden in München: Ein Gedenkbuch* [On the Jews of Munich: A Book of Remembrance] (Munich: Ner-Tamid-Verlag, 1958)

Lapide, Pinchas, *Three Popes and the Jews* (New York: Hawthorn, 1967)

Large, David, *Where Ghosts Walked: Munich's Road to the Third Reich* (New York: Norton, 1997)

Larson, Erik, *In the Garden of Beasts* (New York: Crown, 2011)

Lehnert, Pascalina, *Ich Durfte Ihm Dienen* [I Was Allowed to Serve Him] (Würzburg: Naumann, 1982)

Levin, Nora, *The Jews in the Soviet Union since 1917* (New York: NYU Press, 1988)

Lichten, Joseph, *A Question of Judgment: Pius XII and the Jews* (Washington, NCWC, 1963)

Marchione, Margherita, *Pius XII: Architect for Peace* (Mahwah NJ: Paulist, 2000)

Maser, Werner, *Die Frühgeschichte der NSDAP* [The Early History of the Nazi Party] (Frankfurt am Main: Athenäum-Verlag, 1965)

Merz, Kai-Uwe, *Das Schreckbild: Deutschland und der Bolschevismus, 1917 bis 1921* [The Terror-Image: Germany and Bolshevism, 1917 to 1921] (Frankfurt am Main: Propyläen, 1995).

Michael, Robert, *A History of Catholic Antisemitism: The Dark Side of the Church* (New York: Palgrave Macmillan, 2008)

Minerbi, Sergio, *The Vatican and Zionism*, trans. A. Schwarz (New York: Oxford Univ. Press, 1990)

Montini, G.B. (Venerable Pope Paul VI), "The Difficulties of 'L'Osservatore Romano,'" (1961) in G. B. Montini, *Discorsi e Scritti Milanesi 1954-1963* [Speeches and Writings in Milan, 1954-1963], (Brescia: Istituto Paolo VI), republished online at http://chiesa.espresso.repubblica.it/articolo/169841?eng=y

Müller, Hans, *Katholische Kirche und Nationalsozialismus: Dokumente 1930-1935* [Catholic Church and National Socialism: Documents 1930-1935] (Munich: Nymphenburger Verlagshandlung, 1963)

Müller, Jürgen, *Nationalsozialismus in Lateinamerika: Die Auslandsorganisation der NSDAP in Argentinien, Brasilien, Chile und Mexiko, 1931-1945* [National Socialism in Latin America: The Overseas Organization of the Nazi Party in Argentina, Brazil, Chile and Mexico] (Stuttgart: Heinz, 1997)

Murphy, Paul, *La Popessa* (New York: Warner, 1983)

Murphy, Robert, *Diplomat Among Warriors* (Garden City: Doubleday, 1964)

Newton, Ronald, *The "Nazi Menace" in Argentina, 1931-1947* (Stanford: Stanford Univ. Press, 1992)

Noel, Gerard, *Pius XII: The Hound of Hitler* (London: Continuum, 2008)

Pacelli, Eugenio, *Discorsi e Panegirici (1931-1938)* [Speeches and Panegyrics] (Vatican City: 1956)

Papen, Franz, *Der Wahrheit Eine Gasse* (Munich: P. List, 1952); English trans. entitled *Memoirs*, trans. B. Connell (London: A. Deutsch, 1952)

Patai, Raphael, ed., *The Complete Diaries of Theodor Herzl*, trans. H. Zohn (New York: Herzl Press, 1960), vol. IV

Pfahl-Traughber, Armin, *Der Antisemitisch-Antifreimaurerische Verschwörungsmythos in der Weimarer Republik und im NS-Staat* [The Antisemitic-Anti-Freemasonic Conspiracy Myth in the Weimar Republic and in the Nazi State] (Vienna: Braumüller, 1993).

Pinkus, Benjamin, *Jews of the Soviet Union* (Cambridge: Cambridge Univ. Press, 1988)

Poliakov, Léon, *The History of Anti-Semitism*, trans. R. Howard (Philadelphia: Univ. of Pennsylvania Press, 2003)

Repgen, Konrad and Klaus Gotto, eds., *Kirche, Katholiken und Nationalsozialismus* [The Church, Catholics and Nazism] (Mainz: Matthias-Grünewald-Verlag, 1980)

Rhodes, Anthony, *The Vatican in the Age of the Cold War, 1945-1980* (Norwich UK: Russell, 1992)

Rhodes, Anthony, *The Vatican in the Age of the Dictators, 1922-1945* (New York: Holt, Rinehart and Winston, 1974)

Rhonheimer, Martin, "The Holocaust: What Was Not Said," *First Things* (Nov. 2003)

Rosenberg, Alfred, *Der Mythos des 20. Jahrhunderts* [The Myth of the 20th Century] (Munich: Hoheneichen-Verlag, 200th ed., 1943)

Rosenberg, Alfred, *Die Protokolle der Weisen von Zion und die Jüdische Weltpolitik* [The Protocols of the Elders of Zion and Jewish World Politics] (Munich: Deutscher Volksverlag, 1923)

Ryback, Timothy, *Hitler's Private Library* (New York: Knopf, 2008)

Rychlak, Ronald, *Hitler, the War, and the Pope* (1st ed., Columbus, MS: Genesis Press, 2000; 2d ed., Huntington, IN: Our Sunday Visitor, 2010)

Rychlak, Ronald, *Righteous Gentiles: How Pius XII and the Catholic Church Saved Half a Million Jews from the Nazis* (Dallas: Spence, 2005)

Sale, Giovanni, *Hitler, la Santa Sede e gli Ebrei* [Hitler, the Holy See and the Jews] (Milan: Jaca Book, 2004)

Samuel, Herbert, *Memoirs* (London: Cresset, 1945)

Sandmann, Fritz, *Die Haltung des Vatikans zum Nationalsozialismus im Spiegel des "Osservatore Romano"* [The Position of the Vatican toward Nazism as Reflected in the "Roman Observer"] (Mainz: Lokay, 1965)

Sandmann, Fritz, *"L'Osservatore Romano" e il Nazionalsocialismo 1929-1939* ["The Roman Observer" and National Socialism], Italian trans. A. Cervone (Rome: Cinque Lune: Collection of Histories of the Catholic Movement, 1976)

Schad, Martha, *Gottes Mächtige Dienerin* [God's Mighty Maidservant] (Munich: Herbig, 2007)

Schirach, Baldur von, *Die Hitler-Jugend* [The Hitler Youth] (Berlin: Zeitgeschichte Verlag, 1934)

Schlund, Erhard, *Der Bolschewismus* [Bolshevism] (Munich: Jos. Hubers Verlag, 1919)

Schmidt, Lydia, *Kultusminister Franz Matt (1920-1926): Schul-, Kirchen- und Kunstpolitik in Bayern nach der Umbruch von 1918* [Minister of Education, Religion and Culture Franz Matt: The Politics of Education, Religion and the Arts in Bavaria Following the Revolution of 1918] (Munich: C.H. Beck, 2000)

Schrönghamer-Heimdal, Franz, *Das Kommende Reich* [The Coming Kingdom] (Augsburg: Haas & Grabherr, 1918)

Schrönghamer-Heimdal, Franz, *Dem Deutschen Volke: Deutsche Kriegsworte für das Deutsche Friedenswerk* [To the German People: German War-Words for German Peace-Work] (Freiburg im Breisgau: Herder, 1917)

Sereny, Gitta, *Into that Darkness* (New York: Vintage, 1983)

Shirer, William, *The Rise and Fall of the Third Reich* (New York: Simon and Schuster, 1960)

Singerman, Robert, "The American Career of the *Protocols of the Elders of Zion,*" *American Jewish History*, vol. 71, no. 1 (Sept. 1981), p.48

Spicer, Kevin, ed., *Antisemitism, Christian Ambivalence, and the Holocaust* (Bloomington: Indiana Univ. Press, 2007)

Spicer, Kevin, *Hitler's Priests* (DeKalb, IL: Northern Illinois Univ. Press, 2008)

Spicer, Kevin, *Resisting the Third Reich: The Catholic Clergy in Hitler's Berlin* (DeKalb, IL: Northern Illinois Univ. Press, 2004)

Stasiewski, Bernhard, ed., *Akten Deutscher Bischöfe über die Lage der Kirche, 1933-1945* [Papers of the German Bishops about the Situation of the Church] (Mainz: Matthias-Grünewald-Verlag, 1968-1979)

Staudinger, Barbara, *The Jewish World and the Wittelsbach Dynasty* (*Die Jüdische Welt und die Wittelsbacher*) (Munich: Jewish Museum, 2007) (published in side-by-side English-German)

Stehkämper, Hugo, *Konrad Adenauer als Katholikentagspräsident 1922* [Konrad Adenauer as Catholic Congress President] (Mainz: Matthias-Grünewald-Verlag, 1977)

Stehle, Hansjakob, *Geheimdiplomatie im Vatikan: Die Päpste und die Kommunisten* [Secret Diplomacy in the Vatican: The Popes and the Communists] (Zurich: Benziger, 1993)

Stehlin, Stewart A., *Weimar and the Vatican, 1919-1933* (Princeton: Princeton Univ. Press, 1983)

Steinacher, Gerald, *Nazis on the Run* (Oxford: Oxford Univ. Press, 2011)

Sutton, Anthony, *Wall Street and the Bolshevik Revolution* (New Rochelle, NY: Arlington House, 1974)

Sutton, Anthony, *Western Technology and Soviet Economic Development 1917 to 1930* (Stanford: Hoover Institution, 1968)

Taguieff, Pierre-André, *Les Protocoles des Sages de Sion* [The Protocols of the Elders of Zion] (Paris: Berg International-Fayard, 2004)

Taradel, Ruggero and Barbara Raggi, *La Segregazione Amichevole: "La Civiltà Cattolica" e la Questione Ebraica 1850-1945* [Amicable Segregation: "Catholic Civilization" and the Jewish Question 1850-1945] (Rome: Editori Riuniti, 2000)

Thyssen, Fritz, *I Paid Hitler* (New York: Farrar & Rinehart, 1941)

Toland, John, *Adolf Hitler* (Garden City: Doubleday, 1976)

Turner, Michael, *Historical Dictionary of United States Intelligence* (Lanham, MD: Scarecrow Press, 2006)

Tyrell, Albrecht, *Vom "Trommler" zum "Führer"* [From the "Drummer" to the "Fuhrer"] (Munich: Fink, 1975)

Ulam, Adam, *Stalin: The Man and His Era* (London: Allen Lane, 1973)

Ventresca, Robert, *Soldier of Christ: The Life of Pope Pius XII* (Cambridge: Belknap Harvard Univ. Press, 2013)

Volk, Ludwig, ed., *Akten Kardinal Michael von Faulhabers*, 1917-1945 [Papers of Cardinal Michael von Faulhaber] (Mainz: Matthias-Grünewald-Verlag, 1975)

Volk, Ludwig, "Kardinal Faulhabers Stellung zur Weimarer Republik und zum NS-Staat" [Cardinal Faulhaber's Stance toward the Weimar Republic and the Nazi State], *Stimmen der Zeit* [Voices of the Day], March 1966, vol. 177, p.173.

Volk, Ludwig, *Katholische Kirche und Nationalsozialismus* [The Catholic Church and National Socialism] (Mainz: Matthias-Grünewald-Verlag, 1987)

Volk, Ludwig, *Das Reichskonkordat vom 20. Juli 1933* [The Reich Concordat of July 20, 1933] (Mainz: Matthias-Grünewald-Verlag, 1972)

Wast, Hugo [pseud. of Gustavo Martínez Zuviría], *El Kahal* (1935)

Wast, Hugo, *Oro* (1935)

Wast, Hugo, *Todas Las Novellas de Hugo Wast* [All the Novels of Hugo Wast] (Madrid: Ediciones Fax, 1942)

Webman, Esther, ed., *The Global Impact of the Protocols of the Elders of Zion* (London: Routledge, 2011)

Wichtl, Friedrich, *Weltfreimaurerei, Weltrevolution, Weltrepublik* [World Freemasonry, World Revolution, World Republic] (Munich: Lehmann, 1920)

Wilson, A.N., *Hitler: A Short Biography* (London: HarperPress, 2012)

Wolf, Hubert, *Papst und Teufel,* trans. K. Kronenberg [English title: *Pope and Devil*] (Munich: Beck, 2008; English version Cambridge: Belknap Harvard Univ. Press, 2010)

Wolf, Hubert, and Klaus Unterburger, eds., *Eugenio Pacelli: Die Lage der Kirche in Deutschland, 1929* [The Situation of the Church in Germany, 1929] (Paderborn: Ferdinand Schöningh, 2006)

Zahn, Gordon, *German Catholics and Hitler's Wars* (New York: Sheed and Ward, 1962)

Zuccotti, Susan, *Under His Very Windows: The Vatican and the Holocaust in Italy* (New Haven: Yale Univ. Press, 2000)

Books Without Named Authors
Bayerns Gesetze und Gesetzbücher [Bavaria's Laws and Statute Books]
Bible
Catholic Encyclopedia (New York: Robert Appleton Co., 1907-1912)
Die Tagebücher von Joseph Goebbels [The Diaries of Goebbels] (Munich: K.G. Saur, 2001)
Documents of British Foreign Policy, Series II, vols. 5-6 (1956-1957)
Documents on German Foreign Policy, Series C, vol. 3 (Washington: U.S. Govt. Printing Office, 1959)
Jahresbericht der Görres-Gesellschaft: 1934 [Annual Report of the Görres Society] (Cologne: J.P. Bachem Commission Publishers, 1935)
Official Proceedings, *XXXII Congreso Eucaristico Internacional* [32nd International Eucharistic Congress] (Buenos Aires: Comité Ejecutivo, 1935)
The Protocols of the Elders of Zion, multiple editions

Newspapers and Periodicals
Acta Apostolicae Sedis [Acts of the Apostolic See] (Vatican City: Libreria Editrice Vaticana), Rome
Allgemeine Rundschau [General Review], Munich, Germany
Amtsblatt [Official Bulletin], Archdiocese of Munich, Germany
Argentinisches Tageblatt [Argentine Daily], Buenos Aires, Argentina
Auf Gut Deutsch [In Plain German], Munich, Germany
Bayerischer Kurier [Bavarian Courier], Munich, Germany

Caras y Caretas, Argentina
La Civiltà Cattolica [Catholic Civilization], Rome
Criterio, Argentina
La Documentation Catholique [Catholic Documentation], Paris, France
Germania, Berlin, Germany
Historische-Politische Blätter für das Katholische Deutschland [Historical-Political Papers for Catholic Germany], Munich, Germany
Illustrated Sunday Herald, London, UK
Ingolstadt Freie Presse, Ingolstadt, Germany
Miesbacher Anzeiger [Bulletin], Miesbach, Germany
Moreshet Journal for the Study of the Holocaust and Antisemitism, Tel Aviv, Israel
Münchener Katholische Kirchenzeitung [Munich Catholic Church Newspaper], Munich, Germany
Münchner Neueste Nachrichten [Munich Latest News], Munich, Germany
Münchener Post, Munich, Germany
Münchener Zeitung, Munich, Germany
La Nacion [The Nation], Buenos Aires, Argentina
New York Times, United States
L'Osservatore Romano [The Roman Observer], Vatican City, Rome
La Prensa [The Press], Buenos Aires, Argentina
El Pueblo [The People], Buenos Aires, Argentina
Der Stürmer, Nuremberg, Germany
Time, United States
Vierteljahrshefte für Zeitgeschichte [Contemporary History Quarterly] Munich, Germany
Völkischer Beobachter [*Volkisch* Observer], Munich, Germany

Films
Sophie Scholl: Die Letzten Tagen [Sophie Scholl: The Final Days] (2005)
Triumph des Willens [Triumph of the Will] (1935)

Papal Encyclicals and Documents
Acerbi Animi, Sept. 29, 1932 (On Persecution of the Church in Mexico)
Apostolic Constitution Officiorum, Jan. 25, 1897
Divini Redemptoris, Mar. 19, 1937 (On Atheistic Communism)
Humani Generis Redemptionem, June 15, 1917 (On Preaching the Word of God)
Humanum Genus, Apr. 20, 1884 (On Freemasonry)
Mit Brennender Sorge, Mar. 14, 1937 (On the Church and the German Reich)
Non Abbiamo Bisogno, June 29, 1931 (On Catholic Action in Italy)
Pascendi Domenici Gregis, Sept. 8, 1907 (On the Doctrines of the Modernists)
Quadragesimo Anno, May 15, 1931 (On Reconstruction of the Social Order)
Quas Primas, Dec. 11, 1925 (On the Feast of Christ the King)
Summi Pontificatus, Oct. 20, 1939 (Supreme Pontificate)
Ubi Arcano Dei Consilio, Dec. 23, 1922 (On the Peace of Christ in the Kingdom of Christ)

Index

www.ingramcontent.com/pod-product-compliance
Lightning Source LLC
Chambersburg PA
CBHW071427090426
42737CB00011B/1591